RED DANUBE

A Hungarian memoir

VERA HARTLEY

Vera Hartley

For George and David

First published in 2016 by WriteLight Pty Ltd
For Vera Hartley
Email: vhartley@iprimus.com.au

© text and photographs (other than those listed below): Vera Hartley
Back cover: Shoes by the Danube, from Wikicommons. Photo taken
by Cebete, 22 August 2012
Page 9: Laci and Erzsi posing as statues in Pompeii on their honeymoon, May 1938,
from the author's private collection.
Page 55: Exhumation of the bodies from the Maros Street massacre, January 1945.
Photo taken by Sándor Ék, used with permission of the Hungarian National Museum.
Page 115: Stalin's statue toppled, October 1956. Photographer: John Sadovy.
(Found on various websites).

National Library of Australia Cataloguing-in-Publication entry
Creator: Hartley, Vera
Title: Red Danube / Vera Hartley
ISBN 97809944325570
Subjects: Hungarians—Biography
Jews—Hungary—Biography
World War; 1914–1918—Personal narratives, Jewish
World War; 1939–1945—Personal narratives. Jewish
Communism—Hungary.
Dewey number: 305.894511092

Produced by Victoria Jefferys www.writelight.com.au
Edited by Sarah Shrubb
Design & layout by Julianne Billington
Printed by SOS Print & Media, Sydney
Front cover: Original illustration painted by Lindena Robb www.lindena-robb.com.au

Front and back cover: *'Shoes by the Danube' was created by the sculptor Gyula Pauer in 2005 to
commemorate the 2000 or so people, nearly all Jewish, who were shot into the Danube by the Arrow Cross
(Hungarian Nazi Party) in the winter of 1944–5. The victims were ordered to take their shoes off before being
shot as those could be re-used or sold. The rusting iron sculpture consists of 60 pairs of shoes and is set into the
concrete embankment. According to eyewitnesses, the river flowed red.*

Sometimes visible, sometimes not,
Sometimes devout Christian
Sometimes staunchly Jewish.
Until our inner love fits into everyone
All we can do is take daily these different shapes.
Rumi (1207–73)
(translated by Daniel Ladinsky)

Most of the quotes come from three newspapers:

Szabad Nép, Free People, the daily newspaper of the communist era, like the Soviet *Pravda*.

Ludas Matyi, a satirical weekly like the English *Punch*. The original Ludas had the motto: 'There are no old jokes, all jokes are fresh to a new-born babe.'

Nők Lapja, a weekly magazine for the education of women, much of it unashamedly propaganda.

Note

Many borders shifted over the time period covered by this book. Towns that had been part of Hungary for a thousand years belonged to other countries and changed names after World War I. I have used their historically correct Hungarian names, which no longer appear on modern maps, but in a few cases I have also given their current names.

Pronunciation

Hungarian	English
cs	ch
s	sh
sz	s
c	tz
j	y
zs	j as in the French jour

CONTENTS

AUTHOR'S NOTE

My mother's oft-repeated anecdotes of my birth started this project. At that time it was only a collection of ever-changing stories, but each telling revealed a little more detail which couldn't but pique my curiosity and beg for more questions to be asked ... until there was a book. Tattered birth, death and other certificates, a gallery of photos, 100-year-old postcards and letters from the War padded out the narrative.

Part way through the writing it occurred to me that the ordinary lives of my family were the manifestations of political decisions made on a much larger scale, decisions made within the protected walls of Parliament House, political Party Headquarters or isolated boardrooms, far removed from those who would be deeply affected by them. I then decided to hang all my shards of information on the pin-board of history.

And the consequences of those actions or Acts by powerful people ripple down the line, generation after generation – to when a great-grandchild can no longer fit into context his unnamed fears, his lack of trust. So it falls to us, it falls to me, those who still remember, to pass the information on to future generations to give them the hope of healing.

INTRODUCTION

My mother didn't talk much about her past – that is, until a few years ago, and after she started that was all she could talk about. I found her stories endless, irritating; told her to get over it. With each story I would appeal to heaven for someone up there to stop her. I already knew about the War, about Hitler, about communism; there was nothing new she could tell me. Most importantly, it had *nothing* to do with me.

Unperturbed, she continued, until one day I promised to listen, write the stories down and present her with the manuscript. With a bit of luck, I thought, that would satisfy her and be the end of it for me.

When the promise was made, my mother was 91 years old, and still had a remarkable memory for detail – the name of every place she went to, how pretty or handsome anyone she ever met was, the name and status of every doctor, lawyer or official she ever dealt with. The more I listened, the more interesting it became. Very soon I was hooked.

By coincidence (are these things ever coincidental?), a friend of a friend stayed at my place and, as thanks, presented me with a book – *The History of Hungary in the 20th Century*. It was written in Hungarian, a language I'd hardly spoken, let alone read, in 50 years. The first page took me several hours to decipher but I persevered, and slowly the complicated and devious history of my birth country emerged, like a Wagnerian opera, with my mother singing the personal high notes as history thundered, rumbling its base underlying facts. I now had a performance on a grand scale.

And I realised it had *everything* to do with me.

PART 1

THE GOOD OLD DAYS

1

SIGNING AWAY THE PAST

The decision is made.

When I arrive Erzsi greets me: 'You're always late. I was expecting you earlier.' There is no right time to arrive at my mother's – I'm always late, except when I'm too early and should have waited because she's not yet ready. I timed my arrival with Helen's, imagining Erzsi would need moral support. After two minutes, *I* need moral support.

She's going into the nursing home and she's angry. Angry with Helen, who came to assess her required level of care, angry with her pain, angry with me, angry with the world. There's nothing new in that. That is how I have always known my mother. Now all five foot two inches of her is fuming, toxic words spewing from her mouth in every direction.

She fumbles with the pen as she signs away her freedom, her independence, her home of 40 years with all its memories. This is the end of Elizabeth Káhn, widow and mother of two; soon she will become Elizabeth Room H 208, one of 400 inmates at Montefiore Hostel for the aged, Sydney, Australia.

Her hand refuses to hold the pen.

'What's the point of getting old? Don't ever get old!' she gives me the oft-repeated advice I do not want. *Sure, Mum, I'll jump off the cliff if you like*, I think, but I don't say it out loud.

'That incompetent doctor who butchered my hand,' she seethes through her false teeth, 'he stuffed up the operation, but he is such a good-looking young man!'

'Mum, Helen's waiting,' I say quietly.

'Can't you understand? It hurts. It hurts like hell. All the time.'

Is she still talking about her hand?

'Especially after the second operation. It's nearly useless now. I wanted to tell the doctor it was not right, but he did not see me for two days. He forgot about me. When he came he apologised with a beautiful smile. Hmm. I told him, "You're so handsome, doctor. You could have been a movie star!"'

'Did you tell him about your hand?'

'He was happy with the compliment because he blushed, his whole face went the colour of his bright red shirt. It had a pointy collar that was not sewn well because both ends were rounded, uneven, and a proper collar must have sharp points. I should know! I made enough of them at the factory. They're bloody hard to get just right. It wrecks your fingers trying to turn them inside out when they're done properly. And mine were good. I wasn't fast. I wasn't fast at anything, but I did a good job. A bloody good job. Lili Deutsch, my boss, always told me, "Elizabeth, your collars are perfect." So.'

'But did you tell the doctor about the botched operation? And how much your hand hurt? Did you ask him if anything could be done about it?'

'No. What's the bloody point anyway? I didn't want to have another operation. I couldn't. It can't be fixed. Now it just hurts like hell.'

She abuses Helen's predecessor, Nicky, who promised to call her back but didn't. She has a go at the church hall where a couple of years earlier she attended a lecture and had afternoon tea, and they had closed one side of the double door to the kitchen without bolting it. She leaned against it, fell, and broke the top of her femur.

She should have sued the whole lot of them. She should have got money out of them, it was all their fault, but the solicitor was not so confident of a win and didn't take the case. But they should have paid for it, damn them. If it weren't for them she would still be able to walk without a frame and without constantly falling over. Twenty-nine falls so far. 'Damn the lot of them,' she spewed her frustration into the living room. And 'them' included me, for the crimes I committed today, yesterday, last year and the years and decades before, for being such a difficult baby at times and, even though I was on time, for being late.

'It's because of that bloody broken leg, now mended but not well. The doctor said to me, "You know, Mrs Káhn, it's only one in a thousand people whose body can't tolerate the metal pins, and you're one of them." Why wouldn't I be? If it's bad, I am sure to cop it. And that's why I fell when I was trying to cross the road behind Bondi Junction. I had to hang on to something; the wind was so strong. That's when I grabbed the sign – what else could I do? And it nearly cut my hand in two. It wasn't my fault, there was nothing else there to hang on to. The Council should be sued for putting up the sign and not having a rail or something to help people cross. They should do something about the wind too. How do they expect people to walk in such a dangerous place?'

'Mum, are you going to sign?'

She gives me a look to kill followed by a shake of her head.

'Why do you refuse to understand me? I have no choice, I can't live here any more. How do you expect me to be on my own when I keep on falling over? Do you want me to break *all* my bones? So.'

Her writing before the accident was neat, her letters rounded, all leaning in the same direction but without military precision. They had character, a dance to their neatness. Now she grits her teeth and with determination and supreme effort scrawls her just recognisable signature at the bottom of the page.

A decision is made, but I am not easy. I cannot see her in a home, eating when she's told, behaving as she should, being one of many. I suggest again, not for the first time, that she consider the alternatives. Get a carer to come daily. 'What happens if I fall during the night?' Get someone to live in the spare room. 'What, and you expect me to share the toilet with a stranger? No way.'

The paper is signed and that is that. Two weeks later there is a vacancy. I come to Sydney to help her pack 91 years of life and transport it to Montefiore Hostel. I look out the window of this fourth floor unit on Old South Head Road. My eyes cannot help but follow the large half-moon of Bondi Beach with its fine yellow sand and the infinite variety of blue hues of the sea and sky, interrupted by the odd high-rise. Expansive. Her new home will be a ground floor room, 2.6 x 5.0 metres. She will have only a tree in the courtyard to look at. We start packing in the kitchen.

'Mum, which of these cups do you want to take? Is this one coming?' I hold up a handmade celadon mug with the maker's stamp impressed into the clay.

'That? Ahhh … Your father gave that to me for my 53rd birthday, filled with cherry liqueur chocolates. The sweetest of sweets.'

My father or the chocolates?

'You know, we had such great times together. If I am feeling down, I go and read some of his letters. I can't be as terrible as you all think. He thought I was all right, *he* loved me so much. And I …'

Her grief throbs through the air, fills the kitchen.

'Mum, do you want to stop for a cuppa?'

'What, now? No. You know it's very easy nowadays. But you forget, during the War there was no coffee or tea, no nothing. I had to stand in a queue for hours just to get you …'

How *could* I remember? I was barely hatched during the War. I am sick of the War. Sick of her memories, sick of the repetitions, sick of the past, sick of buying into her pain.

'We have to get on with the packing,' I say matter-of-factly.

'OK, OK. Stop rushing me. I don't want to take the cutlery. I'll have no use for it there, it'll only be stolen. You take it. You know it's antique. I had it valued, and the man said he had not seen anything as beautiful as this for a long time. Lovely workmanship. It was a wedding present for your grandmother Gizka.'

'When was that?' I can't help but ask. I had swallowed the hook that will, again, drag me to the bottom of time.

'Oh, let me see. She was married in 1910.'

Then, realising I've trapped myself, I say, 'Mum, Mum, the packing. We have to finish it today.'

The stories keep on coming. At first the same one over and over until I am ready to scream; yet each telling brings a little more detail. Then others emerge as conversations roll into a story like marbles on a dimpled wooden board, randomly, without order, without connection, jumping from person to person, decade to decade.

'Yes, yes, I *got* that. But who said it? Your grandmother Ernestine or Róza?'

'You ask such stupid questions. How could it be Ernestine? She died when my mother was only two years old. If only just once in your life you would listen to what I say!'

'I don't want to hear, I don't want to know,' I mutter under my breath.

In the end she won; she always did, because it was easier that way. I started asking questions – who, when, where and why, especially why, and drew a timeline through the narrative as best I could.

2

BELLEVUE HILL, SYDNEY AND
PACKING FOR THE NURSING HOME

We start packing in the kitchen – the least memory-filled space – then ease our way through the apartment.

The flat at Bellevue Hill caught Erzsi's and Laci's eye in 1964. Even though it had only two small bedrooms, a tiny bathroom and an awkward kitchen, it boasted a spacious lounge and a sumptuous view. With the large picture windows and balcony the expansive outside felt like part of the little flat.

At first the idea of buying it was only wishful thinking. We could not afford it – but we *had* to have it, even if it meant taking on a second mortgage. Laci's job only paid a bit above the basic wage, Erzsi's was dismissed by the bank manager: after all, she was only a woman, a wife. Eventually we convinced him that *I* could repay it. He was dubious, but in the end, taking into consideration the security of my professional salary in a government job, he let us have the money.

On hearing the news we danced for joy. For the first year our furniture consisted of several tea chests and mattresses on the floor. We skimped on everything, ate simple food, walked everywhere to save on bus fares and bought no new clothes, but Erzsi ordered custom-made built-in cupboards. Laci spent weeks playing with ideas, designing every detail – the number of drawers and their size, the partitions inside, the handles, the desk in the study with its nooks for pens, envelopes, paper clips. Erzsi said she commissioned the best furniture maker in Sydney, Hungarian of course, to make it. The teak-veneered cupboards had a simple, no-fuss line, without handles or knobs but with large fancy keys for each door. The inside was finished with white timber polished to a high gloss. The doors emitted a reassuring 'sssshsssh' as they closed.

The few items Erzsi decides to take to the nursing home are packed. Now we stand in the lounge, in front of the opened wardrobe. She looks at the empty half

Erzsi with grandson David

and sighs – for the past 32 years it's been a daily reminder to her that Laci was gone, that she was alone.

As soon after his death as she could bring herself to, she gave away his clothes – with the exception of a few memory-laden items. An overcoat made for him when he was the newly appointed director of Hungarotex, a government export company, a pair of size 10½ brown hand-tooled leather shoes from one of his official trips to Turkey, half a dozen silk ties from Syria and a stack of hankies with his monogram, KL. These Erzsi kept until her only grandson, my son David, was old enough to wear them. Eighteen years after Laci died and David had been born, at the height of a retro fashion period, the clothes – David's only direct connection with his granddad – fitted him perfectly.

Now I stand awkwardly in front of the open doors. I had never been allowed to touch any of Erzsi's things. A long time ago, as a child, curiosity got the better of me once ... and she knew immediately. A large hanging space on the left is filled with skirts, shirts and frocks hung left to right in order of length. The tiptop order means grouping of skirts, winter and summer, blouses, long-sleeved to short-sleeved, and simple shirtmaker dresses. Everything washed, ironed and hung on its own matching coat-hanger. Truly Róza's granddaughter.

On the right are six shelves above five drawers. One drawer contains scarves sorted according to colour and size; another, her underwear. Erzsi had well-shaped, pert breasts that didn't need anything to hold them up for the first 60 years of her life, and after that, skimpy

Erzsi and Vera, 2002

bras sufficed. She packs her four bras, and her neatly folded undies, which have been placed on a piece of cardboard covered with pink taffeta and tied with a matching ribbon. She makes her selection of clothes – five skirts, ten blouses, all her sporty T-shirts, a couple of dresses and a light overcoat. She'll need some more formal clothes for mealtimes – it's expected.

The wardrobe's two halves will be empty soon. The whole flat, still filled with life and memories, will soon be reverberating with loss, with what was. What remains is the view of the ocean and the blue skies.

3

ERZSI'S STROKE AND GULYÁS SOUP

Though Erzsi had enjoyed good health for most of her life, after she hit her mid-70s she had her fair share of trouble. In 1991 she had a haemorrhagic stroke – a blood vessel burst and flooded her brain. Though she lay in a bed in St Vincent's Hospital and talked to me and sighed heavily, she was not there.

'Mum, what's wrong?' I asked.

'Oh, I don't know how I can finish this job.'

She seemed to be collapsing under the enormity of it all.

'What job? What do you have to do?'

'I have to paint it. This whole huge room.'

'You do?'

'Yes, it has to be all black.'

'Can you ask someone to help you?'

'I have to paint it all black. And the ceiling's so high. I don't know how I can reach it. Even this long ladder here is not going to reach. The ceiling has to be black. Oh, it's a huge job. I don't know if I can manage.'

'Have some rest first,' I tried to calm her. 'The painting can wait.'

'No, I have to finish it today. It has to be done now.'

Mercifully, she fell asleep.

They drained her brain the next day. On the door of the operating theatre there was a sign:

God give me the serenity to accept the things I cannot change,
the courage to change the things I can
and the wisdom to tell the difference.

I have seen this serenity prayer since, but it was most helpful this first time, on the door of a potential abyss.

The operation went well; the nurse said afterwards that Erzsi would recover, but to what extent nobody knew.

I returned the next day, anxious to see how she was. There was someone else in her bed. White-faced, I stood there, grief-stricken, motionless.

The other ladies in the room recognised me and started chirping. 'Oh, don't you worry, dear, your mum is OK! They took her to a different ward, where they can look after her better,' a friendly voice said from the other side of the room. 'The nurses only moved her because she fell as she tried to get up during the night to go to the toilet.' 'Yes, then the nurses even pulled up the railing around her bed, and she still tried to climb over it,' someone else added. 'She is very determined!'

Still recovering from the initial shock, I was a bit slow taking all this in. They saw my confusion and tried to reassure me.

'Your mum's a lovely lady! She's a real sweetie!'

Erzsi *is* very determined, and she is extremely particular about hygiene. But a sweetie?

'I am *Elizabeth's* daughter,' I said.

'Yes, yes, we know.' 'She'll be fine! Such a good eater, she'll get her strength back soon, you'll see!'

Now I was really worried. My mother is the fussiest eater I know: she eats little and complains a lot. This was not her. I thanked the ladies, wished them all a speedy recovery and raced off.

Erzsi was fast asleep on the second floor of the stroke unit. She looked peaceful and I didn't disturb her. The next day my son David and I went together. She was sitting up in bed eating cherries.

'How're you going, Mum? Someone brought you cherries? Aren't you lucky! They look delicious!'

'Yes, they are,' she agreed.

I didn't see her spit out the stones.

'Mum, you are swallowing the stones. You have to spit them out!'

'Oh, thank you, I didn't know there were any stones.'

I pitted the cherries for her. Noticing she wasn't wearing her hearing aids, I suggested she put them in.

'My hearing aid?' She looked confused. 'I don't think I have a hearing aid. I can hear you all right.'

Dinner arrived. The rissoles came with mash, mushy peas and gravy. She managed the food by herself, cleaning up the plate, making approving noises as she ate. She hated hospital food, and she never ate gravy.

'Was it OK, Grandma?' David asked.

'Yes, it was really nice, thank you. And now I am full.'

'Tea or coffee, Elizabeth?' the tea lady enquired.

I thought coffee would keep her awake. 'Have a cup of tea, Mum. It'll do you good.'

'You think so? OK.'

She enjoyed her drink, though normally she hated tea. Erzsi eagerly studied the menu for the next day's meal.

'*Stuffed capsicum with boiled potatoes.* Well, I don't think I'll have that today. *Lecsó.* Oh, I haven't had that for a long time. *Pasta squares with cabbage,* hmm … *Gulyás soup.* That's not my favourite.'

She was 'reading' a Hungarian menu in Hungarian. Noticing that she held the list upside down and was reading it without her glasses, I took it out of her hands and placed an order on her behalf.

'I am a little tired now,' she said, and immediately fell asleep.

Simple, normal conversations. No blaming, no criticising, no complaints. Easy, appreciative. Finally a glimpse of the lovely, beautiful person she must have been. Before communism, before me, before the War. I am glad David was a witness to this transformation.

We could hardly wait to see her the next day. And the next. It was nice spending time with my mother.

David joined me again on the third day.

'Oh, here you are!' she greeted us. 'It's about time too. I've been cooped up here all day by myself.'

'Sorry, Mum, we had to go to work. Anyway, how are you?'

There was no real need to ask, we already knew. 'Well, what do you expect?! You think I'm on top of the world? Fat chance! I had to go to the toilet and kept on buzzing, but nobody came. And I could hear the nurses outside just yakking away. That's all they do all day. I could die in here and they don't care, nobody cares.'

'We brought you some strawberries, they're washed already.'

'What was that? I can't hear you. You're always mumbling. And David's even worse.'

'Put in your hearing aid,' I suggested.

'Can't you see it's in already? I am really *severely* handicapped with my hearing and you can't seem to understand that. I tell you, don't ever get old, it's not worth it.'

I handed her the punnet.

'These? Thanks. Clara brought me some yesterday. They were A1 quality, large, really delicious. Did you buy yours at Harris Farm?'

I nodded.

'Were they on special? Clara bought hers from the Fruitologist on Bondi Road. They have the best. You know what? Take yours home. You have them tomorrow,' she said handing back the punnet.

'Will you have some tea?'

'You should know I don't drink tea. And the coffee – acchh! It tastes like dishwater.'

David and I smiled at each other across the bed. Erzsi was back.

* * *

Ten years later, when I started gathering stories for this book, I wondered: did Erzsi time travel to her grandmother Róza's restaurant? In the days after her stroke, which were difficult for both of us, she became a beautiful, happy, agreeable person. Was that what she was like as a little girl?

4

THE HÁBER FAMILY: RÓZA, IGNÁCZ AND THE BOYS

Both Róza and her husband Ignácz Háber's families were well-to-do wheat farmers, born in the right place and at the right time. In Poland and Tsarist Russia, Jews were forced to live in their own towns – *shtetls* – separate from the rest of the population, and were regularly threatened by pogroms.[1] Hungary was different because of a unique dilemma.

When the lands that became Hungary were ruled in the 9th century by the Magyars, all the many conquered nations were allowed to stay and to keep their traditions and languages. A thousand years later most of the ethnic groups were strongly agitating for independence, and the Magyar aristocrats felt threatened.

In 1867, Hungary and Austria reached a compromise and the Austro-Hungarian Empire was born. It was to have a common emperor/king in Franz Josef, share foreign policy and an army, but otherwise both countries would remain independent. The Jews were

Ignácz Háber, circa 1901

assured of full citizenship and, for the first time ever in Hungary, were allowed to own land. So now in the Jewish population there was a minority who truly

---

1   A pogrom is an organised massacre of an ethnic group. They were carried out in particular on the Jews in Russia and Eastern Europe.

Róza, circa 1873

considered themselves to be Magyars, and with their support, the otherwise small number of original Magyars now became a majority – and were able to hang on to power.

Both Róza's and Ignácz's families prospered under this arrangement and, in turn, were grateful to belong. In fact Róza's family, together with some other wealthy Jews, were ennobled, and became known as Dunai-Fritz, coupling their German family name with the Hungarian Dunai, meaning 'by the Danube'. The Hábers' feet were anchored in the soil, and they wanted to be nowhere else in the world. Hungary was their paradise.

Róza and Ignácz had three sons. Ignácz ran a strict household, with the expectation that children were seen not heard, especially at the dinner table. Here they had to sit up straight and eat in silence: proper table manners were imperative. Róza attempted to soften the harshness imposed by her husband with her wonderful cooking.

On one occasion she made an elaborate dinner, the oldest boy's favourite, as a reward for his having been praised by his teacher: she cooked roast goose, crispy oven-baked potatoes and cucumber salad. While the four men sat at the table in silent anticipation, Róza dished up the food, but she inadvertently overlooked the very child who was being celebrated. As usual the family ate in silence. After the meal she beamed, 'So, how was it, son, did you like it?' expecting an appreciative compliment.

The Háber family. Bela, Róza, Ignácz and Ferike in the front, circa 1889

Instead, the boy muttered that he had missed out on the goose. It's hard to know who felt worse, mother or son.

Not long after this incident tragedy struck the family: the boy died of an infection. Soon after, the youngest son, Ferike, was taunted by friends to swim across the Danube. Although a strong swimmer, he felt intimidated. Nevertheless, he took on the challenge. However, the river was freezing, and within days he caught a severe cold that turned into pneumonia. With no available medication at the time, and aged only 16, Ferike died too.

Their one surviving son, Béla, would become Erzsi's father.

Béla was privileged to finish high school and matriculate. His favourite subject was Maths – like others in the family, he excelled at it. At the time, education past the three Rs was not considered important for girls at all; for boys it was a privilege, not a right. To get into high school a student needed the ability – and some hard work – to pass the entrance exams, as well as the substantial fees. In return, the standard of education was high. The peasants could not see the sense of sitting in a classroom; nor could they spare their boys from work on the farm. For most, one or two years of primary school, mostly provided by the church, was their fill. They were usually semi-literate at best.

Although Ignácz was strict with the boys, he himself gave in to temptation. He was very fond of travel, though his itineraries remain a mystery. He simply disappeared for a while, never taking his wife or family with him, nor discussing his travels with anyone. Although he had inherited quite a large estate, by the time he died, at the age of 56, there was hardly any money left – all had been spent on seeing the world.

'Do you think he had a mistress?' I asked Erzsi.

She blushed, stumped for words. It seemed the idea had not occurred to her.

When Ignácz died, the widowed Róza decided that her skills as a cook and a businesswoman would help them survive. She bought the restaurant at Lipótvár railway station.

Lipótvár was a main rail junction and a transit stop for travellers, and while waiting for their connection many took refreshments or dined at Róza's restaurant. She had a large staff to ensure that patrons were served quickly and could catch their connecting trains; it was the 'fast food' restaurant of its day. On her menu were *Gulyás* soup, Hungary's national dish, a hearty meat soup with potatoes, onions and paprika, *lecsó*, and *stuffed capsicums*. All this was followed by delicious, rich homemade cakes and good strong coffee. The restaurant thrived. One guest in particular left a memorable impression.

The Habsburg Emperor of Austria and King of Hungary, Franz Josef, chose to take his refreshments in Róza's establishment when he travelled through Lipótvár. Róza cooked the meal herself, but neither she nor her staff were allowed to serve it: only those in the emperor's entourage had permission to approach him. However, after the meal, he made a point of congratulating the cook, Róza. In that moment, she became a confirmed royalist, and in the afterglow of the compliment decided to name her not-yet-born grandchildren after the imperial couple, Ferenc (Franz) and Erzsébet (Elisabeth).

The Habsburgs generally were not liked. They were the foreign oppressors, and this latest emperor was no exception. Yet, in time, he became highly respected because of his reliability, strong work ethic and austere lifestyle. The Jewish people were grateful to him as he allowed them to own land, to conduct business – to thrive. But above all, Róza's generation embraced in their hearts the beautiful, sad, eccentric Queen Elisabeth, known to all as Sisi. She had lost her first daughter at a young age and her son, Crown Prince Rudolf, committed suicide (or was murdered) in 1889. To show their compassion, many named their daughters Gizella after the couple's eldest surviving daughter. When Sisi herself was murdered in 1898 the nation grieved with the Emperor.[2]

* * *

The emperor's visit to Róza's restaurant took place only a few years before the unleashing of further, this time international, tragedies. When Archduke Franz Ferdinand, Royal Prince of Hungary, was assassinated in June 1914 by Serb nationalists, it was to honour the Austro-Hungarian compromise of 1867 that the reluctant Hungary, at the time an 'eternal friend' of Serbia, was drawn into World War I.

2 My paternal grandmother, Cina, told me with great nostalgia that she once saw the imperial couple in their carriage on the streets of Budapest. It was the highlight of her young life.

5

ERZSI THE ADVENTURER

In the mid-1800s most of the Eisenbergs, the maternal side of Erzsi's family, lived in or near the town of Pozsony, which had been the political centre of Hungary (now it is known as Bratislava and is in Slovakia). In 1873 the towns of Buda, Pest and Óbuda were amalgamated and formed the new capital of Hungary, Budapest.

Ernestine Eisenberg

The Eisenberg family was rather large by today's standards. They lived in *Felvidék*, the 'Upcountry', in northern Hungary. Erzsi's maternal grandparents, Adolf and Ernestine Eisenberg, had 14 children, of whom eight reached adulthood: two boys and six girls. Ernestine, exhausted by the yearly pregnancies, died at the age of 34. Erzsi's Auntie Stefka and mother Gizka were the two youngest daughters. They did not know their mother at all, being only one and two years old when she died.

After the death of Ernestine, Adolf married Cecilia, a spinster, who took on the care and upbringing of the children. She was both kind and very strict, according to Erzsi, and quite distant. To Erzsi she was simply 'Grandmother'. Erzsi only met her grandfather a few times, but treasured the gold bracelet he gave her on her eighth birthday, in 1921. A year later Adolf died, ignorant of the shivers his given name would send down millions of spines a few years later.

Erzsi's parents, Gizka Eisenberg and Béla Háber, were married in 1910. Gizka's present from her mother-in-law, Róza, was an 144-piece silver cutlery

Eisenberg family, 1903. Adolf on the left, Stefka third girl from the left, Gizka third from the right

set, which included not only a 12-piece service for eight but serving implements with genuine ivory handles.

A year after the wedding Feri was born, at Vágújhely, and two years later, on 13 October 1913, Erzsi surfaced, at Lipótvár. Her mother, Gizka, was a 13th child and the newborn was the 13th grandchild of Cecilia, her maternal step-grandmother. When the old lady realised that Erzsi had 13 letters in her maiden name, Háber Erzsébet, it was all too much, and she registered the birth for the following day. But fate won't be cheated so easily. According to tradition, Erzsi's celebration was always on the 13th, the night before her official birthday.

Gizka, Béla and the two children now moved in with Róza at her restaurant. The two women got along well. Gizka was busy helping to run the restaurant, and looked after the children by herself at first, but later, as was the custom, she hired a German nanny-cum-governess. The Fräulein, who was addressed only by that title, arrived in early 1915, when Feri was three and a half. On being introduced, Feri clicked his heels together, bowed deeply from the waist and, like a young gentleman, introduced himself with serious politeness, 'I am Ferenc Háber,' he said.

Erzsi took one look at the woman, and although she could barely talk yet, lisped, 'I don't want no Fräulein, the thilly Fräulein can go to hell.'

The Fräulein stayed with the family for the next five years.

Erzsi was an adventurer from the moment her feet touched the ground, happy as long as there were people around, space for her to explore and animals to play with. She needed little attention from the Fräulein, and the less she had the happier she was. Being the younger sibling and a girl, no academic expectations were placed on her. Unlike her brother Feri, she never felt the back of a hand – her harshest punishment was being chastised verbally or, in serious cases, not being allowed to go outdoors. She led a charmed life, and in turn, charmed everyone around her.

In the restaurant Erzsi was surrounded by her family, the kitchen staff and Róza's customers. Yet she could also find her own entertainment. Sometimes, a deck of playing cards in hand, she might accost passers-by, innocently minding their own business, and ask if they could play Rummy. A 'yes' meant an invitation to a game; 'no' was met with an offer to teach them. Her victims adored the clever and cute little girl, but if, out of misguided concern for her safety, one would report her to her mother, Erzsi got into trouble. Not for walking on the street by herself, but for pestering strangers. They were safe and happy times.

Meanwhile, Hungary was stuck in feudalism, even as the rest of Europe was beginning to be industrialised. Modernisation was necessary, inevitable, but seemed elusive. The aristocrats owned the land and held the power, but mostly lived the good life at court in Vienna. The gentry ran the country's political life and public administration – anything else was beneath them.

So again the answer was found in the freshly accepted Jews, who would form the new middle class. This status suited them well, as they had always valued education as well as trade. It was the Jews who would be the new doctors, lawyers, teachers, writers, clerks, bankers, factory and even property owners. They would fulfil the roles that the upper crust did not want and the peasants had no education for. In return, the Jews were expected to be good citizens: pay taxes, fight for their country and preferably shed much of their Jewishness. Both sides of Erzsi's family embraced this. They Germanised their name, and as far back as the mid-19th century, all four of Erzsi's grandparents spoke only Hungarian or German. None used Yiddish.

Béla saw himself as a typical middle-class gentleman. In 1915 he bought a property at Mosonújfalu in the north-western corner of Hungary and the Háber family moved there. Although Grandmother Róza continued to run the restaurant in Lipótvár, they saw each other often.

*　　*　　*

Gizka did most of her shopping in Vienna, a large, cosmopolitan city with everything her heart and soul desired, or Pozsony, which, while not as glamorous, was close to the rest of the Eisenberg family and to a good gossip. On one of her trips Gizka bought her daughter a pretty white batiste pinafore with large pockets.

On one visit to her grandmother Erzsi discovered a puddle full of frogs while playing near the station. She filled her new apron pockets with the croaky little creatures, eager to share her discovery, and ran back to the house. 'Look what I have, look!' she enthused as she let them loose in the kitchen – and was most surprised that the maids and patrons showed no delight in her new-found friends. Rather, they squealed and vacated the premises, quickly. The little girl was duly punished.

One rainy summer's day, Erzsi came across a shallow duck pond tucked away in the back of the yard. She immediately fell in love with the ducks and joined them – the best way to get to know them, she thought.

The property at Mosonújfalu was sizeable, with a generous single-storey house. One day two carthorses were standing right against the building. Inside, eye-to-eye with the horses, was the young Erzsi, who could not let such an opportunity slip by. She wriggled through a hole in a nearby window, ready to sit atop one of the horses. Instead, she fell flat on her face under it. Luckily, the well-trained, docile animal did not move and Erzsi scrambled out safely, but she then bore the punishment of not being allowed outside for the rest of the day.

When not running around the yard, Erzsi was learning from her grandmother how to sew and embroider, and it wasn't long before she put this skill to good use. She loved all things small. She had been given a miniature porcelain doll – with moving parts but no clothes – by one of Róza regulars at the restaurant. For the sake of modesty, Erzsi painstakingly sewed a complete outfit for her tiny new friend.

Róza liked everything spic and span and in its right place. Erzsi, just like her grandmother, noticed that indeed, a button had fallen off the old lady's cardigan. She decided to fix it. She fossicked through Róza's large biscuit tin full of buttons. The young girl was bewitched by a *very* special one – a white, shimmering mother-of-pearl button. Whichever way she looked at it she could see the colours of the rainbow dancing in it. This is what she chose, and Róza proudly wore the black cardigan with the one white pearly button until she died, a year later.

6

THE COLOURED TERRORS – RED AND WHITE

Life hummed along peacefully in Mosonújfalu for a while. Béla took care of the management of the property, Gizka of the household and the children; Feri read books and Erzsi found herself in trouble, constantly. All was well.

They regularly spent time with Róza and with the Eisenberg aunts and uncle, but most evenings they invited the two local dignitaries to their home. Gizka was an excellent cook; nearly every night the priest and the notary came to dinner, washing it down with a glass or two of good wine. There was talk of politics or social chit-chat and the Hábers and their frequent guests became close friends.

Béla was so patriotic to Hungary that if ever questioned, he declared, 'I'd rather work in a Hungarian quarry breaking stones than sit in a plush velvet chair in Slovakia.' He was fluent in German and Hungarian, but had trouble with Slovakian, though he tried to honour his guests by speaking in their native tongue. He ushered in his friend the judge with utmost deference, greeting him with, 'You, get in here!' while he growled at his dog Lumpi, forever under his feet, 'Sir, would you please kindly go away!' The judge made allowances for Béla's linguistic shortcomings.

The children of landowners were permitted to not attend school; the Háber children, accordingly, were home educated by the Fräulein. However, an end-of-year school report was still needed. Erzsi sat on the priest's knee while he asked relevant questions, then the notary signed the report card.

The Hábers were happy and content. The Empire became a great power in Europe – unbeatable, they thought – and yet Hungary dreamt of expanding further, trying to gain ports in the Baltic Sea. The 1914 war gave them an opportunity to achieve this, and they pushed north. Erzsi's Uncle Lajos lost his life fighting, leaving behind a wife and three children.

The losses were great and progress was slow, and within a few months everybody just wanted peace. The war continued for another three years, and when it ended, different 'fun and games' began.

In January 1919, Prime Minister Mihály Károlyi declared a republic and ordered all Hungarian troops to lay down their arms and return home. With the country undefended, the Czech army occupied the Upcountry where the Eisenbergs lived, the Serbians claimed the occupied southern parts, and the Romanian Army advanced into Hungary from the east, taking agricultural machinery, train carriages and trucks back to Romania. In that same year, in this undefended chaos, Béla Kun and his troops overthrew the government and set up a 'dictatorship of the proletariat'.

Kun had been captured during the war by the Soviets and 're-educated' in communist ideology and practices. He was part Jewish, fully embraced Bolshevism and was in direct contact with Lenin. After the Russian Revolution he was sent to Hungary to spread the Soviet message. The communists promised utopia – equality for all, no discrimination, no more exploitation. Their ideology appealed to many Jewish people, who, over the millennia, had never fully belonged or been treated as equals.

The Hábers were not so enamoured of these ideas. The ideology was sweet, but for many the reality was different. In the four months of his government Kun alienated the majority of Hungarians and turned their world upside down. The peasants were now empowered, but had not been given land – which was all they wanted. Private property was socialised, redistributed to the government and those with private assets were collectively labelled 'the bourgeoisie' and demoted to the bottom of the pecking order. The government took all large factories and mines; later, financial institutions and even homes were taken, with no compensation paid to the original owners.

When the Romanian army invaded, Kun was forced to flee to Vienna. His short reign had been a maelstrom, later aptly dubbed the 'Red Terror'.

Communist rule cost grandmother Róza her life. Ill with a kidney infection, she had been taken to hospital, but was refused treatment because she was 'bourgeois'. The family took her to Gizka's place in Mosonújfalu but she died within a week. Many people, family and friends, came to her funeral. Erzsi, who was only six years old, enjoyed the 'party', the hustle-bustle of the household, the good food. Afterwards, her mother severely admonished her for her light-hearted behaviour.

A new government was soon formed, but it was not right-wing enough for many, and in August 1919 anti-revolutionaries formed a new extreme right-wing government with the support of the Habsburg monarchy. They managed to reverse the communist policies – and this time jails overflowed with factory workers, peasants and intellectuals. Hundreds of teachers, lecturers and clerks were dismissed from their jobs, and many, together with leading artists, scientists and writers, left Hungary. However, the victors of the war, the Entente, did not recognise this government, as they wanted to neutralise the power of the former Austro-Hungarian Empire.

And there was more upheaval to come. Horthy, the admiral of the Royal Hungarian Navy, formed an independent government at Szeged, in eastern Hungary. His troops terrorised the countryside, lynched and tortured ex-Red Army soldiers and many Jews, regardless of whether or not they had supported the Kun regime. On 16 November 1919 Admiral Horthy famously rode into Budapest on a white stallion; his rule of terror, overseen by his cronies, Pál Prónay and Iván Héjjas, known as the 'White Terror', extended into the 1920s.

To further complicate matters, Franz Josef died in 1916. The new Habsburg Emperor, Karl I, had decided to not interfere in state matters, but did not abdicate, so Hungary officially remained a kingdom, but the king refused to rule. Horthy promptly declared himself Regent of Hungary and appointed a Prime Minister. A stable right-wing government was formed – this one was acceptable to the Entente.

The World War I peace terms were delivered at Trianon in France in 1920. There was no question of negotiations, and the Hungarian delegation, held under house arrest in Paris, was required to accept the terms as they stood. They were harsh. Hungary lost two-thirds of her territory: half of her total population – one-third of her Hungarian-speaking people – were now within the borders of Romania to the east, the newly created Czechoslovakia in the north and Serbia (joined with other Slavic nations and later named Yugoslavia) in the south. Even Austria, Hungary's ally, received a chunk of Hungarian land.

Hungary also lost much of its industrial areas and mines, as well as some of its best agricultural lands. The economy was a shambles, with very high inflation; there were devastating shortages of food, petrol, coal and wood for heating. The influx of Hungarians from other, now occupied parts of what had historically been Hungary made matters more dire: they had no jobs, nowhere to live and no food to eat.

All this spelled the end of the Hábers' bucolic life. Their property, first threatened under communism, was now again at risk. But now, under the pogroms of the White Terror, their lives were threatened as well. In the first few weeks of Horthy's ascendancy, hundreds, even thousands, of people, half of them Jewish, were brutally executed.

The only two Jewish families in Mosonújfalu were the Hábers and the elderly couple who owned the corner shop (who were generally disliked by the locals). As the White Terrorists swept into town, the couple hid in the shop's cellar. Within a short time, they were found, taken to the yard and, at the barrel of a gun, made to dig a deep ditch and climb into it. They were covered with soil up to their necks, had honey poured over their heads and were left to die.

It isn't clear whether the young Erzsi saw any of this or overheard people talking about it, but from that time she suffered nightmares and had an abiding horror of being buried alive.

The Hábers were well liked in the community. Their close friend, the Catholic priest, appreciated the seriousness of their situation far earlier than they did. In the dead of night, at great risk to himself, he bundled the whole family into his car and drove them to Szombathely, on the Austrian border, where they were safe for the time being. The family stayed there a night or two before sending the two children with the Fräulein to relatives near Budapest who had a two-bedroom flat with no room for three extra bodies.

The house guests Feri, Erzsi and the Fräulein, slept on the floor, the little girl and the governess sharing a mattress. Erzsi could not understand the sudden departure; she missed her mother and was anxious in a strange place with strange people. In her distress she wet the bed, and stayed awake all night, ashamed and worried, desperately trying to dry the sheets by lying on the wet spots.

After a few days, the family moved to Budapest, to the home of Gizka's sister, Auntie Stefka, and Uncle Feri. When it was safe enough, Gizka and Béla returned to the estate at Mosonújfalu to sort out their affairs. Although most was lost, they managed to salvage some possessions. Within a few months they lost their town, too, as with the change of borders Mosonújfalu became part of Austria. On their return to Budapest in 1919 or 1920, Gizka and Béla moved in with Auntie Stefka, at 13a Visegrádi Street.

The apartment was not big enough for everybody. The Hábers were now broke and could not afford a place of their own. A few months later Auntie Stefka and Uncle Feri went to live in Zagreb (in Yugoslavia), where Feri leased a large forest plantation not far from the city. The Hábers stayed in Budapest, and a new and different chapter in their life started.

*   *   *

History is strange. What at the time is a horrific experience of upheaval and trauma can turn out to be a lifesaver. The forced move from Mosonújfalu to Budapest saved the family's life 25 years later.

7

LIFE IN BUDAPEST BEFORE 1942

At first, the Fräulein had her hands full with Feri. She felt he often needed to be smacked and she did not shy away from the task. He was not an exemplary student, as he regularly forgot to do his homework – his mind was on other things. Unlike Erzsi, he was an introverted indoor child, a loner.

As the family could no longer afford a full-time governess, the Fräulein was dismissed and Feri started formal schooling in a gymnasium (middle school, for 10 to 18-year-olds). It was not to his liking, but Béla was determined that his son continue his education. School was important for a boy. In the harsh years after the war and pogroms, any boy called up for service without a matriculation would be doing latrine duty or some other lowly job. In those days the life

Erzsi and Feri

of a private was expendable; that of a Jewish private even more so. But with matriculation papers, Feri would become a commissioned officer and have a much better chance of survival.

To help him along, Gizka employed a private tutor. This worthy educator also believed that knowledge was best belted into children, and from then on the boy was the regular recipient of corporal punishment. It appeared to be with his mother's blessing. Erzsi couldn't bear to listen, but couldn't make the beatings stop. She crouched in the doorway, whimpering, hitting the door in frustration and sympathy.

Erzsi also started school. Unlike her brother, she loved it. She wasn't an able student but she made up for that with diligence. When asked to memorise two verses of a poem, Erzsi learnt the whole piece. She had learnt German from the Fräulein and came top of her class. There were no academic expectations of Erzsi, and she was not only spoilt at home, but was also the teacher's pet.

As Hungary was still in the aftermath of Trianon, each morning Erzsi's classes started with a recitation of a nationalistic rhyme:

Csonka Magyarország nem ország,	Mutilated Hungary, no country at all,
Egész Magyarország mennyország!	Complete Hungary – heaven!

The names of Hungary's rivers were memorised through another ditty, despite the fact that by the time Erzsi went to school neither the Dráva nor the Száva was part of Hungary:

Duna, Tisza, Dráva, Száva	Danube, Tisa, Drava, Sava
Törjön ki a lábad szára!	Break your leg!

Hungarian nationalism remained fierce, and the losses at Trianon, now a *fait accompli*, were mourned for the next two decades by flags being flown at half-mast.

＊　　　＊　　　＊

Auntie Stefka's spacious three-bedroom unit in Budapest was a prestigious place to live. It had a massive mahogany dining table and exquisite oriental rugs that Erzsi loved. The main rooms faced the street – significant because facing the street had a higher social status than looking onto the courtyard. All were aware of their place in this myriad-layered society; all made sure everybody else knew it too.

In the late 1920s, Gizka and Béla often travelled to Yugoslavia while the children were in the care of their live-in maid, Panni. She and other maids kept each other company in the evenings and swapped horror stories. With Feri in his room early reading a book, Erzsi made herself invisible, playing silently with a doll in a corner. One night it was Panni's turn to tell a story and it scared young Erzsi out of her wits. She had nightmares and snuggled into Panni's bed for safety. From that day on Erzsi was too afraid to go to the bathroom by herself, and when everybody was busy, she waited for ages before she was able to relieve herself.

A couple of years after they arrived in Budapest, Gizka's father, Adolf, died and left a large timber yard in Vágújhely to his wife and children. The only surviving Eisenberg son, Ödön, paid out his siblings and took over the running of it. Erzsi didn't think her uncle particularly bright, yet under his management the business flourished and he became a wealthy man: he paid more tax than anyone else in the district, which was significant because those who paid no tax were not permitted to vote. Having not long ago lost their own property at Mosonújfalu, the inheritance was well timed for Gizka and Béla, and through Auntie Stefka's generosity – she had no children and no need of the money – they received her share as well.

Once the terror abated, Horthy became a popular leader and remained in power for the next 24 years. His main objective, in line with the desire of most Hungarians, was to revise the Treaty of Trianon. This position meant an increasing cooperation with Germany, despite Horthy's mistrust of Hitler. Although the Horthy regime's initial aggressively antisemitic position was gradually moderated, the position of Jews in Hungary changed dramatically – the 'good old days' were over.

The more successful the Jews became, the harsher the resentment of them, and so the more they felt compelled to assimilate and to perform. They became over-educated, urbanised; they stopped going to synagogue – some even converted to Christianity.

And meanwhile, as part of the rise of Hungarian nationalism, the Magyars became increasingly outraged that the Jews were obstructing their progress by 'usurping' jobs that they, the Magyars, 'deserved'. Antisemitism increased, and within 30 years led to the large-scale denunciations made during the Holocaust.

And yet, during the entire time of the Hungarian regime, most Jews displayed an unshakeable loyalty to the country, including supporting the alliance with Germany to regain the pre-Trianon lands.

Even after Hitler's rise to power in 1933, when newspapers reported the fate of the German Jews, a Jewish leader confidently asserted that such horror could never happen in Hungary. Most Jews agreed. Throughout the Horthy era the Hungarian Jews utterly denied the reality of their situation.

8

HOLIDAYS IN SLOVAKIA AND YUGOSLAVIA; THE CONQUEST OF HUNGARY

The two Háber children regularly stayed with the Eisenbergs in the Upcountry. When Erzsi and Feri went on their own, they were under strict instructions to treat all the aunties equally. Lajos, the first-born Eisenberg son, died as a soldier in World War I, so Erzsi did not know him, but she liked his widow, Palka, best; their children, Ellus and Gyuszi, were her favourite cousins. Erzsi would pay a whirlwind visit to all her relatives and then, against her mother's wishes, travel to her Auntie Palka's to spend the rest of the holidays.

Erzsi's lack of appetite was a constant source of worry and discussion for the family, but only Auntie Palka could fatten her up, which she did with thick slices of home-made bread well spread with goose fat and sprinkled with paprika and salt. It was not a time when one worried about high cholesterol levels. Palka was the envy of all the other aunts in this, and the 'battle' to entice Erzsi to eat fed the healthy sibling rivalry among the Eisenberg sisters.

Lard and goose or chicken fat were the only fats Hungarian cooks used. Every household rendered fat for its own use and kept it in large enamelled pots or metal buckets in the pantry, to be consumed throughout the year. While the fat was still hot, all the children clamoured for the fresh crackling, which they ate with a good sprinkling of salt on a thick slice of potato bread. But it was the liver of the goose which was most prized, cooked in the rendered fat and eaten in thin slices on bread with salt and paprika, the Hungarian way.

*   *   *

Erzsi's other favourite relatives were Auntie Berta and Uncle Nándor. Uncle Nándor was born in Romania. The Hungarians said of the Romanians that they 'don't travel on straight roads', a reference not only to the mountainous terrain of Transylvania.

They had two children, Pali and Enka. Erzsi didn't much care for Pali's company, but a tall and handsome friend of his, who happened to be the son of the mayor of Pozsony, caught her attention. She was attracted to him, mainly because he owned a motorcar – rare in the 1930s. One day he invited her to go on a little trip. She asked no questions and accepted with relish – his wink indicated that it was going to be a fun ride. Off they went.

He sped up the country roads, through villages and then back again. No thought of speed limits. It was a hairy drive because the roads were unsurfaced, and roughly built – for horse-drawn carts – but Erzsi found it thrilling.

When they arrived back, Nándor was darkly waiting in the doorway. He gave them the third degree. By Nándor's reckoning this long trip had been done in too short a time and Erzsi was in trouble – she was not allowed out for the rest of her stay.

As she grew into her teenage years Erzsi showed a natural talent for sports. She was slightly built, light on her feet, well balanced and strong. She excelled at gymnastics, rowing, and she taught herself to swim.

When she was 17, it was agreed that Erzsi was old enough to wear lipstick. All her friends had shiny red lips, in line with the latest fashion, but Erzsi had only a borrowed matte lipstick. She didn't want to be left out and improvised by painting nail varnish on top of the lipstick. She achieved the desired effect, but with a slight drawback – she could hardly open her mouth, let alone smile or laugh. The other girls made up for this – they laughed heartily at her expense.

*   *   *

Feri Neumann, Stefka's husband, a short, slight man with a red nose and a great sense of humour, was born near the Russian border. He had a good head for business, was prudent with his investments and loved luxury – once he returned from a business trip with six made-to-measure pure silk shirts and six pairs of silk underpants.

When he had money to spare he deposited the cash in Swiss banks in his and his wife's names, and later he did the same for his favourite niece and nephew. None of this money was recovered after the War.

Feri's business ventures included leasing an estate, which included a forest, from an earl in Moslavina-Popovac. He managed three large oak plantations in the area and in Drenovac. These were so large and important for the economy – 350 men were employed – that the government built a narrow-gauge railway to transport the timber. The trees were used to make charcoal, which is as much a science as an art. Feri employed the expertise of the neighbouring Bosnians, who always arrived with their families in tow. Each forest supplied timber for five to six years, with strict regulations controlling their management.

The Hábers visited regularly and stayed for long periods. The house was befittingly grand (for an earl) and situated atop a hill, with large gardens sloping away on all sides. A plaster crown, complete with coat-of-arms, sat on top of the roof.

In the gardens were apple, pear and plum trees, bursting with fruit in season. Erzsi spent summer afternoons nestled high up in the fork of the greengage plum tree grazing on the small tasty plums. While she had no great appetite for food, fruit didn't qualify as such in her mind and she ate her fill at every opportunity.

The house was often full. Auntie Stefka regularly had up to twenty for lunch,

the main meal of the day. The large kitchen opened onto a spacious terrace and food was served by the kitchen staff. The children ate first at a separate table. The household dogs, goose and hen invariably jostled for a spot near Erzsi, but the cat sat snobbishly at a distance. Most of Erzsi's meal 'accidentally' fell off the table, and was eagerly vacuumed up by her forever-willing attendants. This worked for all – the animals benefited and Erzsi could show her

Auntie Stefka, Uncle Feri, Gizka and Erzsi on the Dalmatian coast, circa 1933

shiny, licked-clean plate to the adults.

Uncle Feri adored Erzsi, and spoilt her to bits. To help her digestion, every lunchtime he would give her a tot of his special, extra strong and excellent plum brandy, Silvorium, from the locked Wertheim cupboard no one was allowed to touch. She was also the object of Feri's tricks. The family grew most of their own vegetables, including an unusual variety of peppers, the size and colour of cherries, and wickedly hot. Feri once put a bit of it in his niece's soup to 'strengthen her up'. But come what may, each night she managed to wriggle her way into the middle of the large feather-down bed between her aunt and uncle, where she slept soundly.

It was in Yugoslavia that young Erzsi had her first crush. It was Feri's driver, Anton Stokan, formerly employed by the Serbian Minister of War, who was the object of young Erzsi's attention. He routinely chauffeured her around, treating her like a princess, which of course appealed to the 13-year-old girl, but her love for the lovely Buick he drove was even greater.

Erzsi's cousin, Enka Haas, often stayed with them on holidays at Crikvenica in Yugoslavia. The two girls were of a similar age, and fought constantly. Both were born in the Upcountry, but with the new borders, Enka lived in Slovakia and Erzsi ended up in Hungary.

Enka insisted on speaking only Slovakian, which Erzsi couldn't understand – she felt she was truly Hungarian. But when the Hungarians did well in the 1924 Olympics, things changed, and the entire Slovakian branch of the family conveniently remembered their Hungarian origins. To Enka's chagrin Hungary improved at each Olympics and the gap between the achievements of the two countries increased. In 1932, Hungary came 6th and Czechoslovakia 17th. For the duration of those Games, Enka declared herself proud to be Erzsi's cousin.

In 1936, the 'friendly' rivalry had a different face. The 'Nazi Games', held in Berlin, were a political exercise in tolerance. Germany temporarily put aside its Aryan agenda – antisemitic, anti-gypsy, anti-black. Hungary came third after Germany and the US. Thirteen Jews won medals that year, including six from Hungary – for water polo, wrestling, fencing and high jump. Unfortunately, by that time Uncle Feri had died and the Yugoslav holidays were a thing of the past.

But as long as the these holidays lasted, the two girls continued to argue. One point of contention was the story of the conquest of Hungary. In 895 AD Árpád the Conqueror arrived at the court of Svatopluk, the king of the Moravians, and tricked him into giving up the land.

Enka argued that Árpád was unfair and greedy, while Erzsi maintained that Svatopluk was incredibly stupid to allow himself to be tricked into such a bargain. The girls fought so fiercely they drew blood. The legend, as told in Hungary, may have helped their dispute.

The Story of the Conquest

All kinds of people lived on this land a thousand years ago, when our conquering ancestors arrived here. But the only ones that had to be reckoned with were the Moravians and the Bulgarians. The Hungarian chief, Árpád, quickly dealt with the Bulgarians, and then he tackled Svatopluk. He sent the ruler a white stallion with a diamond-studded bridle and a golden saddle. The king of the Moravians was delighted with the presents and asked if the chief wanted anything in return.

'My chief does not want anything at all,' the envoy replied, 'only a canteen of water from the river, a handful of earth from yonder fields and a few blades of grass from this beautiful green meadow.'

Svatopluk was delighted with the swap. 'Tell your chief that I have accepted his presents gladly. I see that he wishes to be my dutiful servant.'

'I will tell him, Sire,' smiled the messenger and rode away.

However, he returned soon after.

'What did you bring this time?' asked the King curiously.

'I am bringing you a message from the chief of the Hungarians. He wants you to clear off his land immediately, now that you've sold it to him.'

'How have I sold it to him?'

'We bought it from you in exchange for the white stallion with the diamond-studded bridle and the golden saddle.'

The Moravian king became angry and shouted, 'I'll have the stallion killed, the golden saddle hurled into the river and the diamond-studded bridle hidden in tall grass.'

'It makes no difference. Our dogs will eat the dead horse's flesh, our fishermen will fish out the golden saddle and our brave warriors will find the diamond-studded bridle in the grass.'

At that the Moravian king blew his horn, but no one came to his assistance – his men had already been scattered by Árpád like hay in a whirlwind, and the Hungarians moved in unopposed.

Árpád not only conquered the land for his people; he also imposed laws so that he could govern it well. He held the first Parliament at Pusztaszer Plains, and divided the land among the conquerors according to their merit. This is how the Hungarian nobility's claims were born and this is how they became all powerful and remained so for the next 1000 years.

*   *   *

Uncle Feri was building a six-storey block of units in Sziget Street in Budapest, and it was left to Gizka to supervise the construction. She was on the site every day and made sure that the concrete was properly mixed, that no short-cuts were taken. Sziget Street was in an elegant, fashionable area on the shore of the Danube, opposite Margaret Island; it was a ten-minute walk to the centre of the city and the building suited the site. Some of the units sold for a good price, some were rented, mostly to non-Jews. The Neumanns kept one of the best flats on the top (sixth) floor, as a place where they could stay when in Budapest.

In 1933 both Béla and Uncle Feri died – within three months of each other. Gizka and Stefka, the two youngest Eisenberg girls, became widows together. They moved into the sixth floor apartment and remained there for the rest of their lives, taking care of each other.

On 30 January of that same year, 1933, Hitler was appointed Chancellor of Germany. In March, the first concentration camp, for sympathisers of the left, communists and other undesirables, was constructed, outside Berlin. A decree abolished freedom of speech and the privacy of telephone calls and mail. The police, meanwhile, were given unrestricted rights of search, access, confiscation and arrest. Though all this happened in Germany, it was to have far-reaching, devastating consequences for this large and close-knit family.

9
FERI AND ERZSI AGAIN, AND LACI

When Gizka was away in Yugoslavia, Erzsi, now a young woman, was in charge of the cooking. She had help from a maid not much older than herself, who was employed to look after the flat. One day, the two girls decided to make donuts. They made a reasonable dough and dropped spoonfuls of it into not-yet-hot oil, and so instead of crispy rings of delight, they produced oil-saturated lumps – but they bravely tried to eat them. Not wasting food had been drummed into both of them.

On another occasion, Erzsi agreed to prepare Feri's beloved rice pudding for dinner. She knew how to do it in principle, but had never actually made it. First she placed several big scoops of rice in a pot, put it on the stove and added a litre of milk. The milk disappeared quickly but the rice was still hard. Erzsi ran to the corner shop, bought a second litre and added that. The rice was still not edible, so a third litre of milk went in. When it was finally cooked it tasted good, and sister and brother tucked into this magnificent feast. However, they had to eat it the next day, and the next and the next. Any hapless visitors were treated to rice pudding, and even the janitor had the pleasure of a large plateful of it.

Feri and Erzsi often went out to parties, dances and nightclubs, under strict instructions to be home by a certain time. They rarely met their deadlines. They had a wonderful time in their late teens and early twenties, with little responsibility and enough money and free time to enjoy themselves.

Sometimes they spent their weekends 'dribbling' down the Danube, lazing in the bottom of the kayak and soaking up the sunshine, wearing only a bikini or trunks. Going downstream was easy. On the way back, of course, they had to paddle against the current. They often walked in the Buda hills or further afield and frequently stayed away overnight in cheap country inns, or found a barn to rent and made themselves a bed of hay, often sharing it with mice or rats.

* * *

One time, Erzsi and Feri planned a kayaking trip with a group of friends. They named themselves Cactus, Capitus, Pictus and Picatus, and Erzsi, the smallest, was simply known as Tus. Feri was a strong man and a very good rowing partner, but constantly bossed his sister around.

He did the shopping for the trip – crusty bread rolls, salami, cheese and fruit – and he also brought a spare set of dry clothes. He was meticulous with the packing; no one else could do it well enough for him. The food was pre-cut into the right size chunks and each meal was packed in special cotton drawstring bags. Each item of clothing was placed in its own waxed japara bag to keep it dry from any splash of the paddles, then tucked into the appropriate nook for easy access and to maintain the balance of the vessel perfectly.

Stepping into the kayak was a closely supervised ritual. Erzsi had to place one foot in the dead middle of the boat, then, mindful of balance, position her bottom on the seat and finally pull in the other leg, slowly.

This time, Erzsi was sick of being told what to do, and with a 'Stop fussing so much!' quickly stepped into the boat, which promptly tipped over. Despite the careful packing, all the clothes were sopping wet. Although there was a cool breeze, Feri insisted they go anyway. In the evening, when they stopped to have a meal with their mates, they found that the bread rolls had swollen to the size of loaves. There were lots of helpful comments, such as, 'One way to save money – pay for a bun and get a whole loaf!' 'It's just as well – now you have enough funds left over to shout us a drink!'

Erzsi had to put up with teasing all weekend; even strangers at the inn chimed in, 'So *this* is the Budapest way of serving bread! Is it as good as it looks? Enjoy!'

* * *

During the week brother and sister often spent their evenings in nightclubs. Both were excellent dancers. Erzsi was never a wallflower, and Feri was there to take her onto the floor or rescue her from any unwanted attention. She relished the many compliments, loved being the centre of attention, confident she was in her rightful place in the world. She had no intention of ever settling down, taking on household responsibilities or having children. Domesticity did not appeal. The whole idea of a burping, smelly baby, stinking nappies and regular feeding times did not arouse any warm or fuzzy feelings in her. Had she been born 50 years later, she probably would never have entered into a marriage, but remaining single was neither acceptable nor recommended in her time.

In 1935, Béla's cousin, an old maid who had to live modestly, pulled Erzsi aside one day for a talk. 'Erzsi, you're 22 already,' she said, 'decide which boyfriend you like best and settle down.'

Erzsi replied that marriage wasn't for her, certainly not yet.

'Do you want to be a spinster like me? With no man to provide for you or to support you? Do you really want to be forced to eke out your own living by sewing and working for other people?' the aunt admonished.

Erzsi at age 24

Working for others, being at their beck and call did not appeal to Erzsi at all, so she promised faithfully that she would be married by the time she was 24.

❋　❋　❋

After the imposed border changes of 1920, Hungary had lost most of its mountains to Slovakia in the north and to Romania in the south-east, and the people of Budapest had only the gentle hills of Buda. There, after a good winter's fall of snow, skiers could be seen weaving their way between the trees.

Erzsi loved the exhilaration of the downhill run, but she was only a beginner, and with this activity, she seemed to have two left feet. On the other hand, one of her very persistent and serious beaus, Bandi Orlik, was an expert skier. He must have had a great passion for Erzsi, because though he could have gracefully gone down the hill in one go, he patiently stopped at every zig and every zag to wait for her instead. 'Are you all right, Erzsi? Do you need any help, Erzsi?'

Left feet or no, she never needed any help.

One day Erzsi finally managed to gain some speed, and felt proud of herself. Her rejoicing was short-lived, though, as she ended up more or less at right angles to a tree, with her two skis part way up its trunk and tangled into a cross. It was her particular bad luck that in that exact spot a camera was ready to click, and the next day the photo of her skiing prowess graced the sporting columns of a local magazine. She never lived it down.

Erzsi met László Káhn, known as Laci, in 1936 at the Danube Sports Club. The Club organised many activities, among them canoeing, kayaking, skiing, hiking and, of course, partying. One of their Club excursions took them to Balatonfüred, by Lake Balaton, the second-largest inland lake in Europe. The threesome, Feri, Erzsi and Laci, went on a walk in the woods there. Feri arrived first at a Y intersection. He stopped, and completely ignoring Laci, announced: 'I am turning left here. Are you coming, Erzsi?'

Before answering, Erzsi looked at Laci.

'Laci, which way are *you* going?'

Without any hesitation, he answered, 'I am going to the right.'

'Then I'll go to the right, too!' she said, and followed Laci.

The relationship between the two men changed immediately – from that day, they hardly spoke to each other again. Erzsi and Laci gradually fell in love, and after they were married in 1938, she faithfully followed her husband for the rest of his life.

Meanwhile, history moved on. In 1936, the German Gestapo was placed above the law, German troops occupied the Rhineland, Mussolini's forces took Ethiopia, civil war erupted in Spain, and in October, Franco was declared head of the Spanish state. In 1937, Stalin purged the Red Army generals and Hitler revealed his War plans.

10

THE HEIMLER AND KÁHN FAMILIES

Laci's mother, Gizella Heimler, the eldest of four daughters, was born on 31 January 1885. She was well educated for the time, having finished middle school and continued to secretarial college. As a young woman she worked as a legal secretary. She met, and fell head over heels in love with, a shop assistant, Rudolf (Rezső) Káhn. Rudolf had little education, no financial means nor any great prospects, and her parents were totally opposed to this misalliance. She was forbidden to marry him.

Gizella could easily have found another match, but she refused to consider anyone else. Without Rudolf, she was looking at a future of spinsterhood.

One by one her younger siblings found partners; even the youngest one, Aranka, who married their first cousin, Ferenc Singer. They had a son, who, at eight months of age was diagnosed with Down syndrome. The boy was given into the care of a nanny, Terka, a country girl from

Gizella Heimler and Rudolf Káhn's wedding.

Kiskőrös, who brought him up. The Singers regularly sent money and he was apparently well looked after and lived into his forties.

Meanwhile, Gizella was still single, and adamant that Rudolf was the only man for her. Eventually her parents relented, realising that her love of her intended was unbreakable, and the two were married in 1907. Rudolf, 12 years older than Gizella, was a gentle and quiet man who adored his wife. His family came from Nagykanizsa in south-west Hungary. Gizella ran their household and their business and did both capably. They had a happy union.

* * *

The four Heimler girls had four cousins, the Kovács boys. When Erzsi married Laci, he introduced his cousins one by one. Each boy was smaller than the one before, and Erzsi thought she'd married into a family of midgets. Sándor Kovács became a friend and our family doctor.

At the time of their marriage Rudolf was working in a shop in Győr, north-west of Budapest. A year later in 1908 their only child, my father Laci, was born. Soon after, the Káhns moved to Budapest and bought a haberdashery shop on the corner of Csáky and Csanády Streets in district V (later known as district XIII). The family lived upstairs in the small, cramped flat. Their business was popular but didn't make much money. To pad out their income Gizella crocheted and embroidered doilies, pincushions, pillowcases and other small items. Her crochet work was exquisite – she used the finest cobweb-like cotton and created intricate patterns which sold well.

She hung one of her cross-stitched samplers in the kitchen. It read: *Akármilyen kedves vendég, három napig untig elég.* (No matter how sweet the guest, a visit of less than three days is best.)

Laci looked at this every day, and just for fun, memorised each word backwards.

When he was young, Laci was made to help out in the shop – much against his inclinations – and he took out his revenge on the customers. He held out a selection of cotton threads on a tray, and as the client concentrated on trying to choose the perfect match, he imperceptibly lowered the tray. As the client bent down a little further, he gently lowered it again. Without being aware, the poor customer found herself nearly doubled over. If she complained while straightening her creaking body, Laci apologised with exaggerated fervour.

Laci was a good student. He was most interested in the sciences and found chemistry particularly fascinating. In 1926, when he matriculated from *real gymnasium* at the age of 18, the first anti-Jewish law – *Numerus clausus*, which restricted the number of Jewish students allowed to go to university and other tertiary institutions – was already in force. Because of these restrictions, Laci could not enrol to continue his education in Hungary. His parents saved and sent him to Chemnitz in Germany to study textile engineering. He specialised in narrow fabrics, ribbons and laces. When he returned to Hungary several years later, he moved back with his parents.

In 1935, Laci's father, Rudolf, developed lung cancer. Like Erzsi's father and grandfather, he died at the age of 56.

❋   ❋   ❋

One of Gizella Káhn's customers was Erzsi's mother, Gizka Háber, who lived a few blocks away. Though of very different temperaments, they chatted to each other during their business transactions. Gizka enjoyed people and was never short of something to discuss or gossip about, while Gizella was more taciturn and more content in her own company. Still, she needed to keep her customers happy.

Gizka also had a small cross-stitch sampler in her kitchen, with the same message as on Gizella's (she may even have bought it in Gizella's shop). It was at eye-level at meal times, and in her boredom at having to look at it several times a day, Erzsi too memorised the whole message backwards.

In 1936, Laci was employed as one of two technical directors at the Reich textile factory. He was in charge of weaving, and his colleague was in charge of braiding. It was a Jewish-owned factory managed by Jenő and Aladár Reich, the two sons of 'old man Reich', who established the factory but by then had passed away.

It was a very large firm – they made shoelaces, ribbons, lace for curtains, elastic for underwear, and such. Laci boasted that there wasn't a single shop window in Budapest where at least one of their products was not on display. But Erzsi cheekily found the exception – the stonemason's in the cemetery.

When Erzsi met Laci in 1936, Gizka already knew him from the shop and of course knew his pedigree. She noticed her daughter's interest in Laci and one day asked Erzsi about her feelings for this quiet, well-educated gentleman.

'He is an unbearably irritating little monkey,' Erzsi burst out. 'As far as I am concerned, he can keep his company to himself. I don't want to have anything to do with him!'

In the end she decided that she liked him because he wasn't a 'yes' man but had well-thought-out opinions of his own, because he accepted rules and believed in customs and traditions, which Erzsi tended to bypass or ignore except when they suited her, and because he was interesting, knowledgeable, and not aggressive. And he adored her.

And when Erzsi and Laci discovered that they could both recite backwards, in their different ways, the sampler's one-liner, they were delighted. Their love lasted all of his life and all of hers.

11

LACI AND ERZSI GET MARRIED, HONEYMOON AND HITLER

Now, Erzsi had to let Laci know she was ready for marriage. It did not take him long to propose.

The civil ceremony took place on 14 April 1938. Then, on 24 April, their full Jewish ceremony was held in the local synagogue. She was 24, just as she had promised her auntie a couple of years earlier. There were almost 60 guests, mostly Erzsi's family.

The newlyweds made a vibrant couple. But as their happiness was on the rise, the world around them was collapsing. On 13 March, a mere month before their marriage, Austria was annexed by Germany; in August the German military started to mobilise. German troops occupied the Sudetenland and the Czech Government resigned in October. The infamous Night of Broken Glass, *Kristallnacht*, when synagogues were set ablaze, 7500 Jewish shop windows were broken and 30,000 Jewish men were taken to concentration camps, was 9–10 November the same year. And Germany was promising to help reclaim Hungary's former lands. Things were getting very close to home.

Erzsi and Laci's wedding, 1938

Even though the political storm was gathering, Erzsi and Laci were too much in love to take any notice of it.

Their honeymoon was in Italy. Laci had prepared well – studied the map carefully, decided where to go, what to see, how long to stay, and booked and paid for the accommodation in advance. He paid for the best he could afford: 'A' hotels. Despite the planning, with the Hungarian pengő of little value outside the country, and the limits on the amount of foreign currency they could take out of the country, things proved more expensive than they'd anticipated.

Venice, for them, was a time of wining, dining, visiting museums, dancing and being serenaded by gondoliers. But it also meant dwindling funds: they sent a telegram home asking for more money to be wired to Rome, their next stop.

On a day trip to Florence they arrived at the station to find it swarming with police and bodyguards. The firm hand of a policeman instructed them to forget about Florence and instead catch the next train to Rome. Later they discovered that Florence had been graced by an illustrious visitor who happened to arrive at the same time they did. This was their first 'brush' with Herr Hitler.[3]

The couple didn't go directly to Rome but travelled through Trieste. Enquiries at the central Post Office for their postal order received the answer: '*Niente, niente.*' ('Nothing, nothing.')

They decided to downgrade their hotel to a 'B' and were given the difference in cash. Once again, a telegram was sent to ask the family for money to be sent on to Naples, their next stop.

Each day their enquiry at the post office was met with the invariable, '*Niente. Niente, niente, niente.*'

They changed to a 'C' hotel. More days passed. In Capri a 'D' guest house turned out to be quaint and welcoming, with good home-made country meals: it was a more enjoyable stay than in any of the higher-class hotels.

By then they were living only on the refunds from the hotels.

From Capri they went to Anacapri, where they visited the home of the then famous Swedish author, Axel Munthe. From there they had a great view of the sea – and were treated to a full display of Italy's naval might, which turned out to have been a special show for Hitler. On their return to Naples the city was on display as a Potemkin village (the idea originating in Tsarist Russia) – only a façade, to mask the shabby poverty.

Laci and Erzsi were completely broke for the last few days of their honeymoon. En route home one evening there was the sound of throbbing music outside a local café, inviting them to dance, but they had no money left for the entrance fee. Leaning against the fence outside they listened wistfully.

---

3   Hitler was in Italy from 3–10 May 1938.

On their last day the only food they ate was a banana each. Then they caught a boat to Trieste and a train home. As soon as they arrived, they gobbled up the generous meal Gizka happily laid on for them.

Their money, it turned out, had failed to reach them because of a ban placed on all incoming mail to Italy for the duration of Hitler's visit.

Laci returned to the Reich factory, working five and a half days a week. The young couple lived with Laci's mother, and continued to go on outings, especially indulging their favourite activities, rowing and dancing.

Gizella and Erzsi did not get on at all; their only point of agreement was their love for Laci. A major difference was in how each woman treated him. Although Gizella brought him up strictly, Laci was 'the apple of her eye'; she spoilt him in many ways and he in turn, doted on her. His mother waited on him hand and foot, and Erzsi was outraged by such pandering. In her family it was the children who fetched and carried for their mother. There was nothing she could do to change Gizella's behaviour towards Laci, but she made sure that *her* family's traditions were maintained with her own children.

Erzsi ran the household when her mother-in-law was away.

One of the first meals Erzsi cooked for her new husband was meatballs with potatoes and salad. Laci took one bite then pushed away the plate: 'It's not like Mother's!'

Erzsi glared.

He pulled the plate back and had another try. 'Well, it's not *really* bad, it's just different,' he declared and went on to eat his words together with his dinner.

When a new law came into effect in 1938, limiting the number of Jews in professional chambers, Erzsi and Laci (and many others) toyed with the idea of emigrating, but neither of them could even imagine living anywhere but Hungary. Laci was a dreamer, but Erzsi was practical and apprenticed herself to a dressmaker, but Erzsi was practical. She apprenticed herself to a dressmaker, thinking that if the situation in Hungary became intolerable and they did have to leave, sewing would be a way to earn money without having to speak another language.

Eventually, reluctantly, they decided to leave. They started to gather the necessary paperwork: birth and marriage certificates, passports, etc. A few months earlier this would've been enough, but now it all had to be translated into English by an official translator. It took a few months. By the time this was done, more anti-Jewish laws in Hungary had been passed: now no Jews were allowed to leave Hungary. But as the rules tightened, so did their resolve to leave. They found an evangelist minister who was willing to baptise them, for a generous fee, and they resubmitted their papers as Christians. It was not enough; the rules had changed again, and no one born Jewish or of Jewish background could leave the country. They were to stay in Hungary for the duration of the War.

In March 1939, German, Hungarian and Romanian troops invaded the Czech Republic. Bohemia and Moravia were declared protectorates of Germany, and a day later, so was Slovakia. Germany returned a large part of Hungary's former lands in the Upcountry – there was great rejoicing. The Eisenberg family was directly affected as this was their land; they were Hungarian citizens once again.

By way of thanks to the Germans, the second anti-Jewish law was introduced in Hungary in 1939. It defined a Jew as someone with at least one Jewish parent or two Jewish grandparents, and most significantly, declared that all such people were not Hungarian (despite their having had full citizenship for the last 70 years). The Act encouraged the emigration of Jews. Tens of thousands of people were affected by these laws, even though they were not fully implemented until several years later – the government was too dependent on Jewish business and expertise.

In 1939/40, Hungary annexed Carpatho-Ukraine and the Germans returned the northern parts of Transylvania to Hungary. As a sign of gratitude, Hungary considered prohibiting intermarriage between Jews and Christians – in 1941 this became the third anti-Jewish law.

The Nazis invaded the western part of Poland on 1 September 1939 and Britain, France, Australia and New Zealand declared war on Germany on the 3rd. Two weeks later the Soviets invaded the eastern part of Poland. The year ended with the Soviet Union being expelled from the League of Nations.

In August 1940, the first German air raids on central London began; the Blitz started in September. Roosevelt was re-elected as US president in November, and Hungary, Romania and Slovakia joined the Axis Powers.

* * *

Life in Hungary went on – as if in a bubble. Erzsi soon found out that she had problems getting pregnant. Though she would've been perfectly happy not to have children, Laci wanted a family. Dr Kovács advised her to bathe in natural mineral waters, and this she did regularly. She was also given injections to help her conceive. She fell pregnant in late 1941.

Erzsi lost her already meagre appetite, and would only eat *Zwieback*, twice-baked crisp bread, consuming half a kilo every day. It was her staple for most of the following nine months.

Laci was very protective of his pregnant wife, but she had no intention of slowing down. She still wanted to walk and row and climb. He learnt soon enough that arguing with Erzsi was useless, so if he thought she was doing too much, he simply scooped her up and carried her.

Then Germany returned some of the southern lands in Yugoslavia to Hungary. To show their gratitude, Hungary transported 16,000 'alien' Jews back to their homeland in Poland and Ruthenia (Ukraine) – and to their death. After this no more lands were returned to Hungary, and there were no more anti-Jewish laws.

The US considered Hungary a vassal state of Germany, so that when the US joined the Allies, it did not even bother to declare war on Hungary. So, on 12 December 1941, Hungary declared war on the US. According to Ciano, the Italian Foreign Minister at the time, a day later a conversation took place between an official of the US State Department and Hungary's representative in Washington. If this exchange did not really happen as it is written, it certainly could have, highlighting the absurdity of the Hungarian situation:

> '*Hungary is a republic, isn't it?*'
> '*No sir, it's a kingdom.*'
> '*So you have a king as the head of the country?*'
> '*No, we have an admiral.*'
> '*Ah, then you have a navy.*'
> '*No, we don't, because we don't have access to the sea.*'
> '*Do you have any demands?*'
> '*Yes, we do.*'
> '*With respect to the US?*'
> '*No.*'
> '*With respect to England?*'
> '*No.*'
> '*Then the Soviet Union?*'
> '*No.*'
> '*Against what country do you have demands?*'
> '*Against Romania.*'
> '*So you are going to declare war against Romania as well?*'
> '*No, sir. We're allies.*'[4]

4   Ignác Romsics. *Magyarország története a XX. században* (*History of Hungary in the 20th Century*). Budapest: Osiris, 2004, p. 255, quoting Hugh Gibson (ed.). *The Ciano Diaries* 1935–1943. New York: Doubleday, 1946, p. 484.

PART 2

THE WAR YEARS
1942–45

12

CONTRACT OF CARE

For the first half century of my being I felt I did not live my own life, but did not stop to question it. Eventually it all became unbearable, and when I had finally peeled back the layers, a man's temporary and very limited love, but love nevertheless, provided the key to the hidden cellar of my being. And in my sixty-somethingth year, this key allowed me access to a couple of old contracts I had no memory of until then:

> *Contract of Care*
> *My soon-to-be-born daughter,*
> *I do not want to have a child, especially not you, a girl. But … if you can be invisible and silent, and if you can be no more than an extension of me with no desires of your own, even better, no existence of your own and, furthermore, if you will serve my needs and are no more than a reflection of me, a favourable reflection of me, then I hereby undertake to look after you physically to the very best of my abilities, even in the face of extreme hardship and danger. I faithfully promise to feed you, clothe you, keep you clean regardless of any or any potential costs to myself.*
> *Your reluctant mother-to-be,*
> *Erzsébet*

What could I do, a not-yet-born babe? I was helpless, dependent *and* I had a strong will to live. I endorsed the contract. Both Erzsébet and I abided by it for the next 60 years.

But, I discovered to my amazement, that there was another contract, a counter contract, made at the same time.

Dear not-yet-born self,
Outwardly I will be silent and invisible, non-existent and an extension and reflection
of my mother or others who will later come into my life. But deep inside myself I
will always remain me. I will protect and cherish the person I am, will never ever let
her be corrupted or damaged or destroyed. I will keep me in hiding, tucked into my
psyche, until such time that I am able to show my existence in public because it is safe.
I will then be able to be myself openly because I am loved and accepted with all my
peculiarities, peccadilloes and faults as a unique human being.
Your loving self-in-hiding,
Vera

On the sly I signed this simultaneously with the first one.

No sooner were they agreed than the above contracts were lost from memory, the only existing copies of them submerged into the realms of my subconscious.

13

THE 'JEWISH QUESTION' AND THE QUESTION OF MY BIRTH

Erzsi was pregnant with me, but I was in no hurry to arrive. No wonder! Ten days before Hitler's speech in Berlin in which he announced his intention to completely annihilate the Jews, the Wannsee Protocol was formulated. One of its key points was the need for the 'forcing the Jews out of the living space (*Lebensraum*) of the German people'.[5] One might think that my imminent birth in Hungary would not significantly crowd the German people, but that's not what they thought – the conquered lands, the annexed territories and the Allies' countries were included in the *Lebensraum* of the Germans, and in their eyes one more Jewish baby was one too many. A suggested solution to the problem presented itself:

> the evacuation of the Jews to the East ... from Hungary 742,800 ... Owing to the prevailing attitudes and concepts, the handling of the problem in the individual countries will encounter certain difficulties, especially in Hungary and Rumania.[6]

No, the 'problem' wasn't that fascist Hungary under Regent Horthy loved her Jews (though he certainly stopped short of wanting to exterminate them), but rather that Jews ran factories, banks, held down important public service positions, were in charge of hospitals, and were some of the most highly qualified lawyers: that is, they were vital to the Hungarian economy. They also had considerable wealth, which Horthy was intent on keeping in the country.

*   *   *

---

5   Documents of the Holocaust: *Protocol of the Wannsee Conference*, 20 January 1942, Section I, p. 251.
6   *Ibid.* Section III, pp. 253–54.

Hungary managed to stay independent for two years after Germany annexed Austria. On 20 November 1940 Hungary finally joined the Axis Powers, but still maintained its own policies. And, although for the following couple of years Jewish men were taken to forced labour camps, Jews were not yet placed in ghettos; nor were they deported.

At first the labour units in Hungary ran along military lines: the men were issued uniforms (but without insignia) and were paid, but were not allowed to bear arms. Later, with the new laws, this changed. The new labour units had two aims: to create a large, free labour force to help with the War effort and to withdraw, gradually, all Jews from the social, cultural and economic life of the country. Eventually Jews would be removed altogether from the face of the earth – when they were no longer of any use. In the Wannsee Protocol the Germans declared:

> *Under appropriate direction the Jews are to be utilized for work in the East in an expedient manner in the course of the final solution. In large (labour) columns, with the sexes separated, Jews capable of work will be moved into these areas to build roads, during which a large proportion will no doubt drop out through natural reduction.*[7]

They were forced to do hard labour, including walking across minefields to clear them for the regular army, did not get paid and had to wear their own clothes, however unsuitable. Some of these men were sent into the bitter Ukrainian winter without proper equipment, clothes or shoes.

True to expectation, a huge number of 'servicemen' perished from 'natural causes':

> *The remnant that eventually remains will require suitable treatment; because it will without doubt represent the most [physically] resistant part, it consists of a natural selection that could, on its release, become the germ-cell of a new Jewish revival. (Witness the experience of history.)*[8]

The 'suitable treatment' in practice meant that the survivors would be shot or sent to the gas chambers.

The situation in Czechoslovakia was very different. On 15 March 1939, German, Hungarian and Romanian troops occupied Czechoslovakia, and Germany declared Bohemia, Moravia and then Slovakia to be German

---

7   *Ibid.* Section III, p. 256.
8   *Ibid.*

protectorates. The gas chambers at Auschwitz were trialled in September 1941 and by June 1942 the full-scale mass murder of Jews by gassing was in operation.

Members of the Czech Resistance, paratroopers flown into the protectorate from England, fatally wounded Reinhard Heydrich, acting Reich Protector of Bohemia and Moravia, on 27 May 1942. Martial law was declared and officially there were more than 1000 executions. Over 3000 more were thrown into prison, beaten, tortured, shot at random.

Heydrich died on 4 June and on 10 June, in reprisals, the Nazis levelled the mining village of Lidice, shooting the men and transporting the women and children to concentration camps. It was rumoured that one of every 10 Czechs would be shot every day until the assassins surrendered. They did not surrender, but after a gun battle they committed suicide. However, the reign of terror continued. All their family members and associates were arrested and killed. On 26 June, the village of Ležáky was destroyed.

After these events Czechoslovakia was a desperately dangerous place for Jews.

Erzsi's favourite cousin, Gyuszi, his wife, Márta, and their 9-month-old baby boy lived in Slovakia. A couple of months after the death of Heydrich – near the end of August – when reprisals came too close to home, they decided to leave. They gathered important papers and a few mementos, bundled up their baby and walked across to Hungary. It was all so sudden, and so quick, that Márta had no time to change before fleeing the country; her shoes were not meant for walking.

They arrived on Erzsi and Laci's doorstep in Budapest in the middle of the night, looking for refuge. Erzsi asked no questions. She was ready to help them, but they could not be housed there safely. Three extra people, particularly a baby, could not be hidden. Gyuszi tried his Auntie Gizka next, but it was too risky for them to stay at her place too. Some of the residents in the Sziget Street house were antisemitic, and it was only a question of time before the family would have been reported to the authorities. To complicate the issue, Auntie Stefka was officially an illegal immigrant from Zagreb (Yugoslavia), and they did not dare risk bringing attention to that. Gizka and Erzsi asked around and found a quiet boarding house nearby, in Falk Miksa Street.

The next day Márta asked Erzsi to help find a shoe shop – quickly. But a ration card was needed to buy the shoes. Erzsi willingly gave Márta her own card and promised to accompany her.

I was due sometime in July, and in mid-August the obstetrician, Dr Balkány, decided that an induction was needed. Erzsi complied with the doctor's wishes and had the injections, but they did not work. I was not in a hurry to come into such an unwelcoming world and Erzsi was delaying the moment when she would need to become a fully fledged mother. We were in agreement.

But now the delivery couldn't wait any longer, so she was booked into the hospital that morning for a caesarean. But there was Márta and the matter of the shoes, so Erzsi called the doctor and informed him that she had better things to do with her time than rush into hospital. The doctor warned her that she was likely to deliver a stillborn child: 'Mrs Káhn, unless you come in within the hour I'm washing my hands of all responsibility for the baby. One does not give birth when it fits in with their social life, but when it's time. And I am telling you, as your doctor, it is time *now*. Madam, you are irresponsible and selfish to risk your child's life, not to mention your own!'

Erzsi could feel me wriggling in her belly and knew I was all right. She answered that as the baby had managed to wait this long, he could wait a few hours more. She then hung up the phone and went to buy shoes.

Márta and Erzsi proceeded to Delka Shoe Emporium, the largest and best stocked shoe shop in Budapest. Márta had difficulty getting shoes that fit, but at long last she settled on a pair and bought it using Erzsi's card. At home she found that the sales assistant had accidentally packed two different-sized shoes. Erzsi gave Márta her card – in itself illegal – and told her to go back the next day and exchange them.

Erzsi, tired out by the day's activities, went home. Late that night two grim men dressed in drill trousers, trench coats and black boots, knocked forcefully on the door. One stayed in the doorway, the other marched straight into the lounge. With a humourless face he demanded to see Erzsi's shopping card. Erzsi, knowing full well that Márta had it, started fossicking for it in her handbag.

Next to her Laci blanched from head to toe. Erzsi stayed quite chirpy and cool, trying to explain that she seemed to have misplaced or lost it. The official stopped her with a scowl as he pulled the card from his pocket.

'Enough of this charade, Madam. I have it here.' Notwithstanding her obvious condition, he said, 'You are to report at 8.30am sharp tomorrow morning to the Office of Internal Affairs on Vámház Boulevard.'

The situation now was life-threatening. Lending a card was a serious offence, but harbouring illegal Jewish refugees was punishable by jail or, more likely, deportation.

Meanwhile, Gyuszi's sister, Ellus, another favourite cousin, had managed to get a pass out of Slovakia – she arrived legally on the night train. The three women, Márta, Ellus and Erzsi met just before 8.30 the next morning at the appointed office. Waiting in the corridor, Ellus literally bumped into a solicitor, a long-time friend of hers in Slovakia.

With real surprise he asked, 'Elluskám, my dear Ellus, what are you doing here?'

The women explained their predicament.

'How much money do you have on you?' he asked.

One by one they emptied their purses and handbags onto a vacant chair. The money was separated out from the odd tubes of lipstick, small pots of rouge and powder, eyebrow pencils, train tickets, hankies and keys. Ellus had a secret compartment in her handbag and now took out of it her emergency money. Márta sorted through the Czech marks and found some Hungarian pengős amongst them, which she added to the pile. Erzsi, already organised for the hospital, had more than the usual amount on her. That, too, went onto the chair. When there was no more, the money was gathered up and handed over to Ellus' friend. With a glance he added up their little hoard and nodded approvingly – he thought it would be enough to grease a useful palm.

The friend told them to stay put. He returned a short while later; it was all sorted, he assured them, then gave the card back to Erzsi.

14

MY ARRIVAL, AT LONG LAST

The next day Erzsi went out to do last-minute shopping. On her way home she phoned the hospital and asked them to prepare a bed for her. No sooner had she hung up than she had the first labour spasm. Nevertheless, she went to have her nails painted carmine, the latest colour, because, she asked herself, 'How could I be expected to give birth without a proper manicure?'

She was waiting for Laci to come home from work, but the cramps increased quite rapidly and she took a taxi to the hospital with her mother-in-law. It was a busy day and the reception desk was frantic, but Erzsi's pain was so obvious that she managed to get through registration quickly and was whisked to the obstetrics ward. Erzsi asked Gizella to leave.

The caesarean was cancelled – with labour pains underway it now had to be a natural birth.

The obstetrician was called as the nursing sister could see all was not going well; the pain grew stronger, until it was unbearable. Dr Balkány arrived, examined Erzsi and called all the other doctors around him. Pointing to her he spoke: 'Doctors, I want you to look carefully. Not so long ago with this kind of labour the mother suffered excruciating agony for three days and then both mother and baby died.'

Instead of the cervix dilating, everything had gone into a spasm: the uterus and birth canal had seized up, cramped. With new techniques, expert medical help and dilatory injections, Erzsi's cervix eventually relaxed and opened up sufficiently. At 10pm I finally popped my head out and the rest of me followed quickly.

'Dr Balkány, a boy?' was Erzsi's first question.

'No, a lovely healthy little girl,' he replied with a smile, but also with chiding undertones of 'not that you deserve it' in his voice.

She didn't like that answer and so she turned to the sister and asked: 'Madam, a boy?'

'No, a beautiful little girl,' was the answer again.

Nurse Julia was then asked, 'Nursie, a boy?'

'A girl.'

It had been a traumatic birth and all Erzsi cared about at that moment was that I was not the hoped-for boy. She turned on her side and didn't look at me. When finally Erzsi did glance in my direction she broke out in a fit of crying. I was long, thin, nothing more than a collection of bones contained in a bag of skin. The doctor explained that the placenta had completely dried up and I could not have survived more than a few hours longer *in utero*.

Despite my emaciated body, the nurses thought I looked very pretty, but so fragile that they didn't dare bathe me without the doctor's say-so. He allowed them to handle me, gently. A few days later, when I had sufficiently recovered from the trauma of birth, they took turns to parade me around the ward.[9]

* * *

As for Gyuszi, Márta and the baby, the maid in the boarding house reported them to the authorities. They were deported and Márta was gassed, together with her baby; somehow Gyuszi survived. Later, well after the War, he remarried, but Erzsi never saw him again.

Before they were captured, Gyuszi's advice to his cousin was, 'If they (the Nazis) take you, don't ever go with the crowd. The crowd will be slaughtered.'

When the time came, Erzsi remembered his words, and it was how she managed to save herself.

As on so many occasions during the War, a person's life depended on the most mundane and trivial of events. Had Márta had appropriate shoes on, or had the sales assistant given her a proper matching pair, they possibly could have left Budapest a day earlier, and she and the baby might have survived.

---

9   After Erzsi told me this story she commented quietly, 'Not all women want children, some simply don't.
      because they don't feel they have enough energy to bring up a child.' I asked her if she felt like that. She
      nodded. 'My body was not properly equipped to have children. It was difficult for me to fall pregnant, and
      when I finally did, it was difficult to give birth. I only had you for your father's sake. He loved children and he
      really wanted a family. It was a good marriage and I had my children for him.'

I was born at Maros Street Jewish Hospital, only five minutes from the Southern Rail Terminus. Because it was such a difficult birth, we stayed for a couple of weeks. Erzsi shared a room with another new mother. A few days later, on 4 September, neither woman had been able to fall asleep, and they were admiring the beautiful clear skies and moonlit night when at 11:30pm they heard a strange whistling sound, the fierce hooting of a steam train and the loud barking of a dog. The women didn't know what the whistling was, but felt it could not bode well. The room-mate was very scared and wanted to turn the lights on, but Erzsi talked her out of it, thinking it was safer in the dark. They stayed in their beds and talked quietly, trying to figure out what had happened.

Later that night, when all was quiet again, the staff went around the wards informing the patients that the railway station had been bombed and the hospital was dealing with the numerous casualties. But this did not make any sense – there was no fighting on Hungarian soil at the time. The following day the newspapers reported that the bomb had been dropped accidentally by Germany on her ally, Hungary. Later on the Germans denied this and claimed (correctly, it seems) that it was a Soviet bomb.

Stalingrad had been attacked by the Germans only a month earlier, in July, and on 23 August 1942 the Battle of Stalingrad began. In this battle, close to 2 million people were killed, wounded or captured. It was a turning point for the Allies.

Erzsi associated all three sounds – the whistle of the bomb, the hooting of the train and the loud barking of the dog – for the rest of her life. Whenever she heard any one of them, she heard all three in her head. Unfortunately, less than a couple of years later, there was more than ample opportunity to listen to the sound of bombs all over Budapest.

Erzsi sustained severe internal bleeding during birth and even after being allowed home from hospital she was ordered to have another two weeks of bed rest. My grandmother, Gizella, whom I later nicknamed 'Cina', looked after both of us while Laci was at work.

One particular incident cemented the deep loathing Erzsi had for Cina. Our bathroom was unheated, there was no running hot water, and by the time we came home from hospital, the weather was already quite chilly. To test the bathwater grandmother used the age-old method of dipping her elbow into it, then adjusting accordingly. She had very high blood pressure, however, and misjudged the temperature. When, a couple weeks later, Erzsi was finally well enough to do the bathing, she realised that my bath was freezing cold. I duly ended up with severe stomach cramps and colic, and for some days was doubled up with pain and cried bitterly. Erzsi spent hours gently massaging me, rubbing my tummy to try to relieve the pain. She never forgave her mother-in-law for this.

Meanwhile, the 'solution' to the 'Jewish problem' was being systematically attended to, just as Hitler had ordered, and was inching closer to home.

15

UNCLE FERI AND LACI IN THE FORCED LABOUR SERVICE

Feri, Erzsi's brother, was enrolled in a driving course which he had barely started when he was called up for service. Feri was a stubborn man – he intended to finish his course come what may. He also thought that it may give him an advantage, as not many people could drive in those days. The family concocted a story and elected Erzsi, the cheekiest of them all, to sell it to the recruiting officer.

She was shown to the desk of the relevant official and stood before him, a picture of innocence and concern. Fumbling around in her handbag, she pulled out Feri's call-up papers.

'Officer, please, help me, I am so worried! My brother went on a hiking trip a few days ago, camping around Lake Balaton. We have not heard from him since and we don't know where he is. The papers arrived yesterday and we don't know how to find him. What will happen to him now? Please, officer, what should I do?'

The man looked Erzsi up and down. He liked what he saw. 'How long is he going for?'

'I don't know exactly, but he said about a month.'

'And he's been gone a week? Hmmm. Right. Madam, I expect your brother right here in a month from today. Good bye.'

Feri took his driving test three weeks later, passed it, and then reported to the recruitment office.

*   *   *

During World War I, and indeed until 1939, Jews served in the Hungarian Army the same as everyone else. In line with Hitler's plan, in April 1939 all

Jewish officers were removed from command and Jews in general were no longer allowed into combat. However, in order to capitalise on all the available manpower, new forced labour laws that applied specifically to Jews were passed and 35,000–40,000 men were conscripted into the service. Their jobs included clearing forests, paving roads, unloading trains. After August 1941 every able-bodied Jew of military age was conscripted into the labour service for a period of two years.

Initially the men were sent to places within Hungary, and the conditions were not too harsh. The men could visit their families if they were close by and were permitted to fast and to celebrate the Sabbath and even to attend a synagogue if there was one in the town. This did not last long, and as the War continued, conditions deteriorated significantly.

*   *   *

My uncle's commanding officer turned out to be a popular nightclub crooner, Pál Kálmár, particularly famous for one song, 'Gloomy Sunday'. He sang its sad notes and emotive lyrics with such conviction that it was rumoured to be the song many had played before ending their lives; it was dubbed the 'Hungarian Suicide Song' and was banned in many countries. Later, the lyrics were changed to lighten their effect.

Feri was sent to Kőrösmező in Galicia (now Ukraine), where Hungary's 'alien' Jews were deported to satisfy the Germans' demands, in order to save the more assimilated Jews of Budapest. Over many decades Hungary had given refuge to Jews from Russia and Poland in particular – escapees from the pogroms in those countries. They mostly settled in the north-east of the country and became part of the Hungarian community. Some had been there generation after generation, others had arrived more recently. These people were treated – and acted – as full Hungarian citizens: they went to school, worked, paid their taxes, and served in the army, just like everyone else. In 1941 the rules changed: every Jew was considered an 'alien' if their citizenship could not be verified. This was nearly impossible for these people to do, because with changes of borders, many of their places of birth had changed countries more than once during the last few years and the relevant documents could not be obtained.

To get rid of all these unwanted Jews to satisfy German demand for dealing with the 'Jewish problem', the government sacrificed, in the strict sense of the word, tens of thousands of 'Galician', 'immigrated', 'alien' Jews. They deported these unfortunates from Hungary to their 'homeland', a homeland they had run from because of persecution, a homeland that they no longer knew and had never properly belonged to. Hungary transported them there and then handed them over to the Germans.

The task of feeding so many now fell to the Germans, but they did not intend to 'waste' any food, so they simply killed all of them. The newly 'resettled' were made to dig a giant hole, then were ordered to take off all jewellery, strip naked, and stand on the edge. Then they were shot into these pits. In this manner, in two days, 20,000–30,000 Jews were disposed of. Many were not killed, only severely wounded; the Germans covered them with lime, effectively burying them alive. According to a few eyewitnesses, the next day the earth was still moving on top of them as they slowly suffocated.

There were some who managed to escape the massacre and hide, and Feri's company was ordered to set fire to the remaining camp and shoot any of their compatriots who tried to run. Having to shoot so many with machine guns deeply traumatised some of the German soldiers. It was decided that a less stressful solution needed to be found, so soon they started to experiment with ways of mass killing that were easier on the Germans. History knows the result.

*   *   *

In April 1944, all Jewish flats and houses had to be registered. They were then listed as *zsidó házak*, official Jewish houses. A large yellow star had to be displayed above the front door of each of these buildings. In November, the Germans created a ghetto in Budapest by building a wall around the old Jewish quarter, which included Klauzál Square and a few surrounding streets. The old and the infirm were ordered to move in there. On his return from the Ukraine, that is where Feri joined his mother and Auntie Stefka. Erzsi and I continued to stay in Auntie Stefka's house, which was a protected (by Raoul Wallenberg) Yellow Star house.

Jews were not allowed to leave the ghetto, but there was not enough food, and people were starving. On one occasion Feri sneaked out in search of some, and he was hit by errant bits of shrapnel. He dragged himself back into the 'safety' of the ghetto, where Gizka found him a doctor. The doctor operated on him in a cellar by candlelight, without anaesthetic. All the shrapnel was successfully removed.

His service time not yet over, Feri was sent to a labour camp in Hungary, but he absconded. After the War he was told by a survivor that because of his departure every 10th forced labourer was shot dead. Feri had to live with this knowledge for the rest of his life.

At the end of the War, in January 1945, the Russian Army was in Budapest liberating the population. Erzsi, Laci and I had now moved from the Yellow Star house to live in a storeroom on the premises of the Reich factory, where Laci had worked before he was called up. But the rest of the family were still in the ghetto, which had not yet been freed. They were barely surviving, on turnips and beans. At least we were free.

In desperation, Feri sneaked out of the ghetto in search of something to eat. He got lucky! He spotted tins of the best export quality goose liver carefully hidden behind a partly bombed wall. First he brought us three tins, delivering them to the factory.

But luck was not on his side for long – before he could take the food to his mother, he was arrested by the 'liberating' Soviets, who made no distinction between captured soldiers and Jewish servicemen. Feri was taken to Archangelsk in Siberia, as a POW. He staged a hunger strike there and was eventually allowed to leave, at the end of 1946, earlier than many of the others, who were not released until as late as 1948.

Laci as a forced labour soldier

* * *

Considering that the labour service was in full swing by 1941, Laci was fortunate that he was only called up a year later. He was taken to serve when I was six weeks old, and we did not meet again until the end of the War. He enlisted in 101/68 company at Szentendre, a lovely historic town dating back to the Middle Ages. The conditions were good, and the commanding officers treated the labourers humanely. Visitors were allowed, as were parcels of clothes and food from home to supplement the Army rations.

For their first wedding anniversary, in April 1939, Laci bought a bracelet and presented it to Erzsi with a charm – a tiny gold hiking boot. Each year after that he gave her a charm representing the past year's activities: a little kayak, a crossed set of skis and so on. From the camp, he gave her a small piece of bread he had shaped into a heart. After the War Erzsi had it framed in gold; she kept it until she died.

Laci wrote home regularly and saw Erzsi as often as he could. These excerpts are translations from his surviving letters. At first they were written on scraps of paper; as conditions became worse, the men were given small cards, and then only cards with a pre-printed message. Mail was censored, though a few letters came via visitors, and may have escaped such censorship.

1 May 1943

Our jobs are quite varied, on Monday we were in Izbég, Tuesday Lerberg, and on Friday we had a lovely excursion to Dömörkapu, etc. From the hilltop forests we load wood onto carts and bring it to town. It's a beautiful place and the work consists only of loading 1m³ of timber onto each cart and then slowing it down by wedging wooden planks against the wheels. Anyway, we don't have to work ourselves to death. The forest is about 10–15 kilometres from here, but we can jump on the cart for most of the journey. On Thursday we sawed and chopped the wood at the timber yard near the station. This too is good work because we can take off our gear. We were three to a saw and worked in shifts. Time goes quite quickly, we don't have much time to think of other serious issues. In the evenings we generally organise lectures peppered with vigorous discussion. They're very instructive and I'm enjoying them. I am healthy and well, only always hoping for news from home. I would love to be with you if only for an hour or two. – Lots of kisses to you all, Laci

15 May, morning

And now the most important thing, something I haven't written before. I love you till death do us part. Not only the outside, but I love the whole person with all my heart. For me you can never become ugly, you cannot become old. You are most beautiful, just as you are. I love you lots. Kisses, Laci

15 May, afternoon

One of my room-mates is Géza Reich. I was at school with him, he has an independent electrical appliance factory. Sándor Mink engineer has a factory, too. Dr Mittelmann is a physician at the Jewish hospital, Neu is a relative of director Kron [director of the company Laci worked for], he returned home only recently from Greece, Dr Steinhoff works at the Bródy surgery, Lichtenthal is a chemical engineer, he has a refrigerator factory, etc. In other words, they're a good bunch of boys, all gentlemen, it's a pleasure to be with them. In our company there are 25 engineers and nine doctors. Totally different from what it used to be before. Despite all this, I would give up this good company if only I could go home. Unfortunately, as I heard from my dear mother, there is not much chance of that.

My dear don't sign anything in my name. I don't trust … at all. He cannot fire me, because of the new laws no one can be sacked while they are in the Labour Force.

There is some hope that we could stay here on the Island collecting reeds, it's good work and I could see you often. But in the end it will be God's decision.

Really we are owed leave, but in the last few days one of the boys absconded and as a punishment they have taken away all leave.

16 May 1943

We work from 7 to 11.30 in the mornings and then 2–5. Before one reaches the centre of the town, here in Szentendre, you have to go across a bridge which crosses a small creek. We have to dig the pebbly soil from the bottom of this creek and build a road with it along the edge. Poor little road, I don't think it will ever be very usable. I'm working wearing a pair of shorts and shirt; we all have a good tan. My shorts are a great success; I'm very elegant in them …

We are starting to be concerned about where they'll send us next, but rumour has it that we'll remain close to Budapest. I wish it were so. The boys are all very nice and in the evenings we have serious and interesting discussions on the most varied of topics.

Our food is quite good … It's a real break from any intellectual activity and a rest for my head, only that I'm missing you. If I could see you more frequently, being here would probably be good for me – for a short while at least.

June 1943

Please send me a good piece of bacon, some sausage and ¼kg of jam … We'll probably be sent to Szentkirályszabadja in a day or two, but it's not for sure … According to the lieutenant we'll fare even better there than here.

While Laci was still close to Budapest things were going relatively well for us. At the beginning Erzsi could visit him regularly and take supplies, and this made the separation bearable. Then his company was moved from Szentendre to Szentkirályszabadja.

1 August 1943 (card)

We're well looked after, we even get dessert! Also butter, cheese, jam, lollies, sugar, raspberry syrup etc. and cigarettes. We have electricity and proper lights. My work is not bad – we're outdoors all day and I have a good colour. I would like my job here to remain as it is, then I'll be able to return home a nice shade of brown. But when?

6 August 1943 (card)

My Dear Little Life [and] my beloved Mother! More than likely from now on we'll only be able to write home once a week, but please, you write to me more often. I want to know everything, tell me all the news. I often look at your photos, only my dear Mother's is missing. As long as we're not over the border I lack for nothing … Hungarian cooks are preparing our meals, so the food is tasty. I've come to love fresh tomatoes.

12 August 1943 (letter)

Lately rumour has it that those of us left behind, after all, will be able to stay here. Of course all of us would be glad of it. Don't worry that our hopes about me being home soon will be dashed … I am amazed at how well you're managing the housekeeping, but am concerned that you're not eating and will waste away. Please don't do that, use some of the borrowed money, somehow we'll earn it back. So far we have always been able to do so. You know, where the need is greatest, help is quickest. The turning point will come for us, too, maybe soon.

16

BOR, YUGOSLAVIA

By early 1943 the German side was not doing well in the War. They urgently needed secure supplies of raw materials, including copper. They took over the copper mines at Bor, about 240 kilometres south-east of Belgrade in Yugoslavia.

However, there was a serious shortage of miners. It was estimated that they needed 13,000 men. The Germans did not trust the Serbs: they saw them as potential partisans. The Bulgarians (Allies) did not want to work there, and the Jews of Yugoslavia and Romania had already been exterminated. So they put heavy pressure on their other ally, Hungary.

Under a new minister Hungary signed a contract with Germany: the Hungarian Government would supply 3000 forced labour men. The companies would remain under Hungarian command; in return for the work, Hungary would receive a number of tons of copper. Later, more men would be sent, against a further payment in copper.

Laci's unit arrived in Bor in early September, and later another contingent of Jewish men was sent there, together with two companies of Jehovah's Witnesses. Before they left the men were given a short furlough so they could collect what they needed in clothes and supplies.

Many of the guards and Hungarian commanders were chosen for their antisemitic attitudes. The men suffered horrific abuse, and in direct contradiction to government instructions, orders were given by these commanders that just before the end of the War the men were to be liquidated. At first the men were treated acceptably – letter cards could be sent and both parcels and letters could be received, but all correspondence was censored. Laci's first note from Bor was a preprinted card with the message in seven languages:

23 September 1943, Bor (Yugoslavia)

'I'm well and healthy.' Above this is printed: *'Nothing else may be said on this card.'*

3 October 1943 (card addressed to grandmother Cina)

Received your parcel yesterday, and was truly happy with it … It gave me pleasure to know that you took the little girl [Vera] to Auntie Aranka's. What did they think of her? Thank God I'm healthy, don't worry about me. Only I'm longing to go home soon, to be amongst you again. Is the little one keeping you very busy? Write to me about her, is she 'talking' yet? I'm impatiently waiting for a photo, too, what's her hair like, you haven't written about it yet.

18 October 1943

… I miss you all terribly.
If it's still possible to send parcels please send me [one].

21 October 1943

… If you're not allowed to send the parcel that I asked for on Sunday, please send the arch supports on their own. I have special permission for them. It's urgent!!!

17 November 1943

I received the parcel … At every opportunity I take out the little one's photo and look at it adoringly. Everybody loves her, don't they? I can just imagine how happily she plays unpacking your handbag. It was my father's anniversary on Friday, I said kaddish for him, but was not allowed to light a candle in the barracks. I've become a great chef – I made jam dumplings. Unfortunately it wasn't the best, there was too much dough, not enough filling, but next time it will be the other way around. I received accolades from Tibor for my potato paprika dish because we're working together on our culinary concoctions. There is a wonderful little stove here. What does my beloved Mother say to all this??

Then in December 1943, Ede Marányi replaced the previous commander. He was outstandingly mean and his brutality worsened after Hungary's occupation. He made his hatred of the Jews known early on.

The guards were encouraged to mete out extreme and cruel treatment to the labourers, even for the most insignificant things. If someone was not properly shaved on a Sunday or did not shake the dust out of his blanket, for example, the punishment was a truss-up[10] or flogging. The guards taunted the workers, stole

---

10 A person's hands were tied behind his back and he was suspended without his feet touching the ground. When the man fainted with pain, after about 10 minutes, he would be revived by cold water being poured on him. The torture could continue for hours.

from them and deliberately made their hard lives miserable. If anyone tried to escape, they were shot.

5 December 1943

Don't be angry with our little one, even if she pulls everything off the table. I would be happy to watch her being so busy, maybe I would even encourage her in the activity. I remember the stories your late Father told us, as you see, history repeats itself. My heart fills with bitterness as I read how you're preparing yourselves for my homecoming, but it's not time yet, there is not much chance of me coming home in the near future. I can only write once a month now. I'm thinking quite a lot about the factory [Laci's job was kept open for him]. I'm planning some innovations …

17 December 1943

My little angel, I miss you so much. I am often at home in my dreams, unfortunately only in my dreams. A Happy New Year to you and the whole family and may God grant us that we spend the next year together in happiness…

9 January 1944

… it is possible that I wasn't in the best of moods when I wrote the last postcard. Some days there is a bitter taste in one's mouth – although there is no serious reason for it … I wish my dear Mother the very best for her birthday, good health and fortitude, and even if I won't be at home as a present for her, she must trust with whole-hearted belief that God will help us and that in good health and happiness we will be able to hug each other again.

Christmas was very restful, we didn't have to work and the military district people left us in peace, too. We played bridge and did the same on Saturday-Sunday in the New Year. No one is getting any leave, no one even talks about it any more. Our little girl must be very pretty, if she has such an effect on our friends.

The men at Bor were housed in huge wooden barracks, each accommodating 60–100. They slept on triple bunks without blankets or mattresses and the floor was trodden down dirt. It was impossible to clean or air the rooms. As the windows were small, the men were always in semi-darkness. The camps were surrounded by barbed wire and every step of the inmates was watched.

A small part of the Hungarian contingent worked on the railway, but most slaved in the mines. They were paid a quarter of a kilo of bread, some cold soup and seven dinars per day. The food was not enough for those doing hard physical labour, and many stole food from the storehouses, particularly potatoes and onions.

Officially they had Sunday off, but in reality they were given no rest. On this day they were forced to do housework.

23 January 1944

I have no need for anything clothes-wise.

13 February 1944

I'm not surprised that money is short for you, I expect prices are high at home and the child would cost quite a lot, too …

Sadly, it's not possible to send any parcels.

I can't say anything new about myself, all is well; I'm healthy, same as before.

The Hungarian guards amused themselves by asking the men if the food was to their liking. A moment's hesitation would lead to a beating. No wonder Laci states in each letter that he's well and that the provisions are good!

It was in the Germans' interest to keep the men healthy and in physically good condition – they wanted the work done – so at times they protected the Hungarian labourers from the extreme cruelty of their Hungarian officers and guards. Some behaved decently; some, Laci remarked, even with kindness.

Those men with any specialist knowledge or usable skills were employed accordingly, rather than in the mine, but it was always with the proviso that 'it is to be avoided in every case that Jewish workers become indispensable in essential production'.[11]

*   *   *

Because of the first anti-Jewish law, passed in 1920, Laci couldn't get into university in Hungary, so he had gone to Germany to study. There he learnt to speak the language fluently and became used to German culture and habits.

When he was in the labour camp, 15 years later, and it was a matter of life or death, his ability to speak German well and his good education landed him a job as a clerk working for one of the officers. Laci was quietly spoken, even-tempered, and intelligent. He and the German officer he was assigned to soon found mutual respect, and though in public played their allocated roles, behind closed doors they often had far-ranging discussions.

In private, the officer called Laci 'Herr Káhn' and not the usual 'dirty, Jewish pig'. He routinely 'forgot' to take the leftovers from his meals with him as he

---

11 Memorandum from Rosenberg File Concerning Instructions for Treatment of Jews (translation of document 212-PS), in *Nazi Conspiracy and Aggression*, Volume III. Washington, DC: USGPO, 1946, pp. 222–25.

attended to some business elsewhere. Consequently, Laci was better fed and less abused than his fellow labourers. Laci's survival was largely down to a thin slice of luck and to this kind man.

The camp's commanding officer, Colonel Marányi, was vicious, and gave a free hand to the guards to do what they liked. Not only were beatings and trussing-ups the norm; so too was psychological abuse of the men – withholding mail or handing over only the empty wrapping papers of parcels sent from home.

The workers were not given uniforms, so when their own unsuitable clothes gave way they still had to wear them. They would be made to work outdoors until December, shovelling snow, often during snow storms, or chopping wood – and this was often on their day off.

To further destabilise them, the men were not told how long they were to stay at the camp. Although the cruelties were mounting, and the treatment severe, 'only' 40 men died at Bor.

17

LIFE IN BUDAPEST 1942–44

Gizka still had a maid one morning a week to help with the cleaning. The woman, who was of German origin and came from Schwabia, adored me. She called me her 'kleine Wachtel', her little quail.

I would often be left by the big bay window overlooking the Danube with the sun pouring in, dressed in the usual baby gear – a singlet, nappies, little vest and bib – and covered with a light blanket tucked into my pram. Yet when Erzsi came to get me a little later, I would be stark naked. No one solved the mystery of how I wriggled out of all my clothes, but I repeated the performance several times.

In general, while food was less available and queues were ever longer, our life went on more or less in the usual way.

But the Germans grew less and less happy with their ally, as Hungary had not taken sufficient measures to deal with the 'Jewish problem'. The two leaders didn't trust each other: Hitler wasn't entirely convinced of Hungary's loyalty; Horthy was certainly no fan of Hitler.

Importantly, Germany wanted the oil wells near Lake Balaton for itself, as oil was crucial for the War effort. Both problems would soon be 'solved' by Germany's occupation of Hungary, which occurred on 19 March 1944. Horthy was forced to remove the Prime Minister from office and then had to choose between selecting a new, more cooperative one or submitting the country to undisguised occupation. Horthy chose the former and appointed Döme Sztójay.

Sztójay legalised the fascist Arrow Cross Party and increased Hungarian troop levels on the Eastern Front. He denounced Horthy's authority and carried out massive persecution of Jews, which, within two months, escalated to wholesale deportation. Horthy, appalled by Sztójay's actions, demanded he be removed as Prime Minister. Hitler refused.

In March Hitler appointed Adolf Eichmann to 'take care of the Jews'. German policy dictated:

The first main goal of the German measures must be strict segregation of Jewry from the rest of the population. Then, immediately, the wearing of the recognition sign consisting of a yellow Jewish star is to be brought about and all rights of freedom for Jews are to be withdrawn. They are to be placed in ghettos and at the same time are to be separated according to sexes.[12]

On 4 April, the Allies started bombing Budapest. There were many air raids for the next few months and after September the frequency increased. The general population blamed the Jews for the air raids.

A new law was passed on 5 April 1944 – all Jews were compelled to wear the Yellow Star. Failure to do so meant the risk of deportation. The Jewish leaders compiled lists of Jews and enforced the ever-harsher regulations as they were announced, hoping, they said, that if everyone cooperated all Jewish lives would be spared.

Eichmann, ruthlessly methodical and effective, divided Hungary into five regions. First the whole countryside was to be made *Judenfrei*, free of Jews, then they would start on Budapest. From the country towns the deportees were to be taken to Auschwitz; from the capital they would go to Bergen-Belsen.

In a matter of a few months, Eichmann succeeded in 'cleansing' all the country towns of their Jews, and he achieved this without panicking the local population. His job was made easy by the super-enthusiastic cooperation of the Hungarian Nazis, especially those in the Arrow Cross Party.

Eichmann had set himself a personal challenge: he wished to topple Hermann Höfle SS-Sturmbannführer's record. This was the man who had organised the deportation of the inmates of the Warsaw ghetto to Treblinka. Despite the worsening condition of the infrastructure during the last year of the War Eichmann won the race – his efforts were crowned with 'success'.

In just 56 days between May and July more than 437,000 Hungarian Jews were taken to Auschwitz-Birkenau. Until then the monthly average number of arrivals for gassing was 20,000–25,000 people. In May that year, ten times as many Hungarian Jews arrived in the camp as in a 'normal' month.

---

12 *Ibid.*

A German officer made the observation that the Hungarians truly did justice to their ancestors the Huns, as in no other country were there as many denunciations as there were in Hungary.

Yet in another absurd twist, following the German occupation the Labour Service became a refuge for the doomed; those called up for service escaped Auschwitz-Birkenau – for the time being.

When the Jews were concentrated into the ghetto at Klauzál Square, curfews came into effect, and they were only allowed to leave their homes between 2pm and 5pm. Food rations were drastically reduced: no more butter, eggs, rice or paprika, and only 100 grams of meat a week. Appalling, when even the *official* ration in Auschwitz was 200 grams a week.

In practice, most of the supplies were gone from the shops by the afternoon. People had to wait in separate lines for meat, vegetables or other groceries. The lines were so long that it was curfew time before one could get to the front of a queue and be served.

By the middle of April, Jews had to make lists of their valuables. These were confiscated. Towards the end of April Jewish shops were closed down.

The Jewish or Yellow Star protected houses were created in early April, and by 24 April all 200,000 remaining Jews in Budapest were ordered to move to these buildings within a week. Each family was allocated just one room. Having had to walk away from their former residences, they were left without basic furnishings – they often had to sleep on the floor.

Auntie Stefka's house, in Sziget Street, became a Jewish house; but the building where Grandmother Cina, Erzsi and I lived was not. Cina moved in with her sisters Aranka and Jolán, a 30-minute walk from us, and Erzsi and I moved to Auntie Stefka's place. We now stayed in the long, narrow maid's quarters next to the kitchen. Four of us lived in the one-bedroom unit. Most of our belongings had to be left behind.

On 6 June the Allies landed in Normandy.

Meanwhile, neutral states were planning rescue actions for the Jews of Budapest. Raoul Wallenberg, Secretary of the Swedish Foreign Ministry, issued thousands of Swedish identity documents and, working with the Swiss consul, Charles Lutz, as well as Portuguese and Spanish legations, created 'protected' houses and a 'protected' ghetto to house the Jews with international identity papers. He is credited with saving as many as 100,000 Jews from Nazi deportation.

Eichmann was now ready to start on the last of his five districts, and had begun clearing the Jews from Budapest. But on 2 July the US Air Force bombed the city again, to try to get Horthy, the Regent, to stop further deportations. The Germans finally submitted to Horthy's pressure and in August 1944, with Hitler's agreement, he was able to remove Sztójay from the Prime Ministership. The deportations stopped, Eichmann left Hungary and there was a reprieve. Horthy, aware that the Axis had all but lost the War, now put out feelers for an agreement with the Allies.

Though the servicemen in Bor were probably told that Hungary had been occupied by the Germans, it's unlikely that Laci knew the details of what was happening.

7 July 1944, Bor

Our little Sunshine is beautiful! Write lots about her ... I'm sorry you all had to leave the flat, I expect we had lost many of our possessions in the process, but from afar I don't see it as being all that bad because in my opinion my dear Mother could be revitalised by being in the midst of her beloved family and my dear Erzsike, you will lessen for her that great loss that she'll experience in having to part from her grandchild by visiting and allowing her to see her little Sunshine often.

May God bless you all.

24 July 1944, Bor

We have not received any mail for a month. I've also not received my summer parcel, I'm no longer expecting it. Do you have any news of the relatives in Komárom? ... My little life, how do so many of you fit into such a small unit? And my mother, how did she organise her flat, who does she live with? ... What does our little girl like to play with? Can she entertain herself, or does she need playmates?

I was 18 months old and my good appetite did not diminish. Dr Kovács, Laci's cousin and our family doctor, told Erzsi that I needed soup with marrow to keep my bones strong, plus vitamin C and fruit and vegetables. But meat was particularly difficult to obtain; Erzsi and Gizka spent every day queuing up for veal bones for soup for me, while also trying to buy other food items. Still, I was hungry all the time.

One day, a Dr Magda Révész, who lived on the mezzanine floor, stopped Erzsi in the corridor. 'Erzsi, what do you do to that little girl of yours that she cries so hard every morning?' she asked.

'Come upstairs and see for yourself!' challenged Erzsi. Dr Magda came and watched.

I was being spoon-fed, and every time the empty spoon left my mouth I cried bitterly until the next spoonful of food arrived. The mystery solved, Magda looked on in amazement and just shook her head.

While there was still a choice, Erzsi was very conscious of what she fed me and how much. Then food became increasingly difficult to obtain, until it was nearly impossible. Erzsi went to the Green Cross,[13] where she was given some semolina, a few small packets of dried onions and, importantly, vitamin tablets.

During my first year Erzsi took me every day to Margaret Island in the middle of the Danube, just opposite where grandmother Gizka lived.

Later on, when we had to wear a Yellow Star, she refused to be restricted in her movements. Jews were no longer allowed in any public parks, so she always left the house appropriately attired with the Yellow Star, but on her way she would find a doorway to hide in and she would take off the coat with the offending star, fold it and place it in the pram. From then on she continued to push me, carefree, like any ordinary mother without a curfew. Had she been caught we would both have been deported.

Vera at 3½

Erzsi was adamant that I needed my daily dose of sunshine – vitamin D deficiency was not uncommon. I was lying in my pram one day and a friend of Gizka's stood near it, casting a shadow over me. Erzsi did not hesitate to ask her to move a few steps, and she obliged, but afterwards she went around the neighbourhood telling everyone who cared to listen, 'Erzsi Káhn wants the sun to shine only on *her* baby.'

On one occasion I was sleeping in the pram on Margaret Island. I was a poor sleeper, and when she saw a couple approaching, Erzsi went to meet them. In horror, she realised that they were Germans. She was not supposed to be there, let alone without her Yellow Star, which was, as usual folded neatly in the pram. There was nothing for her to do but pretend all was as it should be. She asked the couple would they please lower their voices so as not to wake me. It was too late.

I was already awake and looking at them wide-eyed. The woman asked permission to push the pram for a little while. Erzsi was in no position to refuse. With her heart in her throat she casually removed the coat from the pram and allowed the woman to push it. The German Frau smiled at me and nodded to her husband, 'Look Helmut, look at this pretty little girl – fine, curly blond hair, big blue eyes, fair skin, rosy cheeks. *This* is what we mean by true Aryan beauty.'

---

13   Green Cross was a nursing service set up in Hungary in the 1930s for the prevention of illness and malnutrition.

Then she nodded to Erzsi, thanked her, and they were on their way. Erzsi, still shaking, thought grimly that we were only the drop of a coat away from being discovered and sent to an extermination camp. The irony of the compliment about her full-blooded Jewish child was not lost on her.

18

DEPORTATIONS FROM BUDAPEST IN FULL SWING

With the War lost, in August 1944, all the forced labour men in Bor were ordered to leave the mines. It was to be done in two waves; the first went on foot on 17 September, Laci among them. On 10 October they arrived back in Hungary, in the southern town of Baja.

The Nazis' obsession with Jews cut across everything that they did; it was the one element of National Socialist ideology that was not subject to compromise, even though the murder of the Jews diverted massive amounts of resources. The deportations did not stop until 1 December.

Behind Germany's back, in October 1944 Hungary formally sought peace terms with the Allies, largely to try to avoid Soviet occupation. It was far too late. Hitler had anticipated this move and ordered his troops to kidnap Horthy's son. He then forced the helpless Regent to appoint Ferenc Szálasi, head of the Arrow Cross Party, as Prime Minister of Hungary.

Szálasi was an ardent fascist; his government had little intention or ability to do other than maintain fascism in the Nazi-occupied portions of Hungary, even as the Soviet Union entered the country.

Then Eichmann returned to Hungary and began negotiations with the new Hungarian Government to deport 50,000 Jews to German death camps. Szálasi was more than happy to give permission, and the deportations started again from Budapest in late October 1944.

Sometime in October, while they were being rounded up, the Jews of Budapest were not allowed to leave their houses for ten straight days. This meant no food, no medical assistance for us at all. When people were finally allowed out, they found the Arrow Cross roaming the streets torturing and killing, often to obtain wealth they assumed to be hidden. On the night of 16 October thousands of Jewish forced labour men were shot into the Danube by the Arrow Cross.

Auntie Lili, an eyewitness to the massacre, told me the river flowed red.[14]

These actions were in total agreement with German policy: 'An eventual act by the civilian population against the Jews is not to be prevented as long as this is compatible with the maintenance of order and security ...'[15]

On one occasion Erzsi was accosted by a young Arrow Cross man who demanded to see her ID. Showing no fear she handed it to him. The man looked at the paper and barked, 'Kun, that's a Jewish name. Come with me!'

Full of apparent self-confidence she retorted, 'What, don't they teach you to read any more? It's Kahn, K.a.h.n, a German name!'

She was a good-looking young woman, and he was barely out of school. The Arrow Cross man blushed, returned the papers without another word, and quickly went on his way. Erzsi hotfooted it in the opposite direction as fast as she could before it would occur to him that most Jews had German names.

Meanwhile, Eichmann was keen to finish the job he had started in the four country districts earlier in the year. Even if the Germans were losing the War, he, for one, was going to make sure that all Hungarian Jews were eliminated. That was his duty, and, no doubt, his pleasure. He had the overall plan, the Arrow Cross put it into action.

Two fully armed Arrow Cross men would stand outside each Jewish house, take out their megaphone and bellow: 'All Jewish men between the ages of 14 and 70, women between the ages of 16 to 40 come down to the street immediately!' All Jews obeyed. Pregnant women and those with children under the age of three were exempt.

At the same time, other pairs of Arrow Cross men repeated the procedure at all the other Jewish houses in the district. The following day another district was chosen. And, with unprecedented speed and thoroughness, the Arrow Cross also took all money and property from the Jews before their deportation.

Hungarian political life was confused and contradictory, but, bizarrely, for many, life went on as normal. While deportations had already started in the northern districts in Budapest, the government was debating whether Jews with Yellow Stars should be allowed to keep dogs or buy tobacco.

The Budapest Jews knew of the systematic removal of Jews from all the country towns. They knew that sooner rather than later their names would be called, yet, like sitting ducks with nowhere to hide, they waited. But Erzsi

14 Mrs Lily Abasár, née Livia Wassel.
15 Nuremberg trials, 119, 21 November 1945. http://avalon.law.yale.edu/imt/11-21-45.asp.

prepared herself for the worst, even though, according to the rules, she was exempt because of me, a child under the age of three.

By autumn 1944 the situation had turned very grim. There was an increasing chance that she, together with my grandmothers, would be taken, and with Laci in the Labour Service, who would look after me?

A widow lived in the house and Erzsi approached her to ask whether if the worst happened, would she look after me – would she adopt me? She offered payment and, surprisingly, the woman agreed, but only if I was baptised.

Erzsi was now faced with the task of finding a clergyman who would perform this ritual. Finally, an Evangelist minister, Jenő Rimár in Angyalföld, agreed reluctantly – for a large sum of money. It was a warm autumn day as the minister sprinkled holy water on me. Clapping my little hands together in glee I squealed, 'This is so much fun! Can I have some more please!'

But the man of cloth was not amused. He was not at all happy with the whole event and grumbled, 'I don't like you people. You're evangelist on Monday, Wednesday, Friday, Catholic on Tuesday, Thursday, Saturday and Sunday and Jewish every day.'

'If that's what it takes to stay alive, Reverend, then yes,' Erzsi replied.

He was not wrong. After all, Erzsi and Laci had already converted in 1939, when they originally applied for their passport to leave Hungary. When I was born, Laci had registered my birth but had completely forgotten his new-found evangelism and put 'Israelite' for the religion of his baby. The minister who baptised me, after the production of numerous papers and medical records, properly registered our new religion.

The baptism was the first step in Erzsi's preparations. The second was to sew herself a backpack. She took the runner from the hall, a heavy woven carpet made of cotton, and made a pack from it. If she were to go anywhere, it would come in handy for carrying survival provisions. When the others in the house saw her handiwork, they all wanted one. She obliged until there was no more of the rug left. Then people queued up, supplying their own materials.

Soon Erzsi was to make good use of her handmade bag – on the 100-kilometre march towards Bergen-Belsen.

Most Jewish people had their satchel or backpack ready with provisions: food, spare clothes and ID papers showing their names and addresses. If they were lucky, they had a copy with no religion, or a religion other than Israelite, indicated. If they had any jewellery they hid it on their person.

The first time Erzsi was called her bag was packed and ready. When the muster was complete, they were all taken by truck to a holding point at KISOK sportsground. My grandmother was not yet in the ghetto and she looked after me in her flat, but Erzsi was only away for a day. She showed her papers to an official in charge, indicating my existence, and demanded they stick to the law and let her go – and they did. She was tired, it was a long way from where we lived, and her pack was too heavy to carry, so she dragged it all the way home.

A week or two later she was rounded up again and again taken to the sportsground, and once again they let her go.

While this was happening in the capital, Laci made the 450-kilometre journey from Bor to Baja in Southern Hungary on foot and was able to communicate again, after a long break. He had no idea how much the situation had deteriorated.

2 October 1944, Pécs, Hungary

I'm anxiously awaiting your calming letters and would like you to answer mine straight away. I'm well, only worried about you. What is our beautiful little girl doing? I only have one remaining picture of her, where she's offering one of her large cubes to you.

17 October 1944, Baja, Hungary

… Thank God all's well with me, only my feet are hurting a bit. They're looking after me here but it will take a few days before it's healed. My dear, be calm and trust in God that we'll be together soon.

20 October 1944

Unfortunately I have no gear at all. I'm wearing lightweight clothes only, no overcoat. At the moment I don't know how I could get hold of anything I need. I would also need some shoes, though at the moment I couldn't wear them, but there is no need to worry too much about me, the good Lord will help me, unswervingly I believe in him …

25 October 1944

… If you could please send 20 to 30 pengős because the money is all gone.

26 October 1944

I've not been happier for a very long time than I was today on receiving your letter and a card from Mother. It's been three months since I saw your handwriting, or received any news from you.

Meanwhile, I was able to get hold of a little money and may be able to get some essentials from Uncle Rezső. Can you imagine, my total assets consist of a safari jacket whose sleeves barely reach past my elbows, the legs of the pants I'm wearing don't quite make it to my ankles, a flannel shirt (the only item that belongs to me) and a borrowed pair of underwear. I have nothing else, no hat, no shoes, even my glasses have been lost. Thank God the weather's been good until now, so I lacked for nothing. It's possible that

I'll get a pair of glasses from the Red Cross nurse. I've already been given a pair of straw slippers, although three of us are sharing it. But the most important thing is that I'm well.

Please tell Vera to be good and give her lots of kisses for me.

28 October 1944, Pécs

… I'm hoping that my Uncle Béla will look me up, and I will get a pair of shoes and an overcoat from him. Anything else is not important.

My dearest, you've just had a birthday and I haven't congratulated you, but don't think that you are not in my thoughts and for your birthday present I was given, after a very long time, some straw to put under myself in the convalescent home.

While Laci was so desperately trying to contact Erzsi, asking her for money and for items of clothing essential for his survival with winter coming, Erzsi was not allowed outdoors for ten days straight, was herself starving and had the nearly insurmountable task of keeping me fed and washed.

* * *

On 3 November, Cardinal Mindszenty delivered a momentous speech on the radio. He intimated that Hungary's liberation was imminent; the War was effectively over. After this speech, the overseer of the building, a Christian man, asked Erzsi to get on the ladder and remove the offensive Yellow Star. She loved climbing and happily obliged.

No sooner had she taken it off than an Arrow Cross man marched by and demanded to know why was it gone, and who had removed it. Luckily, no one volunteered her name. Had they, it would have cost her life.

On 26 November, Cardinal Mindszenty was arrested for treason.

In mid-November all four of my grandmothers were forced to leave their homes and move to the ghetto. Auntie Stefka's flat was now crammed full of others forced to move from their own homes because they had not been declared Jewish houses. There were a dozen people, including Erzsi and me, living in the two-bedroom unit.

19

FROM BOR TO BAJA: 450 KILOMETRES ON FOOT

In one of his last letters, dated 28 October, Laci continued with a description of their journey back to Hungary.

28 October 1944, Pécs (letter continued)

And now so that you'd have more or less an idea of our route. We left on the 17th, on the day of Erev Rosh Hashona. On the first day we walked 45 kilometres and finally arrived in Belgrade – a week later, after a total of about 220 kilometres. Actually we crossed the Sava River and camped in the Belgrade exhibition pavilion. This is how far we got and for most of it we had good provisions and the people there did themselves proud, they supplied us with heaps of snow-white bread, fruit and other food. There I fasted for Yom Kippur and we set off again on the 27th and eventually arrived at Cservenka. We will never forget the name of this place. From here I walked the rest of the way without any of my gear, barefoot. Eight of us continued on to Zsomborka, then Gara and at long last on the 10th we arrived at Baja.

By the time we arrived here my trousers (ski) were in rags. My coat was still all right. At first I went into the convalescent home, then they transferred me to the hospital. On the 18th we left to come here, where I finally settled. This is my travelogue in brief, but it's not possible to write down what we had to endure, and it's not important anyway. The important thing is that I'm in Hungary and we need to believe in God that he will continue to help us.

By the way I want to just say that from Pancsova to Baja we were given a total of 500 grams of bread [i.e. half a kilo of bread for two weeks]. How did we stay alive? We ate raw corn, squash, beet and we got so used to not eating that on the last day I ate nothing, I was not hungry at all and only had some water.

29 October 1944, Pécs (letter continued)

I lost quite a lot of weight, and had to adjust my belt from the 3rd hole to the 13th and the last day we could only whisper to each other, we had lost our voices. What was amazing [was] that had my feet had not been so blistered, we could have gone on longer. It's beyond imagination how much a human being can bear. Thank god all my acquaintances arrived back with me and only one, Pali Günser, was left behind in Bánát. We don't know what happened to him. Don't say anything to his wife. Meanwhile I've fattened myself up. I have to lie down all day because of my feet and while doing so eat everything I can.

Today I received a card from my mother, she is more diligent in writing than you …
Unfortunately it may take a long time yet before we'll see each other again and we need to be ready for that.

30 October 1944, Pécs (letter continued)

Uncle Rezső didn't show yesterday either, and so I mailed him a letter in which I mentioned everything I needed, so now I just hope that he'll receive it.

My dear Erzsi I had such a beautiful dream – last night we were together, I was so sorry when I woke up this morning …

Today I received 100 pengős in Bella's name, but it was posted in Pécs [Bella was Laci's cousin, Dr Sándor Kovács' wife, and they lived in Budapest]. I'm not sure if I've solved the mystery. Possibly Uncle Rezső is either not able to or not willing to come here and for that reason he is trying to fulfil Bella's wishes by post. I'll see what he answers to my letter.

My dears, do you still have my papers that I kept in the bottom drawer in the wardrobe in our bedroom? Unfortunately, all my work in Bor is lost, although it took a lot of effort and was valuable, but it doesn't matter, life is more important.

And this is some of what Laci left out of his letters, but on his arrival at home told Erzsi, just the once:

On leaving Bor the servicemen were given 370 grams of bread and one tin of food and marched 220 kilometres to Belgrade. They were guarded somewhat less vigilantly by both the Hungarians and the German SS. The Serbian people helped these forced labour men in general, gave them food and encouraged the prisoners to escape.

After leaving Belgrade the horrors really started. They were given virtually no food or water and those found begging for water or raw corn from the fields were shot.

The Germans killed more men who tried to escape. Then the black-uniformed DM (Deutsche Militärpolizei) joined them. The group went past a mound of rotten melons. The prisoners were given permission to eat them and as they went for it, the Germans shot 250 men in the back.

Then they were marched to Cservenka. More men were killed because they tried to drink some water and others because they couldn't walk. One of those men was a gentle Seventh Day Adventist, a quiet, peaceful, religious man who over the months became Laci's good friend. By this stage the servicemen had had no food and no water and in desperation, Laci's friend bent down to drink from a puddle on the road. The guards made sport of him, verbally abusing, taunting him as they kicked him to death in front of the others.

At Cservenka they stayed at a brick factory. The next day they received the news that the Germans refused to approve provisions for them. All day the men were taunted and tortured in a multitude of ways.

In the late evening they were again lined up and ordered to hand over their valuables – this included their wedding rings. Then they were called out, 20–30 at a time, to the edge of a huge pit, dug the day before by Jewish and Seventh Day Adventist labourers, and 700 to 1000 were shot into the pit. The executions continued until 4am the next morning and only stopped because the officers had orders to move on at dawn, before the job could be finished. Laci was in one of the last rooms in the brickworks and so was spared by the dawning of the day.

Less than an hour later those who could walk were forced to march on.

At Mohács, just south of the border, Hungarian guards took over. The forced labour men rejoiced at this, expecting better treatment from their fellow countrymen, but their lot was now even harsher, as the Hungarians tortured them even more than the Germans.

At last they arrived at Baja; seven men were admitted to the hospital – and they may be the only ones from Laci's company from Bor who survived the War.

What was left of the company was herded back to Szenkirályszabadja, once again under the command of the brutal Marányi from Bor, and half of them died en route. Most of those who had survived were in such a pitiful state that they were unfit to work and were shot.

The Germans were so aghast at the condition of these Hungarian men, the ones who were considered to be fit for work, that they fed and watered them. Those who couldn't walk were taken to the hospitals at Győr, but no hospital would admit them, so they too were shot.

Those who were still alive were sent to the front line, then to death camps, and most, if not all, perished.

Laci stayed at Pécs for almost three weeks. These are his last letters from there.

31 October 1944, Pécs

Uncle Rezső has not come yet and I'm worried about ever getting the parcel ...

1 November, 1944, Pécs

... I'm so glad that everybody wrote to me, even a few lines. It's as if one by one you all gave me a hug. My blanket is a rag rug I was given in Baja. I don't know how much I weigh, but I doubt if I'm more than 10 kilograms short of my normal weight. I am looking much better than three weeks ago.

20

MARCHING TOWARDS BERGEN-BELSEN — ERZSI'S STORY

The Szálasi government 'lent' a percentage of Jewish working-age men and women to the German authorities. By December 1944, some 30,000 Jews from Budapest had been marched to German camps and thousands of forced labour servicemen had been handed over to the Germans to build new defence lines in the border region.

Even with the War lost, the Nazis were driven by one thing: the complete annihilation of the remaining Jews. There were no more rules, no regulations, no exceptions; certainly no mercy.

Erzsi was called for the third time on 9 November 1944.

The group of Jews who had gathered on the footpath, including Erzsi, was marched off on foot this time to a collection point. It was not the sportsground, as before, but the brickworks just outside Budapest. They stayed there for three days while more Jews were gathered together, all in all about a hundred. They slept on the ground wherever they could find a bit of space big enough to stretch out. It was already cold and they were not adequately dressed.

The railways were mostly in tatters due to Allied bombing, so the Jews were forced to walk to the border between Austria and Hungary, where they were put on trains and taken to various extermination camps.

These are Erzsi's own words of those life-and-death days:

I look at all these people, worried, restless. I am restless too. I can't sit still. Soon curiosity gets the better of me, especially with all these nooks and crannies asking to be investigated. A woman about my age is standing next to me.

'I'm going to climb up there to have a closer look,' I comment to her.

'My name is Edit.[16] I'll come with you.'

'And I am Erzsi. Let's go. Who knows what we might find?'

'Dead rats probably.'

We clamber up and find a brick ledge. There is enough room for both of us, and dangling our legs in mid-air high above the thronging hordes we feel like royalty. It seems to us that we are in the Budapest Opera House, sitting in a plush balcony box lined with red velvet watching with interest Victor Hugo's Les Misérables unfolding below. Up there in the gods we don't feel part of the play at all.

We both realise at the same time that we're desperate to go to the toilet. There are no toilets anywhere in the brickworks and we're not allowed outside. We climb higher.

'Watch out, Erzsi, the bricks are crumbly!'

'Nah, I'm OK.'

We are now in the chimney. It's not too safe, but there is a hole surrounded by some bricks and enough headroom to stand up. We have found our toilet. Seeing us up there, more women follow.

'Hey, I bet you can't hit the chimney hole square on!' one of them challenges.

'You just watch! Pretty good, don't you think?'

'I can do better than that!'

'Show us!' we all chorus.

We have a good few laughs, caring little what effect our bravado has on the people below.

After a while we clamber down to the rest of the misérables. We had not had anything to eat all day, but Edit and I still have some food in our rucksacks.

An old gentleman shuffles to us and the three of us start talking. He speaks well, with a certain quiet authority ... obviously well educated. It turns out he was a Professor of Hungarian Literature at the University of Budapest. He was picked up by the Arrow Cross unprepared and had no provisions. He's so frail he couldn't have carried much. He tells us he hasn't eaten in three days. Edit and I share our tins of sardines with him. The company is good and the evening passes quickly.

There is a general consensus that the War could not last much longer. The Germans are in retreat and we might be one of the last batches of Jews to be on our way to the camps. 'Well,' I think, 'if this is the case ...'

And my head is buzzing with plans to escape. I don't know how, when or where, but it must be soon. If we are the last or one of the last, then I only need to survive a short time and not fear recapture and vengeance. Only a few days ...

---

16 Even with her impeccable memory, Erzsi could not remember the name of her companion through this ordeal. I call her Edit.

On the fourth morning an Arrow Cross official gives the order, 'All right you bunch of filthy, dirty Jews, you rag-tag heap of garbage. Time for you to get off your lazy arses and use your own withered legs. No taxis here! You have exactly ten minutes. Anyone not in the line outside will be shot.'

Edit and I are ready in five. We march about twenty kilometres before we stop for the night. I am hungry all the time. I have solid shoes on and I am young and fit. I walk fast, quickly overtaking the crowd. We are divided into smaller groups with a Hungarian Arrow Cross officer in charge of each. Every day there's a new officer on duty.

It's quite late when we arrive at Piliscsaba and are herded into a large warehouse. It's empty and all we find is the dirty, half-rotten wooden floor and once whitewashed grey and peeling walls. We collapse on the hard floorboards and use the surrounding field as our toilet. Men to the left, women to the right. Early next morning we are ready to march on.

Before we leave, the commandant orders, 'Doctors, step forward!'

Maybe one of the guards or officers is ill?

'Lawyers, step forward!'

Hah, these barbaric men have an ounce of decency left in them after all. They're showing respect to the educated, singling them out for better treatment. And we soon find out, the doctors and lawyers do, indeed, get special treatment.

'Clean up the whole area. I want to see nothing but grass on the field. The world wants no Jewish shit left behind. You swine! You think you're somebody? I'll teach you who you are! You are nobodies, nothing!'

The Jewish doctors and lawyers pick up with their bare hands not only all the bits of paper and general rubbish scattered over the area, but also the excrement. They have nowhere to wash their hands.

Then we are ready to march the next twenty kilometres. Gradually the Hungarian Arrow Cross men are joined, and later replaced, by German Nazi officers.

We pass one town after another. The local people are used to watching the daily cruelty of the officers against the Jews – we are prodded none too gently with the heavy butts of their guns, with threats of being shot to anyone who falls down or lags behind. And all along the officers are yelling and swearing at us.

Piliscsaba, though in Hungary, is a Swab town. The Swabians are Germans, and are notoriously antisemitic. Still, as we file past, the women line the highway and, from their gathered-up aprons, throw us thick slices of country-baked bread.

'You poor souls. Here, take it. May god save you!'

As the women throw the bread, the Nazis and the Arrow Cross men belt their backs with their guns. It does not stop them. Our captors don't like all this display of compassion and we are being marched through the town at the fastest possible pace. The Swabian women have to trot along to keep up with us. It doesn't deter them and they return to their homes only when they run out of bread.

Cruelty and betrayal, kindness, compassion and loyalty came from unexpected corners during this War.

It's November. And cold and grey and wet. It is pelting down; most of us are shivering. I am still walking at a steady pace; it helps keep me warm. I have the pack I made from mother's rug on my back. In it I'm carrying my ski pants and jacket for warmth, a few tins of sardines and a blanket.

At this stage I am still feeling fit and strong. For me it's no more than a couple of long days of hiking, which I used to do regularly for pleasure, but others around me are finding it difficult. Every so often we are given a break, and I notice that there is a poor hunchbacked woman barely dragging herself along. I met her last night, but we didn't talk. Her bag is far too heavy for her and I offer to carry it. She gratefully accepts. Now I have a pack in the front and one on my back and an umbrella above keeping me dry. Nicely balanced and warm.

Near the end of the War there were many foreigners around in Hungary, 'inside' observers of the political situation, foreign correspondents of newspapers and the curious. Under the Nazi occupation they were free to come and go. They line the open highway taking photos, watching us march along. And here I am wearing a simple, well-cut English suit with my good, solid mountaineering boots, and holding my umbrella high above my head. I was the only person mad enough to carry one. I, and my umbrella, provide a source of great merriment. I hear cameras clicking, as the observers burst into a laugh.

Some of the spectators call out, 'It won't do you much good where you're going! You'll need a bit more protection than that!'

Stuff 'em! Anyway, I wouldn't want to get drenched to the bone and possibly even catch a cold on the way to being exterminated. And I hold my umbrella high.

Another twenty kilometres later that evening, we reach Dorog and head towards the cattle market, now unused. Quite appropriate, I think; we are en route to be slaughtered. By now nearly all of the Hungarian gendarmes have left us and we are guarded mostly by Germans.

'How kind of these lovely Germans. Make us feel comfortable in this palace of bovine fear and death. Getting us gently acclimatised.'

'Yeah ... Preparing us for the camps, the gas chambers.'

'Not me. I ain't goin',' I hiss between my teeth.

Edit and I are still well out at the front of the group. The gendarme in charge of us, one of the last Hungarian guards, is a youngish man, quite good-looking. We seem to impress him; we still have spring in our step, even with little food in our bellies after the third twenty-kilometre day.

He gives us the slightest of nods and whispers as we come to the bridge leading into the slaughterhouse, 'I'll go to the right here, but you two go left. I won't turn around.'

We are afraid to open our mouths, but smile our grateful thanks to him. I can't explain why, but I am not yet ready to make a break for it. It simply doesn't feel right and so we don't take up the offer.

In the morning we are off to the next town, yet another twenty kilometres. There they feed us. We are all starving. A huge cauldron of 'soup' is brought out. It has been made from turnips and water and has a greasy layer of pork fat floating on top. The hungry crowd attacks the food, filling to the brim whatever container they can lay their hands on.

The officer in charge, his face beetroot red, screams, 'You filthy Jews, you're no better than swine, you animals. Look at you swilling at the trough. I'll teach you some table manners!' and he belts the people with his rifle.

'Stand in line! Ask for your meal. You think you have the right to this food? You think you have the right to be fed for nothing? After all you've stolen from us?'

I am starving, but can't even look at the slop and am about to throw up at the sight of it. I have run out of provisions, so the following day I march on an empty stomach to the next stop, a village near Komárom. Hunger is getting the better of us all. At night we are fed again. This time the food looks a little more palatable and I have a couple of spoonfuls.

The following day we march towards Ács. After we leave Komárom, we find ourselves on the shores of the Danube. The officer closest to me is a most unpleasant, brutish-looking man with eyes far too close, a chin far too protruding and a low, wrinkled forehead.

'Are we going to cross the river?' I ask him.

In a raspy, sarcastic bark he answers, 'Nah, I'm going sailing in my luxury yacht with the commandant.'

I take a breath and stop for a minute. Maybe the hunger is getting to me. Then I turn to him and say, 'Please, you go ahead, enjoy the trip! Unfortunately I get seasick. I won't be joining you.'

His glare, not to mention his rifle, were ready to smite me.

During the day, in full view of everyone, the German guard shot a woman because she fell and could not get up again. Everyone is worn out and morale is very low.

Ács is the last town before the Austrian border. I have to escape tonight, before we get to Ács.

It is a dark night, overcast, still raining. While everyone is asleep with hunger, exhaustion and fear, Edit and I slip away. We walk quite a distance. There is nothing here, being November, only fallow fields. No houses, no light, no moon, no sign of civilisation. That suits us fine. After a couple of hours of walking into the nowhere we reach a large haystack. We're dead beat and feel too scared to even know it.

'This'll do us,' we say in unison.

We are soaked to the bone, and it is cold. To make a shelter, a sort of a little cubby for the night, we pull handfuls of wet hay out from the bottom of the stack. We snuggle into it close to each other, and sleep fitfully, shivering through the night. The next morning there is a pitiful sunshine. Looking around, now in daylight, we still can't see any activity, any sign of people. We are so tired that we decide to stay here and rest up a bit. We strip down to our negligees and lay our wet gear carefully on the haystack, hoping to dry it. We fall asleep again, but our ears remain cocked to any noise.

Both during the daily march over the last week and at night I try to imagine everybody's face in the family. My Laci is with me all the time, I can clearly see Feri and Gizka and Stefka, but I cannot conjure up your face and I try and try as hard as I can. It upsets me terribly, but I have no picture of you.

In the morning a soldier comes by. He is possibly billeted in the nearest settlement patrolling the area, as we are not far from the border.

'What are you doing here?' he demands, while turning his head from our near-naked bodies. Grabbing whatever is at hand to cover ourselves, I answer, 'We got so wet last night. We're trying to dry out.'

It's obvious he knows the real reason for our being here. 'Get dressed! I'll take you to the compound.'

My heart sinks. We would be shot or at best marched off to Auschwitz. The soldier has possibly given us a death sentence. I throw my clothes on, stand up and look him straight in the eye. 'I can't see the compound from here,' I say to him. 'Is it far?'

'Over there,' and he nods with his head in the direction.

'Still in Hungary?'

'No, over the border.'

I still have a chance here within the borders. Hungary is my home, Austria is enemy territory. Crossing the border will be the end of us for sure.

I am so petrified, I am not even able to show fear. I start talking, ask what part of Hungary he comes from, commiserate with him about having to be away from his family. He is married and has a little son. I remark how good he looks in uniform. He is a pleasant young man, happy to forget the War momentarily. Then I blurt out, 'You know, I've been told by one of the officers in our unit that the deportation of Jews would stop in just three days.'

'I know of no such thing. Nobody told me that.'

Not listening to him, I continue, 'If we could remain on Hungarian soil for a few more days we'd be safe. Please.'

Edit knows me well enough by now and lets me do the talking. I am the more brazen one, and she throws a pleading look towards the soldier. He takes pity on us. Maybe with the end of the War so near he wants to minimise the burden on his conscience; maybe he is simply a kind man.

'*Turn around and go. On the top of the hill you'll see a road leading to a shepherd's hut. I'll make some enquiries. Wait there and I'll return later tonight.*'

We thank him.

The hut is indeed a typical shepherd's hut, a triangular pyramid contraption with no door and a clay floor covered with straw. To our surprise a woman is already there, and what's more I recognise her.

'*Mrs Klein, of all the places one meets old acquaintances!*'

'*Yes. Well. I could imagine better circumstances,*' she responds, the gravity of the world weighing upon her.

She has lost all sense of the bizarre. Not many have my warped sense of gallows humour. I had met the woman in Budapest, where she ran a sack-patching business. '*So how did you get here?*' I asked her.

'*A peasant saw me in the fields and he directed me to the hut. He said he would return tonight with some food.*'

'*We'll have quite a crowd then. We were found by a soldier and he, too, is going to come back later on.*'

Mrs Klein's face twists with fear. She does not like the idea of this large gathering, especially not the possible presence of the military. She vanishes as soon as it's dark.

It is pitch black when the peasant arrives. He lights a match and finds there is no Mrs Klein, but instead Edit and me. My wedding ring's still on my finger and it glints in the light. He notices it immediately and demands that I give it to him if we don't want to be reported to the authorities. But I am too fast and say to him, '*You must be mistaken,*' while quickly slipping the ring off and dropping it into the straw. '*Look!*' And I show him my bare hands in the feeble light of the next match. '*No ring.*'

He examines my hands carefully. His food deal is with Mrs Klein only. We have to buy his silence. Amongst all the people who helped us, he was the only one who demanded payment for it. In the end he is satisfied with a couple of pairs of nylon stockings Edit had in her pack and I give him some cash I carry sewn into my trouser cuffs. Then he starts to bargain for more payment for the food, which he says he will bring later. We don't trust him and want him gone. We turn down the offer of food. The soldier returns, luckily well after the peasant. He is a decent man.

'*I asked around at the compound,*' he reports, '*but it is not likely that the deportation of Jews will stop soon. Wait here for a few days.*'

'*Thank you, but we haven't eaten anything in days. We won't last that long.*'

'*I'll send someone with food.*'

True to his word, he sends another peasant with provisions in the form of home-baked bread. I am so hungry by now that I can't eat. I have a bad case of diarrhoea and I can't hold anything down. Even the smell of food makes me want to throw up. This peasant, unlike the one the night before, is a kind man.

'Whatever you do, don't go to Ács. The place is overrun by Arrow Cross men. Go instead to the railwaytrack man's house. His wife is a good woman, she's sure to help you out.'

I look at the man in amazement. 'How do you know we are Jewish?'

He laughs. 'Look at yourselves. Look at your clothes: good walking boots and a well-tailored suit. City gear. Who else would be at a shepherd's shack miles from nowhere in that get-up?'

I suppose I had not thought about how incongruous we appear in the landscape. We would have to do something about it. We are very grateful for his warning and his advice.

The watchman lives a few kilometres before the railway station at Ács. His job is to change the sidings manually before the train is due.

By now too many people know of us. We decide not to stay any longer and go in search of the railway man. He is not at home, but his wife is, and just as the man said, she's a good woman. She gives us clothing that would be worn by the locals, a simple blue cotton dress, a headscarf, more suitable shoes and a basket. No self-respecting peasant woman is ever seen travelling without her basket. Despite this passable disguise, we still have our own work cards with us, showing not religion, but our correct names and Budapest addresses. Heaven help us if anyone ever asks to look at them.

Dressed to kill, we walk to the railway station in Ács, my new (too small) shoes making the journey agonising. We spot a man outside the waiting room, a local, and I start to chat to him, though even that is risky – I don't have the right local accent. I ask him if there is a homestead nearby. He says, 'Yes, there is.'

'What is it called?'

'Csillagtanya.' Star homestead.

My accent tells him we are city people and he probably can guess that we're on the run. I have nothing to lose. 'If anyone asks us, would it be all right to use you as a reference?'

Without any expression on his face he shrugs his shoulders as if to say, 'What's it to me?' By now it is getting dark, but luckily it's not raining. I've had enough rain for a while and we are dressed in lightweight clothes.

We sit down in the waiting room. The train is due and by now a few people have gathered. From here on I decide not to talk unless I must.

Two Arrow Cross men enter with only one torch between them. There are two old women sitting on the bench, not looking up, minding their own business. The officials demand their papers. They hand them over.

'You're Jews. You're wasting your time trying to get away from justice. You'll all go down the tube sooner or later! Get outside!'

Edit and I stare at our shoes with great interest. We don't get involved. Maybe if we don't see them, they will not notice us. But our time comes soon enough. The Arrow Cross men systematically check everyone's ID. It's my turn. He takes my card and reads out loud: 'Mrs László Kohn – Jew.'

I do my trick again; it worked before! And I angrily raise my voice at him. 'No it's not. Didn't they teach you to read? It's K.á.h.n – a German name.'

The man is embarrassed in front of a waiting room full of people and especially in front of his colleague. He returns my card without another word. After looking at Edit's papers, he sends her outside to join the two old women. With feigned indignation, she demands, 'But I am from Csillagtanya. I came with the man waiting over there,' indicating the person we asked earlier to be our alibi. 'Why are you sending me out?' Edit is allowed to stay.

We notice the two old women are taken away.

At that moment we hear the shrill sounds of an air raid warning siren. The torches are turned off and we're all too scared to move. But we need not have worried; Ács is a very small station and unlikely to get bombed. At last the train arrives. We get on and are on our way home.

A man of about my age sits opposite and keeps making eyes at me. I am worried in case he can smell my fear. But no, he's simply interested in making conversation. Despite my wedding ring, he's trying to pick me up!

He starts to chat and asks if we could go out somewhere. I blush, keep my eyes to the ground and only harrumph yes or no. I don't dare open my mouth because of the accent.

At 4am we arrive at Budapest's Eastern Railway Station. The place is crawling with Arrow Cross men. There is a curfew until 6am, so the two of us sit on a bench and pretend to be asleep. We could certainly use the rest, but are far too anxious to take a nap. One of the officials is about to 'wake' us, but the other takes pity on us.

'Hey, Zoli, they're only a couple of peasant women. They're tired. Let them be,' and to our relief the uniforms walk away. At 6 o'clock we start on our way home. Our path leads us to Üllői Road, right past the Arrow Cross headquarters. Again we are spotted and our papers checked. Amazingly, we are allowed to pass – two countrywomen with Budapest addresses.

After that Edit and I part company and we never again see each other.

I am too tired and unwell to make my way home and decide to seek asylum for the day at an acquaintance, Blanka's. She is a Christian woman – the person who attended Vera's baptism only a few months ago.

She lives nearby, only a few minutes away, but has to be at work by 8am. She won't let me stay in her flat alone, so we leave together at 7.30. Now I have to drag myself another ten kilometres to get home.

At last I arrive. No one recognises me. Mother of course is in the ghetto with Auntie Stefka. I've lost 9kg in the nine days, I look gaunt, feel ill and exhausted and I am still *wearing my peasant's garb. They don't want to let me in; they are sending me away. But you come running to me.*

'Visszavagy a katonáéktól, Anyukám?' (You're back from the soldiers, Mummy?)

A relative, who came to visit me in Budapest, told me years later what happened to my group. They were marched directly to Bergen-Belsen, one of the most notorious concentration camps. One of the guards told me en route that it was originally built for 5000 people, but they crammed 50,000 in there. The conditions were so awful, typhoid fever broke out and the whole place had to be burnt down. Everybody in my group perished.

On 18 November I arrived back home and a few days later Laci's last letter from Pécs arrived:

13 November

… Next week I'm likely to leave the hospital, but I don't know where I'll end up. It's a bit unsettling to hear the news that the forced labour companies in Pest are being taken away. But I believe in the good Lord that he will continue to help us, even though not straight away, but we will meet again and will never again have to part from each other. This hope gives strength and stamina. You, too, my dear, trust. – Many kisses your Laci

PS. I have no news of the parcel so far.

Laci had been waiting in vain for his uncles Rezső and Béla to bring him clothes. He was oblivious to the fact that by July all the country towns had been 'cleansed' and their Jewish residents sent to the extermination camps.

21

THE WAR COMES CLOSE TO HOME; CELLARS

In the second half of November Laci returned from Pécs to Budapest, hoping the War was just about over. It was not safe for him to stay with us because he should have been with his company, and rumour had it that the Germans were looking for escapees.

Before the War, Pista Kovács, Laci's cousin, ran a walnut-shelling business in an Ötvös Street cellar. To get to it one needed to go down a set of steps and then negotiate a heavy metal door with a crossbar. There was only one small window for air, light and ventilation, and towards the end of the War, in 1944, when the Kovács family hid there, even this window was covered. After Laci returned from Bor, afraid he might again be taken away, he was given shelter by Pista.

The cellar was not well equipped – there was only a small electric hotplate, a few provisions and some large barrels full of walnut shells. A toilet had to be improvised from an old barrel, and all activities, including cooking, took place in complete darkness. They slept on the floor on hay, sharing the warmth and comfort with the local rats.

One day there was a noise outside and, thinking it was the Arrow Cross, Laci quickly hid between four drums. It was a false alarm, but when he tried to clamber out, he found himself stuck, and the barrels were far too heavy to move. The others threw him a sheet which he twisted into a rope. He hung onto it while everyone pulled him out.

Erzsi went to visit Laci whenever she could. Mostly she waited until nightfall to sneak in but sometimes she arrived during the day. She was risking her life breaking curfew. For Erzsi the conditions in the cellar were difficult to bear even as a visitor, but her love for her husband overcame her revulsion at the dirt and the rats. Erzsi had been obsessively clean and tidy from the time she was a child; given a choice between spending her last pengő on food or soap, she said, memorably, 'Soap, of course!' and meant it.

One day, while waiting for the tram, a policeman appeared in the unpleasant company of two uniformed Arrow Cross men. They marched up and demanded her papers. She kept her cool.

'What papers would you like? I have my complete life history here in my handbag.'

The policeman smiled and said her ID would do. That was the only document she had on her. The policeman took his time studying it, all the while carefully shielding it from his Arrow Cross companions. He gave her a knowing look and wished her a good day. The three officials went on their way but Erzsi, very shaken, retreated to spend some time with her husband in the cellar.

By late December, it was no longer safe for Laci to remain where he was, as too many people knew about the hiding place. He managed to go somewhere else, where he stayed until the liberation of Budapest in mid-January 1945.

❋   ❋   ❋

Although now a designated Jewish house, Auntie Stefka's place had many Christian tenants and even owners of apartments. Before the War they all got along fine, but when Stefka and Gizka were evacuated to the ghetto in November and many Yellow-Starred strangers were forced to take up residence in the house, the tension between Christians and Jews became serious, at times explosive.

In April 1944, when the War first came to Budapest, I was too young to understand what it meant. It became part of a game I played with a new friend, a little boy my own age. A favourite and oft-repeated scenario was to imitate the frequent warnings on the radio. I'd call, 'Air raid Veszprém, air raid Veszprém! Let's hide quickly!' and we'd both scuttle under the table.

I had no toys, but Gizka had a large collection of buttons of all shapes, colours and sizes. After tipping the contents of the box onto the floor, I spent hours sorting them. Erzsi was chastised for allowing a young child to play with such small items, but I didn't put things into my mouth.

Then the bombs began to come closer to home. Like most blocks of flats, the Sziget Street house had a large cellar that could be used as a bunker. When the raids got closer we went down there. Despite being a poor sleeper, the air raids must have been very familiar by then, because at times I slept right through them.

On one occasion I started to play with another child, Éva Éber, an Arrow Cross chief's daughter. Her grandmother pulled her away immediately, saying, 'Évike, dear, don't play with the little girl, she has a bad cold.'

I was in perfect health. Erzsi's blood boiled as she thought to herself, 'Being Jewish is neither a disease, nor infectious.' She couldn't let it go, and remarked, 'This little girl doesn't have a cold; she was simply born in the wrong place at the wrong time.'

With the frequency and closeness of the bombings, tensions increased. In the end the Christians commandeered the bunker to the exclusion of the Jewish residents. Next to the bunker was a small windowless box room, and when it was not possible to stay upstairs the Jewish children slept there. There was so little room we lay shoulder to shoulder – if one child turned during the night, all children had to turn. The adults slept sitting up, if they managed to sleep at all.

The Sziget Street house had seven direct hits, one particularly bad. When the siren sounded, a Jewish man living on the fourth floor tried to pick up his toddler granddaughter to rush her to the cellar. As he reached out a bomb hit him. The little girl survived; he didn't. The staircase in front of their unit collapsed and wasn't fixed until the bombings stopped. His dismembered body stayed in the rubble until the end of the War.

Most of the Jewish residents went hungry. But not me – I had Erzsi.

Erzsi made a 'stove' of sorts from the metal buckets in which she'd stored rendered chicken fat before the War. She cut a piece out from the rim on one side and turned the bucket upside down. She fed the 'stove' with match-sized bits of bamboo from a broken chair and used the top of the bucket as the cooktop.

She made me semolina pudding or soup from veal bones, the latter taking more than an hour of constant feeding of the fire. All of this took place in the backyard between raids, with a chorus of hungry onlookers. Erzsi guarded the pot vigilantly, sometimes with tears rolling down her face from hunger.

For dessert she made me a drink of hot water with a dissolved vitamin tablet and a spoonful of sugar and, if she had one, a biscuit. While I was relatively well fed, the rest of the family was starving.

On 27 November the Arrow Cross closed down the protected houses with the excuse that the protection papers had been falsified – nearly 20,000 Jews were sent from those houses by cattle train to Germany. The Red Army, who had first come into the city at the end of October, resumed its offensive on 19 December and a week later a road linking Budapest to Vienna was seized by Soviet troops, completing the encirclement of Budapest. As a result of this, nearly a million people, soldiers and civilians, were trapped within the city.

Budapest was bombed by the Allies, and urban warfare increased. Food shortages were more and more common and soldiers and civilians had to rely on finding their own sources of sustenance. Some resorted to butchering frozen horse carcasses in the streets. Towards the end of the War daily rations consisted of melted snow, horse meat (if lucky), and 150 grams of bread.

By this time some Hungarian soldiers who had been captured by the Russians had defected, and fought on the Soviet side, but the Germans refused to surrender and defended every street and every house, on Hitler's order.

Around Christmas 1944, Erzsi was at home in Sziget Street when she heard the sound of gunfire very close. She crept out onto the balcony and lay on her stomach to peer through the gap between the concrete floor and balcony railing.

People were being shot below her on the street. The gunmen were wearing Arrow Cross uniforms and only stopped when the small group in front of them were all crumpled on the ground. The scene etched itself into Erzsi's memory – lying dead in the street were an older gentleman with a small goatee beard, a woman dressed in a beige tartan skirt, and a very young man, maybe only a child, with a pair of large spectacles. They were all wearing Yellow Stars on the left side of their coats.

This small group of Jews, for one reason or another, had found themselves on the street close to the 5pm curfew. They had hurried to the nearest house with a Yellow Star – our house in Sziget Street – hoping to find safety and shelter for the night. They had knocked on the door, but nobody had answered. They knocked harder, louder, with more urgency. Surely somebody would let them in!

The Christian couple employed to look after the house could not see who was at the door. They were hiding an Army deserter – a cousin – and so were too scared to let anyone in until they were sure that all evidence of the fugitive was out of sight. The husband peeked through the curtains and blinds and was about to open the door when ra ... ta ... ta ... ta. Fourteen innocents paid with their lives for that delay.

Being winter, it was now dark, and the dead were left on the street. The night was cold, the snow had turned to ice by morning. At dawn the able-bodied occupants of the house, Erzsi included, were ordered by the Arrow Cross to dig the dead out of their frozen beds. It was very hard work, but with the uniformed men barking orders at them, joking and shouting denigrating remarks about the deceased, the residents dug the murdered out of the ice as fast as they could and then, without dignity, unceremoniously, tossed them onto an open cart.

Many Jews from the Yellow Star houses were made to do work around Budapest – dig trenches, clean up bomb sites or, like Erzsi, dig the dead out of their frozen temporary tombs.

At the end of December a new edict was issued: any Jews found outside the ghetto would be killed. Meanwhile, many of those who were still in the protected houses, and who had been granted diplomatic protection by Raoul Wallenberg and Carl Lutz, were murdered. All of these houses were within a block or two of us.

The ghetto in and around Klauzál Square was established in November 1944 and remained until fighting on the streets stopped, less than three months later. The area was completely sealed off from the outside world: rubbish and waste were not collected, the dead lay on the streets and piled up in the bombed-out storefronts, and the buildings were over-crowded, often with 40 to an apartment that had one kitchen, one toilet. Disease spread rapidly. The Jewish leadership managed to send in only one slice of bread and a thin soup once a week, for the children.

More than half of the people forced into the ghetto were sent to death camps. On 1 January 1945, the Battle of Budapest began, and a couple of weeks later the Soviets freed the streets where the protected houses were. On 6 January, because of Wallenberg's intervention, the deportations stopped. Meanwhile, the fighting continued at Buda, and the Arrow Cross continued to murder. All the patients and doctors of the Maros Street Jewish hospital, where I was born a couple of years earlier, were shot.

The remaining defenders finally surrendered on 13 February 1945. Budapest lay in ruins, with more than 80 per cent of its buildings destroyed or damaged, the Hungarian Parliament and the Castle among them. Before they left, German troops destroyed all five bridges spanning the Danube.

The Soviet 'liberators' sent 30,000 Germans and half a million Hungarians to the gulags, including many Jewish forced labourers. In some villages the entire adult population was taken to labour camps in the Donets Basin, and many died there. In the Battle of Budapest the final tally of casualties was huge: 150,000 Germans and Hungarians dead, wounded or captured, 80,000 Soviet troops dead or missing, and a further 240,000 wounded and/or sick, as well as 38,000 civilians dead.[17]

Almost 50 per cent of Budapest's Jewish population died during the Holocaust. When the returned tried to reclaim their property, they were resented and rejected by the non-Jewish Hungarians. They no longer had a homeland.

---

17 Krisztián Ungváry. *The Siege of Budapest: One Hundred Days in World War II.* New Haven, CT: Yale University Press, 2005.

22

THE TAIL END AND THE AFTERMATH
OF THE WAR

It was December 1944; the Axis had lost the War. However, the gold of the deported Jews was still arriving by the truckload at warehouses all over Hungary. The carefully sorted items were repackaged and transported to the so-called Gold Train, to be moved to Germany for 'safekeeping'. All was to be returned to Hungary after the War.

There was one slight problem, though: there was no available engine to pull the train across the border. Finally a private German company offered to take it – for a fee. To add further insult to injury, in 1947 the Soviets put in a claim for five-and-a-half million pengős, the total value of the confiscated Jewish money. They felt it was rightfully theirs as they had liberated the Jews, and with not much choice, the Hungarian Government paid it. Neither the money nor the gold was returned to Hungary and the surviving Jewish people were not compensated.

The number of people robbed, the amount of wealth taken, and the speed with which it all happened made the economic annihilation of the Hungarian Jewry unique in the Holocaust.

* * *

Sometime in late January, Laci came out of hiding. Poor Laci had not seen me since I was a newborn babe, and now he was welcomed by my fists and kicks. I was pummelling this stranger that Erzsi referred to as 'your Daddy'.

As soon as the fighting stopped, we moved into the Reich factory's warehouse on Váci Road. There was no space for a bed so we all slept on large, lumpy bundles of shoelaces, but at least we were together. When the factory opened again, Laci had his old job back.

Later we rented a flat, further down Váci Road, which was owned by a Kovács cousin, Sándor. It was well situated for us – just opposite Lehel market, and only a ten-minute walk from my grandmother Gizka's place in Sziget Street.

The 1944–45 winter was bitter, and we, like everybody else, had no heating or cooking facilities. Erzsi noticed that in the Sziget Street cellar, among the mounds of coal dust, there were still a few lumps of coal left – using a bed frame she sifted it and lugged the few buckets' worth of coal back home for us to use in our small stove.

Szálasi, the leader of the Arrow Cross Party, fled the city early in December 1944, well before the fighting stopped. After the War he was captured: he was hanged in 1946 in the yard of Markó jail.

The Regent of Hungary, Miklós Horthy, was in German captivity at the end of the War. He was about to be tried for war crimes when the Americans took him to stand as a witness at the Nuremberg Trial for war criminals. When the trials finished he moved to Germany, then emigrated to Portugal, where he published his autobiography. He died in 1957, aged 89.

Eichmann was captured by the Americans in 1945. He escaped, was given false papers by some Franciscan monks and then settled in Argentina. But he was found by the Israeli secret agency Mossad in 1960. In 1961 he was tried and executed in Israel. He took no responsibility for his actions: his claim was that he was just following the orders of a legal government.

After the Soviet Army liberated the city, Wallenberg was seen on 17 January 1945 being taken to a Soviet prison. No one knows what happened to him.

*   *   *

In the middle of January all my grandmothers returned from the ghetto. Cina and Jolán moved into their sister Aranka's house, each in her own little flat. Gizka and Stefka shifted from the sixth floor to the second floor, as they could no longer walk up six flights of stairs when the lift was out of order.

When the War was truly finished, communications resumed and a tally could be done: Gizka Stefka and Erzsi were faced with the aching loss of 23 members of their close family. I expect that on Laci's side, the count would be similar.

*   *   *

There were thermal waters in Buda, and in the streets near the Danube on the Pest side too. Some of the Russians now occupying Budapest were stationed on Margaret Island, just opposite Gizka's flat in Sziget Street (later renamed

Hegedüs Gyula Street), and they walked across the bridge to Sziget Street to get hot water. Gizka, who spoke fluent Slovakian, could understand Russian. One day a young soldier came over and she asked him, 'Kolya, my boy, you're so very young, why did you enlist?'

'For tovarish Stalin' (for comrade Stalin), he proudly replied.

Another Russian, a young woman called Svetlana, being away from home, feeling lonely and lost, became a regular visitor at Sziget Street. Svetlana had a baby, but she had no idea how to care for it. Her baby was kept wrapped up tightly in bunting, hands and feet so bundled up that the poor little boy couldn't move at all. Gizka taught Svetlana how to look after the child: to allow him to move freely and to feed the baby properly. The young Russian woman found herself a kind and capable surrogate mother in Gizka.

When they first met, Gizka praised the Russians for fighting for Hungary, to help bring an end to the nightmare of the past year. Svetlana shook her head and said, 'You just wait with your praise, Auntie Gizka. Your whole life will change soon. You will not have time to go and chat with the other women in the house or help your daughter with the baby. They will send you out to work. There will be lots of rules. You won't be able to sleep, your whole life will change. Just wait and see, Babushka.'

Svetlana's predictions came true. After the communist government took over, Gizka – then 60 – had to get a job. First she shelled walnuts, then she worked as a parking lot attendant and finally as an inspector on a coal-delivery truck. She had to work to the age of 70 before she finally became eligible for the pension.

In 1946, the Soviet POWs started to return home. Every day Gizka and Erzsi went to meet the trains at Budapest's Western Rail Terminus, searching for Feri. One day Erzsi grabbed her mother's arm and said, 'Look, Mother. Look at that poor man, he's nothing but a walking skeleton!'

It was Feri. They rushed him to hospital, and he stayed there for a couple of weeks. Gizka made him two litres of soup every day and Feri devoured it in minutes in front of her, and soon recovered, physically at least. Oh, the power of mother-made soup!

When he was better, he met Éva, a young, cheerful woman, whom he married. Feri was an odd, sullen, morose sort of a man, but he had a kind heart, and he remained very much in love with Éva to the end of his life.

23

MY MEMORIES OF THE WAR

I had no memory of the War. It happened a long time ago. It happened to others, not to me. And yet I was reminded by two events that showed me that even if the mind does not remember, the body does, and the experience is not forgotten. Had this body-remembering not happened to me personally, I would have vehemently denied its validity, thought of it as the figment of someone's over-active imagination. But it did happen.

I was reading *Child Survivors of the Holocaust* by Paul Valent, a Sydney psychologist, in which ten Holocaust survivors tell their stories. I did not connect with any of them, but when, at the end of the book, the author summarised the behaviour of severely traumatised children, to my great surprise, I recognised myself.

I was intrigued, and went to a meeting of the Child Survivors Group in Sydney. We finished late, and as I don't live in the city, one of those present, Sylvia, a total stranger to me, very kindly suggested I stay the night at her place. Uncharacteristically, I accepted. She served me home-made chicken soup for dinner. I listened to Sylvia's memories of the War, of the loss of her parents, and the long-lasting effects it had on her life. It was not until the small hours that we finally went to bed.

My room was comfortably cosy. I felt extremely tired and yet could not doze off. After a while I was aware of lying on my side, my body knotted into a tight ball, hands clenched into fists, stomach hard and tight. I wanted to throw up, but was not able to move. Despite the warm doona I felt cold. My head was empty. I couldn't let go, couldn't relax, couldn't sleep. My feelings had no name.

I stayed like this for a long time, maybe hours, while continuing to shiver uncontrollably. When finally my body was ready to let go and started to relax, the old and frequently recurring childhood nightmare of a Nazi pointing a gun at my family came back to me.

The next day I returned home, but was listless, agitated and distracted. The following day was no better. At lunchtime an overwhelming feeling of exhaustion took hold of me and I felt completely depleted for the rest of the day, as if I'd just returned from a week of hard labour.

Sometime later I talked to a counsellor, and on describing the incident she said, 'You had a classic case of post-traumatic stress syndrome.'

The War was 60 years ago, what was she talking about? And I have no memory of it. Reading my mind, she explained, 'Even after this time. The body remembers.'

'What does my body remember?'

'Fear. I expect you relived the fear of the War. You were too young to remember, you were pre-verbal, so have no words to describe what you may have felt. But the fear remained entrenched in your body.'

The second reminder was when, in bemoaning the fact that I never feel loved, the counsellor suggested that as an adult I could find the unloved little girl in me, pick her up in my arms and try to love her to bits.

My instant reaction was, 'I can't. It's not possible!'

She insisted, 'But you *do* love your son, you love other children, other people – you are strong enough to learn to love yourself.'

For homework she told me to write about 'Loving myself'. Like a good student I tried, but couldn't. The little me kept on pushing the big me away. Then a grey image appeared.

I am four to five years old, running in the streets of Budapest. Behind me the buildings are crumbling as they are being bombed. There is dust everywhere. There is an all-permeating stench in my nostrils while gunfire fills the air, and I keep running and running on the uneven cobblestones of the city. I have the expression of Edvard Munch's haunting painting, 'The Scream', a terror so absolute it has no words. I step into this picture as an adult to try to stop the little me from running. I pick her up, try to hug her, try to have her close to me, clutch her tight to my body, while soothing the frightened little girl, 'You're all right. I'm here now, I'll protect you, keep you safe.'

She doesn't hear me, she can't, her fright is too great. My small girl feet keep on running, kicking in my arms. Her little face is turned back towards the crumbling city, and she kicks, punches her way out of my arms, and keeps running.

I realise that inside me I have not stopped running ever since I was a little girl. The fear has never gone away, it is still too great. The War I can't remember lives on as a part of me.

PART 3

COMMUNIST TIMES

24

BATHS AND A LITTLE BROTHER

We had no showers, but bathed once a week. If the boiler didn't seize up. If there was enough coal. If there was any coal at all. If Mrs Kovács, the janitor, was at home and had the energy to get it all going. I hated to get wet, but once I braved the tub you couldn't entice me out of it until I was wrinkled like an old woman. Instead of a rubber ducky, I took a little putt-putt boat with me, which ran on candle power. On those occasions when Erzsi lost track of time I continued navigating the rough seas of the bathtub until the water was freezing cold.

It was a different story at my grandmother Gizka's place. She lived on the shores of the Danube and, as the Buda half of Budapest lies on top of hot thermal springs, she had the sulphury steaming water piped right into her flat. Here I could luxuriate in the smelly bath to my heart's content. I slept well on those nights.

When I was about six years old, my mother insisted I learn to swim. For me there was no pool like the Palatinus, named after one of the Roman emperors. The Palatinus was special because it sported an artificial wave-creating machine, a piece of modern technology for modern indulgences. Every half an hour the waves would start, small at first, then bigger and bigger. For my generation, who had no concept of the ocean, it was the best entertainment in the world! We jumped up and down in anticipation or dived right into the waves. We could not ride them, though – the pool was always too crowded for that. In fact there was a nasty little ditty doing the rounds at the time:

'*Aki a Palatinus vizét issza, saját vizét issza vissza.*' (When in Palatinus' waters you dip, your own and everyone else's water you sip.)

It didn't deter any of us.

The instructor Erzsi found was a fitness fanatic, wiry, tough. He used none of today's gentle persuasions to tempt me into the water; there was no shallow pool to dip into for coins. Learning to swim was serious business and the sooner he got it over and done with the better. I, on the other hand, was scared, and was not going to let anyone rush me.

The instructor encircled me with a wide woven belt, hooked to a strong line, which in turn was attached to a rod.

'Get in the water!' he commanded.

I didn't move. When he gave me a stern look, I stated the obvious: 'I can't swim!'

'You're safe at the end of this. You'll never learn without getting wet!'

I didn't trust him. What if he looked away and didn't see me drown? I started to cry, and looked to Erzsi for sympathy. She told me to listen to Mr Instructor and not to make a fuss. He in turn sent Erzsi away to sit at a distance, out of earshot. He was not going to have any nonsense.

'Sit on the edge!' he ordered.

I sat on the edge.

'Hop in!'

'No! No! I can't!' I pleaded.

He did not argue with me. Holding the rod in his right hand, his left gave me a quick shove and I was in deep water, dangling at the end of the fishing line, kicking furiously.

Now he barked down from the dry above, 'Keep on kicking! Good work!'

Screaming, I swallowed what felt like half the pool's water.

'Good! Use the energy in your lungs!' he encouraged. 'Kick harder!' Then he added, helpfully, 'If you close your mouth and breathe through your nose, you'll drink much less!'

I hated him.

After only a few swimming lessons, Erzsi took me for extra practice. I found myself in the outdoor pool of the Palatinus, drowning. She, though heavily pregnant, jumped in the water to rescue me.

I panicked and held on to her with all my might. Through panic my hands became like a clamp and soon she was gasping for air as she desperately attempted to remove my cramped fingers. We were going to drown! Another swimmer noticed our plight, gave Erzsi her arm and pulled us out. We were safe.

Now relaxed, I tried to snuggle up to my mummy, ready to be loved and to celebrate our survival, but she angrily pushed me away. When she finally caught her breath, she screamed at me, 'You stupid girl, don't you have any common sense?'

'But Mummy, I was scared! I can't swim!'

'Why have I been paying for your lessons all this time if you're not even trying? You nearly drowned me!' she yelled.

I was ordered to return to the instructor. He now had full permission to take no pity on me and to keep at it until I learnt to swim, even if it killed me. It did not kill me, but it killed any trust I had in my mother. I listened to and obeyed Erzsi, but had no confidence in her. I knew that what I longed for in the pool was to be saved, comforted and hugged, not to be yelled at. I desperately wanted my brother to be born quickly so I would have someone to love.

It took many lessons, but in time I became a good swimmer. In 1955, aged 13, I joined the newly formed Kilián György Swimming Club. It was the first time I officially belonged to anything, and I had got there on my own merit. We were given Club colours, a tracksuit and a soft, blue terry-towelling bathrobe on permanent loan. For a child who had hardly ever had any new clothes, something new and the *same* as everyone else's was super special. I felt part of the team, I felt important. However, shortly afterwards Hungary and I parted company and my gear had to be returned.

I trained regularly several times a week in Hungary, and later in Canada. I was not fast, but I was a decent distance swimmer, and won several medals at my club, mostly third place. They were part of my one-briefcase of luggage when I left Hungary.

*   *   *

In 1943, Erzsi fell pregnant. She decided to terminate the pregnancy. After the end of the War she found herself expecting again. This time she contracted German measles (rubella) and Dr Kovács advised her to abort. But I still wanted a brother, and I nagged, cajoled and pestered her ceaselessly. She finally gave in.

One day she uttered the magic words as we walked side by side on Csáky Street. 'Vera, we are going to have another baby.'

I skipped and jumped for joy, and afterwards, every morning on our way to my kindy I turned to Erzsi and offered, 'If you like, Mummy, we could talk about my little brother now,' and often we did.

Nine months was a long time to wait: I wanted him to arrive *now*.

'Is the stork bringing him today?' I pestered.

But he, like me, was in no hurry to come.

*   *   *

At his work Laci was the boss, and every couple of months he treated his immediate colleagues to dinner at our place. Erzsi was already a few months pregnant, and my parents were waiting for the right moment to announce the coming of their second offspring. I helped them with this decision. In front of the assembled company I demanded to know if Erzsi had already started making the baby's clothes.

She gave an embarrassed laugh, 'No, not yet.'

'Well, Mummy, really, you'd better start sewing right now. Do you want my baby brother to be born naked?'

From then on Erzsi was teased mercilessly. But soon she did start sewing, and later my brother was born – naked.

It was well past the due arrival date, and after ten months this baby, too, had to be induced. The doctor ordered Erzsi into hospital. Although they had tickets to the opera, this time she obediently followed his instructions, while insisting that Laci should attend the performance on his own. At the end of each act he called to see if there was any news. Gyuri took his time.

The gynaecologist – Dr Marius Hancsók – was beset by questions as the induction was taking effect. It was not the labour or the baby that interested Erzsi, but his name, not a typically Hungarian one.

'What do they call you at home Doctor? Marius? Mario? Hancsi?' she impertinently asked him.

'Madam, don't you worry about my name. Instead, concentrate on giving birth to your baby,' he retorted humourlessly.

Eventually the injections worked, but the birth was excruciatingly painful for both mother and child. It was a difficult delivery because the baby weighed 4.5 kilograms, and Erzsi lacked the appropriate hormones and had a small pelvis. Afterwards she kept on losing blood. She was very close to death when my brother finally arrived at 6am the next day. It was a struggle for him too – his eyes were bloodshot with the effort.

He was duly named György (Gyuri or Gyuri) Iván. György, because we liked it and it was universal; Iván because it was a common Russian name, and because by that time Soviet-inspired communism had taken hold in Hungary. Erzsi thought it was politic. She was not unique in her reasoning – 50 years later I found it amusing to meet many Boris Gonzaleses, Kolya Ramoses and Vladimir Castillos in Cuba.

When Laci told me the news, I wanted to see Gyuri immediately and knew he would want to meet me too. I puffed up with pride at being a Big Sister.

'Be patient. Maybe I can take you tomorrow.'

I didn't understand why I had to be kept waiting. After all, it was I who wanted a brother – he was ordered especially for me!

On the trip to the hospital I fidgeted, jumped up and down and talked incessantly. Finally we arrived. Hand in hand Laci and I walked down the corridor in the basement of the hospital. It was poorly lit, unwelcoming, even spooky – in contrast to the sparkling lights, shiny decorations, lollies and firecrackers I had in my heart for Gyuri's arrival.

Erzsi's room was to the right. She was wearing a cloth over her mouth and holding a bundle in her arms. 'Stop there! Don't come any further! The baby!' she anxiously called out to us.

I stopped, still holding onto Laci. 'Why can't we go in?' I asked.

'Gyuri is very sick. We have to be extremely careful not to give him an infection. We need a face mask, like your mummy is wearing.'

We were in the isolation ward, with Gyuri hovering between life and death. Soon a nurse handed Laci a mask. There wasn't one for me.

'So, how are you, my little angel? Are you all right?' Laci cooed to his wife. 'When can you come home?' the questions tumbled out of him.

'Can I have a mask too?' I whimpered at the door.

'They are for the adults only,' the nurse said curtly as she left.

Erzsi took pity on me and my misery. 'You can come a little closer and look at the baby.'

I was still too far away and couldn't see him properly. In my frustration I kicked the bed.

'Stop it! Don't shake the cot!'

It was the only time Laci had raised his voice to me. I was deeply offended and retreated to the doorway.

'I will hold him up for you to look at. Here. Say hello to your brother,' said Erzsi, holding up the bundle. 'You can look, but only for a minute!'

I had seen other babies. They were plump, pretty, with rosy cheeks and hair. What I saw was a bright-red-faced, bloodshot, wrinkled, hairless, small wizened little old man the size and look of a monkey.

'I want to go home now.' I had had enough.

* * *

Gyuri cried and cried and cried. A woman from the next room in the hospital came in to make a personal inspection of the unhappy child. He had reasons to cry. He had a cold, he coughed, he sneezed and he couldn't breathe. At a moment of ill-fated inspiration the nurse gave him an aspirin without checking with the doctor. Gyuri had an allergic reaction and was very ill. His little tummy gurgled as he suckled and as the milk went in at one end, it all came out the other as diarrhoea. Mother and child stayed in hospital for eight days.

Once at home, there were problems with feeding as well. Mrs Pápa, a friend of Erzsi, who lived only a few blocks away, had had a baby at the same time, and she had milk to spare. Erzsi walked to her place every day to collect expressed milk for Gyuri.

But he continued to cry. Miss Friedmann lived next to us on the third floor, in Unit 2. One day she knocked on our door and reported rather sourly that Gyuri cried for a minimum of seven and a quarter hours every day. Erzsi was more than aware of that fact. Gyuri, however, was too ill to be taken out to a park to give us or Miss Friedmann any peace.

Dr Petényi, the head doctor of the Green Cross, examined him and said, 'Mrs Káhn, you will sweat as much blood with him as 14 other mothers with their children but you will reap that much joy as well.' In her old age she told me rather bitterly that the first half of the prediction came true, but not the second.

Gyuri needed three blood transfusions in the first six months of his life. He was on constant medication, which Erzsi delivered day and night for many months. I was not allowed near my brother for almost a year.

His birth was the first huge disappointment of my young life. Instead of a playmate and someone to love, I had lost whatever little time and attention my mother had for me. And as she had to wake up several times a night to look after Gyuri, she was permanently tired and cranky. I kept away from her as much as I could. I was now truly on my own.

25

SNOW WHITE AND MY FIRST LOVE

A little while before Gyuri was born Erzsi sent me away on a holiday. It was probably done to give herself a break. I was booked into a private house at Göd. I did not want to go despite the promise that there would be other children of my own age for company. I didn't want to go away by myself, and I did not want company, but her mind was made up.

Of the three other children there I knew one – Jancsi Valkó. The others were a boy and a pretty, petite spoilt brat, Marika. I didn't like her at all, probably because I would have loved to be the spoilt one. The adults got us to put on a play, *Snow White and the Two Dwarfs*. I had no acting ability, was tongue-tied and petrified of uttering a word in public, yet wanted to be the beautiful heroine. Instead, I was given the role of the ugly stepmother. My costume – Erzsi's long red velvet dressing gown – set the tone for my dark mood and behaviour. I was so petulant and difficult on stage that I ruined the performance.

Snow White and the Two Dwarfs. Jancsi Valko on the left, Vera next to him as the Ugly Stepmother

So much so that after the play the woman in charge commented loudly – in front of the audience of parents and children – that I had no talent, and would never become an actress. She commiserated with Erzsi for having such an unpleasant and difficult child. My mother concurred with the woman and accepted her sympathy. Now I was embarrassed *and* humiliated.

But I told myself I didn't care if the children would never talk to me again. I knew I would not go back to that place, and I didn't need their friendship. But that was not quite true, because there was something wonderful about that unhappy week – I fell in love. At the ripe old age of five, the dwarf, Jancsi, became my first true love.

He was a good year older than me and he could read. I was desperate to learn, but due to the near-catastrophic shortage of schools and teachers, no child under six could be enrolled. I was five and illiterate. I considered my options. School was out for now but perhaps I could persuade Erzsi to teach me? She refused. I enticed, cajoled, then reasoned, and finally tried to trick her into admitting I was old enough to learn.

'Mummy, how old were *you* when you started school?'

'Well, I didn't really start school properly until I was 8. I had the Fräulein until then.'

'But you could read, couldn't you?'

'I wasn't interested in reading. I preferred to climb trees and chase animals.'

That strategy clearly didn't work, so I tried another. On a No. 6 tram on St István Boulevard, one day, I pointed to the a huge neon sign blinking at us, 'Mummy, what's that squiggly letter called, the one that goes up and down like a zigzag?'

'Oh, you mean the M?' She fell for the trick.

I was thrilled. M became my favourite letter!

'And mummy, next to the M, does the circle have a name?' I knew I was pushing my luck.

'You'll have to wait until you start school. What if I don't teach you properly? The teacher will be upset with me.'

I adored stories, but no one had much time to read to me. Laci was away a lot, travelling, and Erzsi was always busy, particularly once Gyuri arrived. I hardly spent any time with my grandmothers. Cina only came once a week on a Wednesday to cook the main meal of the day.

Jancsi Valkó lived one floor above us. I often sat on the steps below our landing, out of my mother's way, a book in my hand. My heart thumped a little faster whenever Jancsi went past me. He always said hello and once he even asked me to read to him! Of course I couldn't. A few days later he knocked on our door to see if I would like to read a story with him.

The two of us selected a comfy step halfway down the flight of stairs and we sat there side by side, two fair, rosy-cheeked children. I hung on his every word, often looking over his shoulder to try to correlate the sounds with the print on the page. We made this a regular experience. Sometimes Jancsi supplied the book, sometimes I did, but the story was not as important as being read to.

I was in love.

'You look so handsome, Jancsi!' I exclaimed one day.

'And you're very pretty!' he replied in kind.

I loved Jancsi because he enjoyed being with me, and because he had time for me. I decided then and there that we would get married, have two children, with whom I would spend a *lot* of time. And, naturally, I would teach them to read as soon as they wanted me to.

'I will marry you,' he said, 'but what a shame that I don't have a sister instead of a brother. Otherwise she and Gyuri could have married, too.'

Very soon after this, Jancsi's family had to move and he disappeared from my life.

I missed him terribly and nagged my mother about bringing us together, to invite Jancsi to our place or to let me visit him. But Erzsi laughed at the thought of me being in love and dismissed the idea with a wave of her hand. 'You can't always have your own way. The sooner you get used to that the better.'

I didn't get used to it, and for years mourned the loss of this good friend who had had time for me. My grandmother Cina was far more sympathetic, even romantic, and she took my loss seriously. She did some detective work, and found the Valkó family. Behind my mother's back she organised for us to meet again. I was eleven by the time she succeeded in her efforts.

Under Cina's watchful eye I washed myself with a flannel from top to toe. Then she dressed me in a clean, freshly ironed dress. She brushed my hair until it shone, checked behind my ears and inspected my nails. She gave instructions on how to behave like a young lady. When she reckoned I was suitably presentable, she took me to the appointed rendezvous site, two blocks from my home. I had butterflies as big as bats in my belly. What if Jancsi and I didn't recognise each other? What if he didn't like me any more?

We were both very shy. Jancsi was also neatly dressed and the perfect gentleman. We walked hand in hand around the local streets with Cina following us like a proper chaperone. I was bursting with pride, especially as Cina referred to Jancsi as 'your young man'.

With Cina's help we tried to meet again, but politics intervened. I discovered why my mother hadn't let me be with Jancsi in the first place. The Valkó family were, to their advantage, communists, which gave them a level of immunity. I expect Jancsi's parents genuinely believed in the ideology – many people did in those early years.

Dr Valkó was a chemical engineer and Jancsi's mother, Angéla, had worked as a high-level official government translator, which included translating English newspaper articles into Hungarian. Some of the work she did was quite sensitive, and straight after the Valkós moved from our house, Angéla disappeared. No one knew what had happened, but it was possible that Angéla was in jail or had been executed. Those who climbed high had a long way to fall, and in the early 1950s many people did. The Valkós' association with the party put at risk anyone who knew them.

When Erzsi found out about Cina's surreptitious matchmaking, she was furious – our family could have been put at risk – and absolutely forbade any further contact with the Valkós. I lost the love of my life a second time.

Jancsi and I met only twice more. The first time very briefly, a few weeks before I left Hungary, at the age of fourteen. I was at home alone soaking stamps when there was a knock on the door. It was Jancsi and Dr Valkó. I looked a mess, my room was a mess with the bowls of water and stamps all over the place and I was embarrassed. I talked to the two men through a crack in the door. It wasn't just my own personal shyness; by then I understood politics and didn't dare risk letting them in. When Erzsi came home I told her about our visitors.

'Why didn't you let them in? It was downright rude of you to leave them standing in the doorway.'

'Well, I wasn't sure if I should.'

'Of course you should have. They'll think I didn't teach you any manners.'

Obviously, politics – or the Valkós' situation – had changed.

The next time Jancsi and I met was more than 50 years later. The truth about his family was much more mundane than Erzsi had conjectured. Sadly, his mother had had cancer and died. At his brother's 60th birthday, remembering their childhood, he mentioned me and the loss he had felt when they moved from our house.

26

A LITTLE POLITICS: LIFE IN BUDAPEST – COMMUNISM IN ACTION

(Country grandmother telling a new version of the *Five Little Pigs* to her grandson)

This one became a tractor driver,
This joined the Co-op,
This one became a builder for the Danube Steelworks,
This one enlisted to be a soldier,
And because of all of them, this little one will be able to live well in peace.
Ludas Matyi, 18 January 1951

Propaganda:
Five-Year-Plan – good living standards, peace, freedom.
Ludas Matyi, December 1949

Reality:
(Two men talking in front of a Co-op office)

'Do you already have this year's plans?'
'Of course! And last year's plans, too … we haven't touched them yet!'
Ludas Matyi, 26 January 1956

By 1945, we all desperately wanted peace. Though it meant that Hungary had lost both the War and the regained territories, and the Soviet presence was yet another occupation, at least there would be no more fighting. For the remaining Jews this meant liberation, the gift of life.

The Soviets – with tacit agreement from the Allies to do as they liked – were stationed in Hungary as overseers. The Kremlin appointed Mátyás Rákosi as First Secretary of the Hungarian Working People's Party in 1945. Parliament effectively became a one-party system free from any opposition, and by mid-1949 all power was firmly in communist hands.

Nationalisation had started well before that, and by the end of 1949 everything was in the hands of the government. Originally we were led to believe that compensation would be given, but the promise was not fulfilled and soon the whole idea was forgotten.

With nationalisation came the centrally organised planned economy. The Three-Year Plan and then the Five-Year-Plan were implemented. By the end of the 1940s official ideology controlled all aspects of personal life. Hungary had truly become a totalitarian state, with a system of terror enforced by the ÁVO (National Protection Agency, modelled on the Soviet KGB) keeping people in constant fear. The former multi-layered and class-conscious society's language had finely nuanced titles and addresses of respect: all these terms were now replaced by one – *elvtárs* (comrade).

Life in Hungary had gone through a blender: those who had been up were now down, those formerly unseen and unheard were now in the limelight, what had been accepted as good was now deemed evil or subversive, and the communist threat many had feared between the War years was now a reality.

* * *

Positions in the hierarchy were marked by special symbols of prestige. While they preached equality for the people, those at the top exempted themselves. They lived in spacious villas in the Buda hills in the midst of an overwhelming housing crisis. They travelled in Soviet cars, while we hung like bunches of grapes on overcrowded trams. This upper circle also had exclusive holiday resorts available to them, hand-picked tailors and prioritised hospital treatment.

At the top of the heap was Mátyás Rákosi. He had participated in the short-lived communist government of Béla Kun, and after its fall he had fled to the Soviet Union, where he was indoctrinated into Soviet-style communism. Rákosi described himself as 'Stalin's best Hungarian disciple' and his 'best pupil'. Unfortunately for us, he had learnt just a little too much.

Rákosi was respected and adored by the Hungarian people, or so the propaganda machine would have had us believe. What we thought in private was nobody's business. Our adulation for the Soviet Union and Stalin appeared boundless, too:

Every friend of progress who has the peace and happiness of the people in his heart,
who is ready to fight against imperialism and the terrors of the warmongering new
imperialists, sees in [Stalin] a leader and surrounds this man with love, who today,
as always, sacrifices his life to the cause of the workers and the liberation of nations.
Szabad Nép, 30 April 1948

Meanwhile Stalin quietly, imperceptibly, had had millions of Soviet workers,
peasants and intellectuals tortured and murdered – anyone his paranoid mind
considered a threat. But of course the propaganda did not inform us of that.

With unprecedented anticipation the Hungarian people are waiting for the first volume
of the selected works of Stalin.
Nők Lapja, 20 October 1949

The Hungarian people would indeed have liked to be holding their collective
breaths until that volume of Stalin's work came their way. It's just that they were
barely able to breathe under the weight of communism as it was.

27

THE *KOFA* AUNTIES

(Sick man in bed greeting Death in the doorway)

'Oh, it's so good you came! The Co-op ran out of scythes ages ago!'
Ludas Matyi, 26 January 1956

(An inspector in the *kulák*'s attic,[18] where eight leg hams are hung for smoking)

'You fat peasant, did you kill two pigs when you only had a permit for slaughtering one?'
'I only slaughtered one.'
'And did it have eight legs?'
'Please, comrade, I don't know. I don't have time to be counting pig's trotters.'
Ludas Matyi, 23 January 1951

We lived on one of the main roads into the city – it was from this road that I watched the Russian tanks thunder into Budapest to quash the revolution in October 1956. Our home on Váci Road was spacious and in a good position. One afternoon Erzsi saw our neighbour anxiously fidgeting in front of her door. She'd locked herself out.

'Did you leave your lounge window open, Miss Friedmann?' Erzsi asked.

'Yes, I only left the flat for a moment and the door slammed on me,' she answered despondently.

'Don't you worry, I'll let you in. Please keep an eye on my little boy for me, would you?'

---

18 A *kulák* is a Russian peasant wealthy enough to own a farm and hire labour.

Erzsi went out onto our balcony, and, with three-storey-high aerial acrobatics, swung herself across to the neighbour's little balcony, climbed over the railing and opened the door from the inside.

* * *

We did our shopping at Lehel Market, diagonally opposite our place. The vendors, whom we called *kofa*, had their home-grown goods spread out on checked cloths. They usually sat on small stools with their broad bottoms uncomfortably hanging over the edge. Their calf-length black skirts were protected by many aprons and topped with black long-sleeved shirts. Underneath were thick dark stockings and lace-up boots, and on their heads a trademark patterned scarf.

To be called a *kofa* in the city was not a compliment: 'Don't you give me any lip, young lady, I did not bring you up to be a *kofa*!' Their loud words and expressions were not generally used in Budapest. Accents and dialects were regional – this had caused Erzsi such distress when she was evading the Arrow Cross dressed as a peasant. Only six or seven years earlier, many of the *kofas* who were now selling at the markets would have been all too eager to report Jews trying to escape their Nazi-intended fate.

I knew nothing of this. I loved the *kofas* and they loved me in turn, but mostly I was just fascinated by the bargaining rituals. Erzsi was not fond of them, but Gizka and I relished them. I learned the rules and rhythms simply by watching my grandmother.

It began with the buyer deciding how much they wanted to pay ... let's say it is a small amount of sour cream. As soon as the *kofa* gives you her price, you shake your head, declaring you've never heard anything so ridiculous. She's defiant. 'It's the best price for that quality of goods, better than anyone else's. Go on, go on, you taste it and tell me if it's not the best,' she says, offering a sample.

You feign distaste at the bit off the end of her spoon and then offer half the asking price. She shrugs it off in disgust. 'Well, missus, if you don't want the best ... Not all appreciate quality!'

You walk away and look interested in someone else's sour cream. She calls after you, ready to bargain. You don't budge. Then loudly, within earshot of all around, she tells you her little boy is gravely ill and needs an operation and oh, may the Good Lord help her, how will she be able to afford to pay for it? You are softened, so you return and offer a bit more. You agree on a price, buy your sour cream and she blesses you for your kind heart.

But ... the conversation continues.

Invariably, Gizka would respond and tell the woman that *her* poor daughter has to work two jobs to keep her family going and that Gizka herself had only just recovered from a heart operation, but she has to go on ... to help her children.

'You poor soul!' the sour cream seller replies. 'I hope Jesus will bring you and your family good health.' Then she continues and mentions that her husband passed away last year, may his memory be blessed, and that her brother-in-law, a scoundrel and an alcoholic, is trying to kick her out of her own home. When finally you're ready to walk away with tears in your eyes you wholeheartedly wish her the very best, hope her hens lay well and her one and only cow produces lots of milk. And, most of all, that her little son grows up healthy and lives to a ripe old age.

It is full of drama and, possibly, lies. But it's tradition. And the reality was that the peasants, who were meant to be protected, were some of the worst hit by the communist policies. One of the aims of the first Five-Year Plan was the collectivisation of all land. If anyone opposed it or couldn't pay their taxes, the police – or, much worse, the ÁVO – searched the house, invariably found something illegal and the peasants were given a hefty fine or were thrown in jail. As a newspaper article proudly proclaimed:

The Workers' Tribunals in Budapest meted out 850 years of combined punishment to agricultural wrong-doers during the first half-year of their operation.
Szabad Nép, 3 January 1948

The co-ops were so inefficient that a country once famous for its exports of wheat and excellent wine now had to import these goods. At times, all of us were on a near-starvation diet.

Gizka and I believed the *kofa* aunties, if only because they told their stories so well. I loved that they were ready to share their troubles – they were open and unguarded, unlike most of us in the city.

After a few trips to the market I took over the bargaining from Gizka. Although under communism there was no official class system and all people were supposed to address each other as 'comrade', many of the old ways remained. The peasants knew their place in 'the big city'. They addressed Gizka as 'Madam' and Gizka spoke to them with respect and demanded I behave similarly. Once I was ill-mannered or dismissive, and she gave me a dressing down, to the loud and grateful appreciation of the women. She only had to do it once.

The *kofas* liked me because, unlike many city children, I was polite and skilful at bargaining. But what they liked most about me was my rosy cheeks, bright blue eyes and curly fair hair.

'Is the little girl with you?' a *kofa* would ask Gizka.

'Yes. She's my granddaughter,' she'd answer with pride.

'Jesus help me, I swear she looks like the Virgin Mary … All right. All right, Lady, take the apples for only 1 forint, but only because she's the spitting image of our beloved Virgin!'

With that, the *kofa* would clap her hands together and all the other *kofas* within hearing distance would echo, while shaking their heads from side to side, 'Just like the Blessed Virgin Mother! The exact image of her.'

In the end both the buyer and the vendor were happy with the deal and the wheels of the world were oiled for another day.

And for the rest of the week I glowed in the compliment. Not bad for a Jewish girl to look like the Virgin Mary, I thought.

28

A LITTLE MORE POLITICS: A NATION OF IRON AND STEEL; INFLATION, SHORTAGES AND RECYCLING

(Hoarding)

> *'Look here, Csaba, the Jones' bought five hundred mouse traps. Do you realise how much more practical that is than your half a truckload of pipe cleaners?'*
> Ludas Matyi, 18 January 1951

> *'Take pride in yourself, my little cast-iron pot. If you behave well you may even become a tractor!'*
> Ludas Matyi, 18 January 1951

(Waitress to a customer in a café)

> *'I'm sorry, yesterday we had ice cream. Maybe today you would like to order an espresso, because that we won't have tomorrow.'*
> Ludas Matyi, 26 January 1956

By 1950, the relationship between the Soviet Union and the US was near breaking point, and both sides were preparing for war. The Soviets needed their satellite countries to provide food and weapons in case the Cold War became hot. Moscow demanded the establishment and maintenance of a large army. Hungary was ordered to increase her heavy industry – to an extent that was beyond reason – so that it could, at short notice, be modified to manufacture armaments.

To achieve this, local consumption was drastically limited. Hungary 'proudly' declared herself to be 'The Country of Iron and Steel', without having any significant iron reserves or suitable coal for the making of coke. As all resources went towards production, and there was no money or time invested in the maintenance of industrial or agricultural machinery. It was all about production; quality was never mentioned, only quantity, quantity, quantity.

The country was broke. Hungary had massive reparation payments to make to the Soviet Union: in the couple of years after the War at least a third of all Hungary's national expenditure was sent to Moscow for repayments to the Soviets. Polish black humour best summarised this situation: 'First we gave them our steel, and in return, they took our wheat.'

The currency experienced marked depreciation, resulting in the highest historical rates of hyperinflation known anywhere in the world. My stamp collection illustrated this quite poignantly.

The official Hungarian currency was the pengő (P) and fillér (f). At the beginning of 1946, a series of older stamps worth from 20 to 80 f were re-used, but they had to be over-stamped to 8–10 P. After that, a new series came out with the value of 4000–800,000 P. Still in 1946, the next batch was worth 1–50 million P, then 100–50,000 million P, then 100,000–500,000 million P and finally 20,000–500,000 billion P. At that point, the currency was changed from pengő to forint, Ft (at the rate of 400,000 quadrillion P to one Ft) and the numbers became sensible again.

People were paid monthly. On pay day Erzsi waited for Laci at his workplace, and as fast as their legs carried them they ran to the shops, hoping they could still buy something with Laci's wages.

Whether Hungary liked it or not, by 1949 the Soviet Union had become the country's most important trading partner, with the rates set for Moscow by Moscow.

As the years under communism ground on, the wheels of commerce became more and more rusty. Amidst slogans, flags and statues of joyously striving workers proudly holding sickles and hammers, our very own Big Brother and occupier, the Soviet Union, dictated that manufacturing steel for weaponry was more important than catering for everyday survival. Regular shortages and never-ending queues continued.

To compensate, there developed an unofficial information line through whispering women. 'Hey, Zsuzsi, guess what I heard? They're selling green beans at the Co-op on the corner of Pannónia and Victor Hugo Streets!'

'Really? I'll tell Györgyi straight away. And guess what? I heard that a whole batch of safety pins have arrived at the Corvin store.'

'Thanks. Jutka, my neighbour will be happy to know. I'd better get some too, while they last.'

Everybody bought everything because it could be months or years before that particular item would be available again. If a person found herself with a surplus, it could be traded for other, more immediately useful, things.

At times, there were queues even for potatoes. When I visited Hungary 15 years later, in the late 1960s, nothing had changed. The inner city's majestic buildings were grey, still full of bullet holes, but instead of safety pins the housewives now queued for matches, shoelaces or sugar.

The government's propaganda in the *Women's Magazine* enthused about the 'much healthier' new dishes – based on whatever happened to be available at the markets that week. You too, dear Mrs Comrade, can follow our great Soviet leaders and join the fight for the proletariat. You, too, can now use eggplant for your chicken paprika. Down with the bourgeois chicken! Long Live Comrade Stalin! Long Live Comrade Rákosi!

Gizka found ways of making beef gulyás without beef, cakes without eggs. Not even realising, we kids ate Csabai sausage made from horse meat, and bean and lentil dishes became our staples.

But we had a good diet – pulses are an excellent source of protein, and at times vegetables were easily and cheaply available. Children were given vitamins and supplements. The thought of cod liver oil by the spoonful still turns my stomach. In unpalatability it is only surpassed by castor oil, which we used as a laxative.

Communism espoused equality of the sexes. In theory, it was great. In practice, it meant that women could, just like men, be laying bricks, working as labourers in heavy industry or digging roads for the glorification of a better socialist state. There were not enough able-bodied men after the War, and of those still around, many were in the army. The shortages were not only in food, housing, safety pins and men; they also included clothing, which was always utilitarian, and paper, which was virtually unavailable.

And amidst these shortages, there were unimaginable wastages through the centralised distribution system. Here is a letter from a reader:

'We requisitioned equipment for the Mining with Explosives Trust. It turned out that scalpels, tweezers, syringes, artery clamps, needles for repairing torn blood vessels, etc. were on the list of approved items. Not only that, but we are allowed meteorological instruments as well … Unfortunately, with today's mining methods, we find it difficult to use the scalpels.' Endre Oberlander, Ministry of Energy and Mining
Ludas Matyi, 19 February 1953

We were recycling everything, especially metals. We 'young pioneers' were encouraged by slogans and cartoons to scrounge around the countryside, in rubbish heaps and in our mothers' kitchens to collect and re-sell useful finds to the MÉH, the official government recycling authority. Small children were gently quizzed through games and 'Show & Tell' activities to find out if their parents were hoarding any illegal materials.

On his first day at kindergarten, Gyurika came home proudly reporting that he told his teacher we had lots and lots of gold at home, and sometimes we even ate using gold spoons. The teacher, very interested in his story, patted him on the back.

Erzsi had a terrible night and the next morning rushed to the school with Gyuri to explain that obviously her little son had confused silver with gold, and that we only had an old silver cutlery set which had been given as a wedding present to her mother Gizka, many years ago. We escaped being denounced and possibly jailed.

29

STARTING SCHOOL; WARNINGS

The land belongs to the people, the factories belong to the people, and now the schools will belong to them, too.
Szabad Nép, 13 June 1948

And the more honest

He who has control of education has control of the people.
Szabad Nép, 3 June 1948

It was the schools' job to not only teach the usual subjects, but also spread communist propaganda. This latter goal was immediately put into action when the educational institutions were nationalised.

Many textbooks were eliminated, all teaching of recent history stopped, and subjects such as sociology and psychology were no longer taught. There were major changes to the curricula as well. In science, for example, the (false) theories of the Soviet geneticists Michurin and Lysenko were hailed, but not the (accepted) theories of Mendel. Students could now learn any living language as long as it was Russian and later, Russian officially became compulsory in the last four years of elementary and all of high school.

Religious instruction ceased, all denominational schools were nationalised, and only a few church schools and one Jewish high school were allowed to remain. In retaliation, Cardinal Mindszenty forbade all Catholics to work in these new government institutions, and many of the teachers obeyed. He was jailed, but the already enormous shortages of teachers had been exacerbated.

The shortages had arisen in part due to the large number of extra students (the children of the proletariat) and because, more than a year after the end of the War, more than a thousand teachers were still prisoners of war in the Soviet Union. Despite the noble sentiment of education for all, the short-term effect was a considerable lowering of standards.

University courses changed, too. To achieve mass education, speeded-up courses at colleges and universities were introduced – it now took only two years to become a technical expert. These pressure-cooked qualifications were considerably inferior to those before the War. At the same time, power was taken from the professors and given to the party seretaries, who excluded many students because of 'ideological unreliability'.

In just a few years, this lack of thorough teaching of subject content and enforced adulation of all things Soviet became the trigger point of the Hungarian Revolution.

I found learning Russian fun and easy, as it is phonetic, like Hungarian.

❋   ❋   ❋

School started for me on 1 September 1948 on the corner of Pannonia and Ipoly Streets. I walked happily the seven blocks from home, considering myself oh so lucky to squeak into that year by only a few days (enrolment cut-off date was strictly 31 August). We attended school in shifts, boys from eight in the morning to 12 noon, girls from 1pm to 5pm, six days a week, swapping after each term. Our school equipment consisted of a blackboard, chalk, and maps for history and geography – and, most important of all, competent and dedicated teachers.

I fitted very well into this new environment, although I was disappointed that I did not learn to read on day one. And finally there was peace at home. I loved school, and Erzsi was happy to have me out of her hair so she could concentrate on her son.

It took more than six months for Gyuri to get better and to look and live like a normal baby. His wrinkles smoothed out, his red face softened to a creamy white and his scrawny fingers plumped out. He became a handsome little boy. I loved him. Then, at just nine months old, he became sick again. He was not a good eater, but now he didn't eat at all. If he finally managed to swallow anything, he couldn't keep it down. The local doctor thought it was nothing serious, maybe an upset stomach. Erzsi knew there was more to it and made an appointment with the head doctor at the Children's Hospital on Üllői Road.

Erzsi was right: the specialist diagnosed Gyuri with German measles and admitted him. He had penicillin injections every four hours and a twice-weekly blood transfusion from Erzsi, as well as vitamin injections for strengthening. By the time he came home, both his little thighs were bruised black and blue. Gyuri was so used to being woken to pain, that for many months afterwards he cried every four hours in the night. Erzsi was there, day and night, to comfort him. To help replace the red blood cells, the doctor prescribed red meat – easy to prescribe, difficult to get. Erzsi queued for hours for horse meat, the only meat she could buy.

No sooner did Gyurika recover from the rubella than there was a serious threat of his contracting pneumonia. He had a chest infection which, in his weakened condition, was heading directly to his lungs. The doctor explained that as long as he was kept upright, water could not accumulate in his lungs and he'd be all right. During the day Erzsi did her chores while she kept her baby vertical by tying him to her chest with a large towel. At nights she slept seated, propped up with cushions and pillows, except when Gizka came to relieve her. After ten days, Gyuri was well and safe.

He was a bright little boy from the very start and was constantly up to mischief. He had an explorer's instincts for the forbidden and dangerous, discovering every corner of a place. But it was impossible to be angry with him – he was far too cute.

On the days when Gyuri was not well enough to be taken to the park for his daily dose of fresh air and sunshine, he spent time on the balcony. One day when he was about 18 months old, some movement caught Erzsi's eye on the street below and she looked down. Meanwhile, Gyuri, too, saw something interesting and colourful flapping in the wind. He figured it required further investigation and off he went to have a closer look. It was the flag displayed in its special holder on the third floor, between our balcony and Miss Friedmann's.

The balcony's railings had been destroyed during the War. As builders or tradesmen were impossible to find and materials for repairs unavailable, Laci had made it childproof by fixing it with a strong rope pulled taut. Obviously, it was not Gyuri-proof, because he managed to wriggle until only his nappy, caught between the strands of rope, held him three storeys above the pavement. Erzsi nearly had a heart attack, while Gyuri grinned happily at the attention and excitement caused by his latest adventure.

❋   ❋   ❋

To my great disappointment, I contracted scarlet fever while still in my first year at school. It took six weeks' isolation at home before life returned to normal.

Auntie Margit was my first-class teacher. She was a sweet, kind, but quite strict old lady, more like a grandmother than a teacher. She had been a nun, but was forced into the school system when convents were abolished under communism. Despite the discipline she insisted on, she used praise and encouragement as rewards and made us comfortable.

From the very beginning of my school career, I was regularly in trouble for chatting in class. The lessons never moved fast enough for me. I did my work, offered to help anyone else, which I wasn't supposed to do, and giggled a lot.

Each child had a little booklet of blank 'warnings' printed on unrefined brownish paper. After a sufficient number of verbal instructions to behave, an official warning was sent home to our parents, describing our misdemeanours in detail, asking for their signature and support in disciplining us. Parents were supposed to have a heart-to-heart with their children. Many girls found themselves in serious trouble at home and were walloped by their fathers. They soon became the quiet ones in class.

I received many warnings, always for the same reason: 'Vera talks too much in class.' But Erzsi, having constantly been in trouble herself as a child, did not chide me too harshly. If this was the worst of my sins at school, she could live with it. But to act the part of a proper parent, she put on a serious face and, wagging her finger at me, told me to pull my socks up and mend my ways. I looked at the floor, promised to behave better and kept on talking in class. Obviously, I was incurable. After three warnings, Erzsi was called in to see the Principal, Mr Hegedüs. She was not happy. 'Comrade Principal, what can I do? Vera is a chatterbox. I am sorry she disturbs other students, and I will talk to her again, but surely, it's not a major crime. After all, she is a good student.'

I was present in the room and stood with my eyes lowered. I was not used to being hauled in front of the Principal, and even less to being given moral support by my mother, especially when I was clearly guilty. The Principal expected a more humble mother. As if talking to an idiot, slowly, in a measured voice, he explained to her how disruptive my behaviour had really been, that it was not appropriate for a budding 'young pioneer' with social duties to her classmates to behave in such a manner. How could Mrs Comrade Káhn expect her daughter to become a good party member later on if she condoned the child's selfish behaviour now? He indicated with his words and a raised eyebrow that he required Mrs Comrade's full co-operation in getting me to see the error of my ways.

Seething, Erzsi took a deep breath and agreed that she would do what she could to stop me chatting. Unlike me, she realised that there was a masked threat between the Principal's words. He could have reported her to the party for having old-fashioned reactionary ideas and sabotaging the education of the working classes with her bourgeois attitude.

But even though Erzsi secretly enjoyed my being a chip off the old block, that evening she had words with me. She told me with deadly earnestness that she had no intention of being dragged in front of the Principal again, and that it was up to me to make sure she wasn't. For my part, I continued to talk in class, but was careful to have only *two* more official warnings in my book for the rest of the year.

The authorities were serious about education. A system of study partners was initiated. Each child was encouraged to match up with another and do their homework together after school, at whoever's home had the space.

Anna Varga and I were an excellent match. We were not close friends, so we spent the afternoons studying, not gossiping. Anna was good at Geography and History, and I at Hungarian and Maths. We learnt a lot from each other.

Space was not the only problem for students. Many families who had grown up in poverty could not see the benefit of education. To overcome this attitude, the families themselves had to be re-educated. The overworked, underpaid teachers, earning 20 per cent of their pre-War salaries, were designated to do this. Regularly they went and visited their pupils' homes, insisting that the household be rearranged to foster a good study environment. After each visit they sent in a report.

As a child I was deeply impressed by the care the government took. I felt strongly that education was vital to the wellbeing of a country, and, of course, of an individual. But as always, there was a hidden agenda – teachers were used to spy on their students' families, their possessions, and their commitment to the communist ideology, and the reports were filed in dossiers for future use. This may seem far-fetched, but the government kept dossiers on a million of its citizens.

30
GYURI'S NOSE BLEED AND MARIKA

(In a London classroom)[19]

'So, son what came first, the chicken or the egg?'
'Well ... first we didn't have any chickens, then there were no eggs.'
Ludas Matyi, 2 February 1951

In early 1951 Gyuri caught a cold. He sneezed once too often, his nose started to bleed and Erzsi stuffed it with cotton wool. Later, when she removed it, the sight of his own blood frightened the little boy.

Vera and George

As she was getting him dressed, he pushed her away and said, 'I'll bbbbbutton it up!'

'Speak properly!' Erzsi admonished, thinking he was playing a silly game.

For the next couple of days he didn't say anything, and when asked a question only answered with 'yes' or 'no'. Erzsi was worried and took him to a child psychologist, who then referred the little boy to a speech therapist.

---

19   The only way to get past the censor was to set the joke somewhere other than in Hungary. We all knew it was about us.

The therapist had a cupboard full of books neatly placed on the shelves, with only the spines visible. The doctor took a book off the shelf, opened it at a certain page and asked Gyuri to name the drawings in the picture – train, car, truck, uncle, auntie, etc – trying to find out which words or letters gave him trouble and started off his stutter.

The following week they went back. High up on one of the shelves, Gyuri recognised the book the doctor had used the previous week and, pointing to it, asked for it. The specialist gave his verdict: 'Mrs Káhn, you have a very bright little boy. Don't worry about his stutter, he will work it out for himself. I would recommend, though, a complete change of scenery. Let him stay with friends or relatives, but don't accompany him.'

Erzsi immediately wrote to the family in Kiskőrös who had looked after Auntie Aranka's son with Down syndrome. After grasping the problem, the daughter, Terka, a slight, quietly spoken woman, came to see us in Budapest, and spoke directly to Gyuri.

'Gyurika, would you like to play with a puppy?'

'Ye-ye-yeth.'

'A kitten?'

'Ye-ye-yeth.'

'What about a baby calf?'

'Ye-ye-yeth.'

'We have all of them at the farm. Would you like to come with me?'

'Ye-yeth.'

A month later he returned home well fed, healthy, happy, and without a stutter.

But he didn't come alone. Terka brought a bantam hen as a present for us. And what a present! We were supposed to have her for dinner, but Mari became part of our family instead. She stayed in a cardboard box in our kitchen, in a little nook next to the ice-chest. Within a few days, under Erzsi's patient tutelage, she was fully toilet trained and did her droppings only in the designated box. Mari took after Erzsi in the cleanliness department, and she let us know with a loud, most indignant voice if the lining of her box needed changing.

Every morning Erzsi or I took Mari, snuggled under our arm, down to our none-too-bantam-friendly yard. She roamed around, scratching wherever she could, flattening herself under the fence into next door's yard where the pastures were much greener, and managed to while away the day, chicken fashion.

Every afternoon after work Erzsi stood in the doorway to the yard and called loudly, 'Marika! Where are you? It's time to come home!'

On hearing her name she would waddle-run towards us at full speed, then sit, ready to be picked up. Once upstairs, she went back into her cosy little nook in the kitchen.

Five times a week Mari laid an egg, and on every occasion she was immensely proud of herself. As by now eggs were nearly unprocurable, we delighted in her efforts, and at the bantam's behest, we were happy to make egg-laying a proper, full-fledged celebratory event. The normally quiet and sedate little hen became a veritable noise machine.

'*Kot, kot, kot, kot, kotkodács! Kot, kot, kot, kot, kotkodács!*' she cackled at the top of her voice, '*Kot, kot, kot, kot, kotkodács! Kot, kot, kot, kot, kotkodács!*'

All right Mari, all right, we heard you. 'Thank you, you're a good girl, a clever little hen!'

Then Erzsi or I stroked her for this amazing achievement, and gave her a handful of corn. Mari self-righteously pecked it up, as it was her just and well-earned reward. With her permission we took away her treasure, and after all the ceremony she was ready to settle down quietly until the next time.

Sadly, after she had been part of our family for about a year, Mari came to an untimely end, after something became stuck in her throat. Erzsi tried her best to remove it with a pair of tweezers, but couldn't. Mari had to be killed by the butcher.

We have two different endings to this story. Erzsi says she gave the meat to Mrs Kovács, our janitor, but I remember that we had chicken paprika for our evening meal. I was suspicious, but Erzsi assured me it wasn't Mari. Unfortunately for Erzsi, as I clearly recall, she was unable to have any dinner that night because, out of the blue, she had developed an upset stomach.

31

TIDYING MY ROOM, PHOTOGRAPHY, AND THE MYSTERY OF THE WARDROBE

Erzsi took great pleasure in seeing herself reincarnated in her son. She took considerably less delight in me, and we had a very difficult time with each other. She was often distressed, tired, and irritable. Laci was away regularly for three to four months at a time, and she was stuck with running the household and taking care of two children. She had a short fuse. I was a well-behaved child, but, according to Erzsi, lazy and messy. My room was never tidy enough.

And I was not easy to live with. If Erzsi asked me to do something I decided that later or tomorrow would be the perfect time to get on with it. By the time I was six, 'lazy' was my middle name.

'Morgen, morgen, nur nicht heute, sagen alle faulen Leute' ('Tomorrow, tomorrow, just not today, is what all lazy people say') was quoted at me *ad nauseam*.

In my defence, I thought many of Erzsi's jobs for me inane, unnecessary and useless. And anyway, whatever I did I ended up being criticised, so why bother?

The bathroom sink was one bone of contention. Every time I washed my hands, I had to wipe it dry using the cloth set aside for the job. 'But mu-u-mmy, this is a basin … a basin is meant to be wet!'

'Not *my* basin. *This* one has to be wiped dry.'

'But why?'

'Because I say so.'

I angrily wiped the basin and hoped it would shatter.

On one occasion she was on a roll and continued, 'And while we're at it, your room's a mess. Again. When you have finished here, fix it up. I want it tidied.'

'It's not too bad. Everything is on the shelves,' I answered back.

'Yes, but look at those shelves! I want them sorted and tidied properly.'

She was adamant and I knew there was no stopping her. I heard the other children playing in the backyard, and went to the window to see what they were up to. I had plans to join them.

After a few minutes Erzsi came in, checking up. 'What? Did you not hear me?' she shouted at me.

Her face turned red with anger, her voice rose to a high pitch, she lifted her arm up and whack! 'Maybe that'll get you going!'

Whack! Whack! Whack! She was strong and her iron hands hit hard. I shrank away from her reach and petulantly whimpered, 'But I don't know where to start!'

Her fury was not yet spent. 'You don't? Here! Let me help you.'

Now her rage had reached a crescendo. With her whole arm she swept everything off the shelves, one after the other, until all the toys and books tumbled into a jumbled messy heap on the floor. 'There's your start. And you're not leaving this room until it's all done.'

She slammed the door behind her as she stormed out.

I sulked. If I didn't know how to tidy up before, I had no idea where to begin now. I cried, mostly in anger. How dare she?

Sitting on the floor I played with my Chinese sticks. Erzsi pushed my dinner into the tiny space between the two panes of glass in the double-glazed windows. Not able to face my horrible task, I crawled into bed and cried myself to sleep.

The next morning I noticed that the mess was still there.

One by one I picked up the books and calmly placed them on the third shelf in order of size, the big ones at the end, the smaller ones in the middle. The pile in the centre of the room dwindled noticeably and I started to take pleasure in the job. My larger toys I put on the bottom shelf so that I could simply slide them off. The soft toys went on the top. I had a few dolls, and the most beautiful one had been given to me by Auntie Piroska, Cina's old customer, who was now living in Canada. I never played with them, but I really liked my hard-stuffed little teddy with his cold, beady, glass eyes.[20]

I was proud of my work and enjoyed the order on the shelves. With my head high I walked out of my room. Erzsi greeted me with a menacing, 'Have you finished tidying?'

'Yes, of course!' I answered haughtily.

She did not like my attitude, and I didn't like hers. Why could she not be like other children's mothers: soft and kind and hugging, and not so obsessed with cleaning and tidying? Before breakfast my shelves were inspected. They

---

20 Erzsi brought teddy to Australia and David, my son, inherited him. Together we named him Fred Bear, due to his furry body having been rubbed shiny and threadbare by love.

were perfect, so it took her a while to find any faults. 'Those books are not in line. Fix them!' she ordered, a little hesitantly and in a somewhat subdued voice.

I picked up a ruler and pushed them all back in line. I couldn't win. *Nothing* was ever good enough.

*   *   *

It was a different story with my Dad – we had some wonderful times together.

Laci bought himself a Leica camera in the early 1930s. It was his pride and joy. He took posed shots of his bride, Erzsi, a whole album of photos on their honeymoon in Italy, then more of us kids as we appeared on the scene, and of his travels in the late 1940s and early 1950s.

I wasn't photogenic and hated to pose for him, but I loved what followed. We developed the film together in the bathroom, which was perfect for the job as it had no outside window. It was good and dark. Laci was the magician and I the sorcerer's apprentice. No wonder I became a chemist.

The newly emerging photos had to be protected, so we replaced the normal bulb with a red one. The atmosphere was set. And the best thing was that the door had to be locked – the bathroom became a fortress, a safe house, a sanctuary. Erzsi's constant urgent chores and nagging simply had to wait.

Laci projected and enlarged the pictures onto photographic paper, timing it carefully with a home-made stopwatch. When they were ready, I quickly but carefully slipped each into the developer tray and waited. Nothing. Still nothing. Then, as if someone had mumbled the magic abracadabra, an image of Gyurika or me grinned back at us. From the initial vague outlines, the picture quickly firmed up, filled out.

'Now!' Laci instructed urgently.

With tweezers, I fished the picture out of the tray and dropped it into the next one, the one that could twist your nose off with its vinegary smell. After a few minutes, we rinsed it and put it into the half-full bathtub to join the other faces already floating there. They were then pegged to a temporary clothesline. When dry, they were smoothed out between the pages of a phone book with a heavy old iron doorstop on top. Finally, Laci trimmed the edges with a small guillotine.

*   *   *

To the left of the dining area was my parents' room, which I mostly kept out of, with a bed on one side and a huge built-in wall-to-ceiling wardrobe. On one of its doors was a curtain accessing a section of the cupboard concealed by the wall. For me it held all kinds of mysteries, although in reality it only contained old suitcases. But the suitcases had seen the world, as the badges and name tags with foreign destinations attested. They stored the wonder of stories from outside Hungary, of different lands and different people. I discovered the cupboard's real treasure only recently.

When I was back in Hungary in 2006, I could not work up the courage to see my old home. The following year I was visiting again, and that time I called Tamás, my second cousin, who lived there with his wife Klára. He seemed happy to hear my voice and we arranged a time to meet.

Everything was as I had remembered it, except that my room had shrunk. How could a bed, a table and chairs and a wardrobe fit in there? In the lounge I recognised the light fittings – they were still the same. The balcony seemed smaller too, but the view to the church and the little hill around it had the same magic as before. The market had been covered and painted a garish yellow, and looking at it from above, all its old character was gone.

The memories flooded back. I remembered the sofa that opened up to a double bed, where I would cuddle up to Laci as a little girl, a desk angled to the corner with bookshelves behind glass on the front, a coffee table with comfortable armchairs. And near the entry to the room was my special piece of furniture, a beautifully crafted walnut timber Orion radio with a record player on top.

Tamás led me into the bedroom. The built-in wardrobe was still there, untouched for 50 years. 'You know the mystery of this wardrobe?'

My eyes opened wide. 'It has a real mystery?' I asked, stunned.

'During the War, at the end of 1944, your father hid from the Arrow Cross in the top of that wardrobe. He was crouched there for a number of weeks.'

'How? Where?'

'Behind the curtain is a false ceiling with a trapdoor. Every day Uncle Laci climbed up and stayed there during the day in case they came looking for him. That's how he survived towards the end of the War.'

So I owed the life of my father to that wardrobe. I don't recall anyone ever mentioning anything about it, but as a child I must have overheard something because that feeling of mystery had always been with me.

32

BALATON HOLIDAY AND ILONA

In the summer of 1951, with Laci away again, Erzsi, Gyuri and I went on holidays to Balatonvilágos. Our hosts were the Bornemissza family – Béla, the husband, owned a spacious villa there. It was on the main street of the town, with the back of the house overlooking Lake Balaton. Our host's brother was a minister in the government, which I suppose is why their villa had not been nationalised, even though Béla abhorred communism.

Although Béla was a large man, possibly even scary to a small child, Gyuri took a shine to him. The two of them, the giant and the little mosquito, liked to walk along the side of the lake hand in hand.

Our room had a bed for Erzsi, a bed for me, and a small sofa for Gyuri. He was out of nappies already, but Erzsi decided he needed them at night, just in case. Gyuri saved her the trouble, putting it on for himself. First, he folded the nappy properly into a neat triangle on the bed, then he carefully positioned his bottom right in the centre. He picked up the talcum powder and shook liberal amounts of it onto the nappy and on himself. He

George 1951

wriggled until he felt he was exactly in the right place, folded the nappy properly, tucking over the edges, and pulled his rubber pants over the lot. All of this was done with intense concentration. Every evening Erzsi allowed two of the guests to watch the ritual. They stood peeping from behind the door, silently laughing themselves silly. Gyurika was gorgeous.

At the time, there were 16 paying guests staying at the villa. We all sat around one table at mealtimes. My little brother was spoilt rotten by the entire company and was a constant source of entertainment to all.

Nobody used Gyuri's name, they called him *Baba* (Baby). The guests enjoyed teasing him.

'Baba, do you know my name?' one would ask.

He couldn't say 'r', so he lisped, '*Mááya néééni*' ('Auntie Maria'), and '*Iyénke néééni*' ('Auntie Irene'), for the next person.

He went around the table, correctly giving everybody's name.

One of the men was also called Gyuri.

'Baba, do you know *my* name?' he asked.

'*Baba bááácsi*' ('Uncle Baby'), he answered, to everyone's delight.

At lunchtime one day the hostess, Mária Bornemissza, announced, 'We are expecting another guest tonight. Her name is Ilona Osváth. She lost one arm in an accident. I'll sit her next to you, Erzsi.'

'Please, Mária, don't.' Erzsi pleaded, 'I won't be able to look after Ilona – it's enough for me to feed Gyuri; he still needs to have his food cut up.'

At the evening meal Ilona was seated next to Erzsi, who was somewhat annoyed that Mária had taken no notice of her objections. But Ilona needed no help. She was perfectly self-sufficient.

The following day after lunch, Erzsi put us to bed for a nap and she and Ilona went for a walk to the next little township along the shores of the lake. They treated themselves to coffee and flip, a chocolate liqueur. On the way back they met a peasant woman, who greeted them with the traditional 'Jesus Christ be praised!'

Ilona, being a Catholic, automatically responded with the standard, 'Forever, Amen!'

Erzsi didn't answer, just mumbled something. When the woman was gone, she said to Ilona, 'I'm going to ask you something. Please answer truthfully or not at all … Are you an antisemite?'

So many Catholics were. Ilona ran ahead, then turned back, bright red in the face and replied, truthfully, 'Erzsi, understand this. I was, I am and will always be an antisemite.'

'Ilona, did they ask you before you were born what you want to be, Hungarian or German, a boy or a girl, Christian, Muslim or Jew?' Erzsi persisted with the questioning.

'How can you ask such a stupid question, Erzsi?'

'Well, then, you did not choose your faith. You could have been born Jewish yourself. What right do you have to be an antisemite?'

After this little exchange, they both thought it was worth getting to know each other better.

Ilona was about 13 when she had an accident on Kossuth Lajos Street. The heel of her shoe stuck in the tram line, and the tram came and crushed her right arm. She was taken to Rókus Hospital in Rákóczi Street. All the way, she remained conscious, and through the pain she kept asking in a panicky voice, 'What will my mother say? What will my mother say?' Her mother responded very quickly by learning to write perfectly with her own left hand.

Ilona and Erzsi remained friends after the holiday and met frequently at home. Ilona was an elegant, cultured, good-looking woman with a degree in economics. Ironically, her third husband was a converted Jew. They lived in Arany János Street, a prestigious address close to the Science Academy building, overlooking the Chain Bridge on the Danube. Once a month Ilona held an open house and Erzsi had a standing invitation. Ilona knew many important people, including government officials. Politicians liked her soirées and often attended, but dyed-in-the-wool communists were not invited, because she and her husband both whole-heartedly hated the regime.

The friendship worked for both of them. Erzsi helped Ilona as much as she could because, after all, her new friend only had one arm. And Ilona, a well-balanced, happy person, presented an interesting challenge to Erzsi.

We hardly ever entertained in the 1950s, but Ilona was one of the very few we invited to dinner, and in her honour the extension table in the dining room was pulled out to its fully glory. I remember the occasion well, as it was one of the few times we used our best crockery and the silver cutlery, dining with great decorum. Ilona, with her Swiss finishing school charm, had that effect on people.

33

GIZKA AND HER TENANTS

My room in the Váci Road flat was originally meant for the maid. When we moved there, we could hardly afford food or clothes, and maids were out of the question. It was a long, skinny room with a window at the narrow end opposite the door.

One day in 1951 a man came uninvited to our flat, pushed his way in and without even looking around announced, 'I will requisition this room. It's a bit small, but will do us for now.'

He was a working-class man with a family and, like so many others, they were desperately in need of somewhere to live. Somebody must have reported us to the authorities.

'This is our home, there are four of us living here. We have no room to spare,' Erzsi retorted, also looking after her own.

The man demanded to speak to the block commander. Erzsi told him that *she* was the block commander. He left, beaten.

Because of acute housing shortages after the War, the government sanctioned the move of homeless families into other people's flats. To ensure that no one was forcibly moved in with us, Laci bricked off the end of my room, making it too small to be requisitioned, and then rendered the wall so the alterations were not obvious.

*   *   *

Auntie Stefka was the only one in the family who retained her faith. She sent regular donations to Israel, for which she always received brightly coloured stamps that decorated the mirror on her dressing table, and she was strictly kosher. This meant that anything dairy had to be cooked separately from any meat dishes, and no pork was allowed.

Gizka's favourite meat was pork. She loved bacon, roast pork and especially scones made with crackling. So Gizka had to accommodate Auntie Stefka's special needs and her own tastes. The small kitchen and the kitchen sink were divided into half, one side strictly kosher, the other not. It was barely manageable. And then the government requisitioned one of the two rooms in their apartment for a Catholic couple, Mária and Zoltán. Mária was a blonde, bubbly 8-months-pregnant 17-year-old; her husband, Zoltán, was much older. Gizka and Stefka had to move into one room. It had a couple of sofa beds, and doubled as the bedroom at night.

Grandmother Gizka and Auntie Stefka, 1948

Now a third area had to be created in the kitchen for yet another way of cooking. The young bride was taught never to touch anything in Auntie Stefka's section, in case she contaminated it. She tried hard, but sometimes forgot. To keep the peace, Gizka never dobbed her in.

The four of them, and later the baby, were the most mismatched of house mates, but with goodwill and some quiet frustration, they managed, without coming to blows. Gizka became a surrogate mother to Mária, who knew little about housekeeping. She taught her how to cook, how to look after the baby and, very importantly, how to budget.

After about a year Mária and Zoltán found more appropriate accommodation and moved out.

34

BOOKS, MUSIC AND SMOKING

I needed to get away from my mother's constant nagging, criticism and anger; daydreams were my passport, the key to escaping the not-so-golden cage that the country had become for all of us, and that Erzsi had created for me at home. The magic carpet to take me was books, the destinations were supplied by stamps, and en route music soothed my battered soul.

During the first years of the new regime, the government began to systematically screen the stocks of book stores, on the lookout for reactionary or 'decadent' titles. Many Western authors, and classics such as Grimm's fairy tales, and crime fiction, were out, Dickens was questionable, Freud or Wittgenstein were off the list, and even Attila József, one of our home-grown and well-loved poets, faded into the background. However, a must-have volume was the red cloth-bound *Lenin's Collected Works*.

New books arrived: many translated works, mostly from Russian, technical and literary works, instruction manuals and always propaganda. At the top of the list were the *Short History of the Soviet Communist Party* and the three volumes of *Das Kapital* by Marx. It was provident for all households to have at least some of these titles.

The most common daily newspaper was the *Szabad Nép* (Free Nation). Like its Soviet counterpart, *Pravda* (Truth), its name was a euphemism for the opposite. A new satirical magazine, *Ludas Matyi* (Matty the Goose-herd), was born in 1945, and on 29 October 1949 the first issue of *Nők Lapja* (Women's Magazine), was published. It unashamedly proclaimed its purpose:

We welcome you the readers … This publication is going to try to bring you into a friendly, intimate closeness to the country, the great Soviet Union, and to its people, who stand at the forefront of humanity fighting for peace, so that you can get to know the lie of its land and the artistry of its people.

Even the crosswords were filled with 'helpful' ideology. The following clues are from a typical crossword:

This is what a reaper does
Soviet chain of mountains
Simonov's [a Soviet author's] story made into a film
Soviet seaport
Symbol for iron
One of the heroes of productivity

The paper had no information about world news, no geography, literature, art or science, and especially nothing about our history. When I left the country at 14, I did not know that Hungary had been an influential nation before World War I; I did not know of the thousands of soldiers whose lives had been wasted for the sake of expansionist policies in the early 20th century. I knew nothing of the Holocaust. Erzsi had mentioned that the 'bloody Arrow Cross', in collaboration with the 'rotten Nazis' had taken her away, and that she'd escaped en route, but I didn't ask any questions. Not until I reached Canada did I realise the extent of my ignorance.

*   *   *

For most of the 1950s, equipment in homes, and whole buildings – everything, it seemed – was broken, falling off, grey and decrepit. There were no spare parts to be had, no capable tradespeople to repair anything. A once-vibrant cosmopolitan city astride the Danube, Budapest was now in a sad and sorry state. No one seemed to care; lethargy ruled. People hardly noticed the dirtiness of the streets, bullet holes left by the War in stately buildings, or broken venetian blinds dangling at half-mast on dirty, un-openable windows.

In our home there was a music system, a majestic, dulcet-toned light oak Orion radio with a record player on top, the crème-de-la-crème of audio equipment. Despite the disarray of the times, it actually functioned. Erzsi couldn't ever sit still long enough to listen, but Laci and I relished the quiet comfort and the music.

Though he was not a regular smoker, Laci would sometimes light his pipe, stuffed with deeply aromatic rum-flavoured tobacco, after a good Sunday lunch. We would all join him as he settled in the lounge and, in the glow of the afternoon, turned on the radio or played a record or two. There were never many played, nor for too long. So soon after the War, one could only take small, measured doses of pleasure.

Every so often, with a sleight of hand Erzsi conjured the pipe from Laci's mouth, taking a cheeky puff while snuggling up to him on the sofa, and he lovingly enveloped her in his arms. She had been a regular smoker as a chic young woman, but Laci did not like it, and for the one and only love of her life she willingly gave up the habit. Not wanting to be left out, I asked my father if I could have a few puffs. 'Sure,' he said. 'Try it!' and handed me the pipe.

I was quite taken aback, but beamed at being allowed to be so grown up and cautiously blew into the glowing pipe.

'No, no, no, no!' he objected, 'You have to do it properly. Don't *blow* into the pipe. Draw on it, draw deeply, pull the smoke right into your lungs!'

Tentatively following his instructions, a sudden burst of coughing and spluttering overtook me as my face turned puce. I returned the pipe very quickly. That was the beginning and the end of my smoking habit.

The record player, predictably, followed the law of entropy and packed up before long, never to be fixed, but the radio remained functional into the mid-1950s when, during the few heady days of the revolution, we were able to tune into the illicit shortwave broadcasts of the BBC and *Radio Free Europe*.

There were two stations – Radio Kossuth and Radio Petőfi, named after two of Hungary's most patriotic sons. The first was named after Lajos Kossuth, a politician and statesman and a fiery orator. He had been the leader of the Hungarian revolution in 1848, during which he had advocated independence from Austria and the Habsburgs. Kossuth lived to the ripe old age of 92. Sándor Petőfi, on the other hand, a contemporary of Kossuth's, did not fare so well. He was only 27 when he died fighting in 1848, but his exquisite lyrics and deeply patriotic poetry, among them the Hungarian National Song, survive. The poem encouraged Hungarians to fight for their freedom against the Habsburgs (and the Russian Army, which had been called in by the Austrian Kaiser – Emperor – to support the Habsburg cause). Even though it was banned during the communist era, as we marched to the tune of *L'Internationale*, we all knew Petőfi's stirring poem by heart.

Talpra magyar, hí a haza!	Rise up Magyar, the country calls!
Itt az idő, most vagy soha!	The time is here, now or never!
Rabok legyünk vagy szabadok?	Should we live as slaves or free men?
Ez a kérdés, válasszatok! –	That's the question – you choose!

A magyarok istenére	God of Hungarians,
Esküszünk, Esküszünk,	We swear unto Thee, we swear unto Thee
Hogy rabok tovább nem leszünk!	That slaves we shall no longer be!
(*Sándor Petőfi*)	(Translated by Adam Makkai)

We kids had trouble relating to the sentiments of the poem, because we were not slaves. Daily we were reminded that our powerful friend and protector, the Great Soviet Union, had liberated us. We were free to choose communism, the only possible choice for a truly free people. And because we Hungarians did not yet know how to *be* free, we were lucky to have our big brotherly Soviet comrades teach us the true meaning of freedom, which they did with the help of their troops in our small country.

The refrain, 'God of Hungarians, we swear unto Thee, we swear unto Thee – that slaves we shall no longer be!' appealed to us kids more in its bastardised version than in the original. With great conviction and gusto we recited, instead, *A magyarok istenére esküszünk, esküszünk, hogy babot tovább nem eszünk* (God of the Hungarians we swear unto Thee, we swear unto Thee – that bean-eaters we'll no longer be), every time our mothers dished up yet another plate of beans or lentils for dinner.

There was another problem with Petőfi's verse. We had been taught that there was no god, so obviously there could not be a special god of the Hungarians. These early communist years, with their extreme hardships, left many of us without much doubt of it.

Radio Kossuth, appropriately, had as its theme Berlioz' *Hungarian March*. This was easy to remember. It went something like this:

Vak Pali,
Vak Pali,
Vak
Vak
Vak

As the more serious of the two stations, Radio Kossuth broadcast the in-depth, though much-censored, news and parliamentary debates and the heavier classical music.

Radio Petőfi had lighter music, folk tunes and current hits, which we called by the German name *Schlagers*. I liked both stations and listened to them for hours every Sunday. Occasionally we would all go out as a family, but often I was left at home by myself. So, while doing chores or reading a book, I listened to music.

Hungary was well and truly behind the Iron Curtain. Our borders were closed, and all art, literature and news was heavily censored. But through music, I could soar on the wings of a song; I could frolic in cold mountain waters with Schubert's *Trout*; I could *Blue Danube Waltz* my way through the ballrooms of Vienna or perhaps take a polite curtsy in a salon with Vivaldi, Scarlatti or Telemann. I could be a Hungarian country wench stepping out the *csárdás* in my seven short skirts and red-tulip-embroidered bodice. I could be Katyusha, a Russian working girl boating down the Volga, or a slave girl on the Mississippi with Paul Robeson. I could ebb and flow with the swelling waters of Smetana's Moldau or be fired up with heroic thoughts, if not quite deeds, to Beethoven's 9th. And if I really felt alone, there was always the music of the beer halls – *eins, zwei, g'suffa*!

But even music was not exempt from social criticism. The party's attitude to a piece of music was determined by that piece's contribution to the cause. Communist Robeson's deep black honey voice was like a balm on the pain and injustice of Red Hungary. Because it was based on Hungarian folk songs, Kodály's music became best accepted. Bartók, considered decadent, was no longer performed in the Opera House; nor were many other major classics of the former repertoire.

Lyricists found it difficult to please their ideological comrades and kept any of their deviant ideas under lock and key. No one wanted to antagonise those in power and risk a jail sentence.

Jazz, old marches and rock 'n roll were outlawed and replaced by the new productivity songs. We heard songs with titles such as 'Up Reds, Proletarians', 'We thank you, Comrade Rákosi', 'Happy Pioneer', 'The Tractors Roar'. These blood-stirring songs were taught at all school levels. One particularly encouraging song that we sang during our morning breaks at school went like this:

Hegyek között, völgyek között	Amongst hills and valleys
Zakatol a vonat,	Clatters the train
Én a legszebb lányok közül	Of all the pretty girls
Téged választalak.	I choose you.
Egy a jelszónk, Tartós béke!	We have one slogan, Lasting peace!
Állj közénk és harcolj érte!	Join us and fight for it!

But of course reality hit home soon enough and a modified version became more appropriate:

Amongst the hills and valleys
The train has gone kaput
Passengers have disembarked
And are tearing their hair out …

35

VISIT TO A SYNAGOGUE

Gizka had grumbled for years that I wasn't being taught anything about my background, that I was growing up without context, and one day, surreptitiously, she took me to the local synagogue in Csáky Street – to hell with the consequences.

To my utter indignation I found that women and children had to stay upstairs on a balcony, separated from the men and the action. I wanted to be in the centre of it all! I was not ready to be a second-class citizen; communism had taught me that men and woman were equal. It was only many years later that the inequalities in our Brave New World were unmasked for me.

The second, and much more profound, impression was of the cantor. In the original Jewish ceremony all the congregation was meant to sing the prayers. But Jewish people had scattered all over the world, and now most could no longer speak, or even understand, Hebrew. So they chose one person, a man, to sing for them; he then became the cantor. No matter where in the world he lived he had to speak Hebrew, be educated nearly as well as a rabbi in biblical studies and have a classical operatic voice and training. The cantor sang and took care of the service, and the congregation only had to mutter a few words or an *Amen* every so often.

The cantor in Csáky Street was a large man. He sported a beard, wore a black cloak and *yarmulke* (skullcap), and had a deep, resonant baritone voice. The sound mesmerised me. It was as if I was hearing some primordial heartbeat: every cell in my body vibrated to the tune. I had never heard anything like it before – religious broadcasts were not allowed by the regime. I wondered then (and now) whether this cantor singing appealed to everyone, or was it that, regardless of neglect and denial, it was part of me and my people … or was I part of it?

In 2007, on visiting Hungary I tried to meet up with friends I hadn't seen for 50 years, revisit the flat on Váci Road, and recall some of my old experiences. For most of the seven weeks I was there I stayed with Kati Szenes from my primary school days. My memory of the synagogue was still strong, and I wondered if I could re-experience the warm glow of such a long time ago. I asked Kati to come with me.

'Go to a synagogue? I haven't been there since *Nagyi* (Grandma) dragged me to the one in Csáky Street when I was nine.'

I wanted to go, felt I had to go, but it was not unlike wanting to go to the dentist – a mix of compulsion and fear. And Kati felt it even more. She had informed me, on the day I arrived, that she intended to leave the past well and truly in the past. And we didn't, as it happened, make it to main synagogue on that Friday or the next. The following Friday we were in Holland, and the one after that I fell asleep in the afternoon and we missed it again, but during the last week of my stay in Hungary we did finally make it.

The Dohány Street synagogue is one of the premier tourist attractions of Budapest. The best architects of the period had competed against each other for its design, and the magnificent Moorish/Byzantine creation was the winning design of Ludwig Förster, an Austrian architect. The temple has two large towers with gilded onion domes and delicate stone decoration. It was built in the mid-19th century, and became the symbol of both the religious and cultural traditions of the then thriving Hungarian Jewish community.

The word 'synagogue' is the Greek mirror-translation of the Hebrew *bet knesset* (house of assembly). The synagogue is not a house where God resides, as is said of the ancient Temple of Jerusalem, but a place where God can be among the people. The main reason for building synagogues is not that God needs a special place to be worshipped, but that people need to feel the presence of God among them.

All synagogues have a threefold purpose: prayer in a community, religious services, and learning. In 64 CE, the then High Priest, Joshua ben Gamla, decreed that a school must be built in every Jewish community. It was the Jews who first put free public education into practice, for boys from 6 to 13. And a school was considered even more important than a synagogue: if a community does not have enough funds to build both, it is the school that should be built, because one can pray there just as well.

Over the years, the temple at Dohány Street had been used for activities other than religious observance – concerts, often with famous musicians such as Liszt and Saint-Saëns, who had both performed on the synagogue's organ.

During World War II, when the ghetto had been cordoned off in the Jewish quarter of Budapest, about 70,000 people were crammed into the synagogue and the surrounding few streets. Today, a memorial park has been constructed nearby for those who died in the ghetto, and in commemoration of those brave foreigners, such as Raoul Wallenberg, who, risking their own lives, helped the Hungarian Jews.

I was amazed at the scale of the synagogue – it can accommodate around 3000 worshippers; such a size may have been appropriate when it was built, but not any more.

A young man near the entrance said, 'Definitely no cameras. I need to search your handbags and please, empty your pockets too.'

'Is this what going to a Jewish service has come to?' I whispered sadly to Kati.

Inside, the ground floor space was divided into three areas, and one level up there was a balcony that stretched around three sides of the building. I remembered the balcony from when I was a child, but on this day no one sat there.

When we entered, the service had already started. There were maybe a hundred or so people inside. We found a spot with a good view of the podium, but then an old man, an usher, directed us: 'This area is for the men only. Please, ladies, over there, on the side.' It was too dark for him to see our embarrassment.

Most women were bareheaded so we didn't bother with scarves, but two or three rows in front of us sat a group of women with lacy head covers. Nodding towards them I said to Kati, 'I'll crochet you a pretty pineapple doily like that one.'

'Thanks,' she retorted. 'It'll be handy when I come again in 55 years.'

In the row behind us sat a group of women chatting.

On the large podium in the front left corner was the organist and his page turner, and on the right were four or five men in a group. A short, stout man of about 60 sat on his own, and the cantor stood in the centre at the front, with his back to the congregation. The choir was pre-recorded.

I listened for a minute or two. Tentatively at first, tears started to roll down my cheeks, then more and more insistently they came, until the cantor's voice again reached that primordial depth within me and I was shaking silently and uncontrollably. Kati felt it, and put a comforting hand on my back as she started to cry, too. The two of us heathens sat in our seats in the Great Synagogue of Budapest, weeping, weeping, weeping.

The women behind us had not stopped their chatter right through the service. We could hear them discussing their children, parents, partners, giving each other unwanted advice. They were loud and annoying, but perfectly within their rights to talk.

Kati nudged me between sobs. 'Does all this singing interfere with their weekly gossip, I wonder?'

We giggled silently while the tears kept on coming.

Next to us, in the aisle, a young woman held a baby in her arms. She stood there for quite a while, cooing to the child, waving with him until the man on his own on the podium – granddad, perhaps, smiled and waved back at them. He was the rabbi.

Towards the end of the service, the cantor turned to face us. His operatic voice soared straight into my heart and wrenched more tears from my eyes. Though we understood nothing of the service, as it was conducted in Hebrew and Aramaic, the women in front obviously did, as they kept standing up and sitting down. We two bobbed up and down following them, the tears still not ebbing.

'This is not a service for the frail and non-athletic,' Kati commented as she wiped her face with the damp and raggedy remains of my last tissue.

36
KATI SZENES AND GIZKA

During these years, the early 1950s, Erzsi and I continued to be at loggerheads. Her two perennial complaints, my untidiness and my laziness, bothered her more over time. If my room was messy she gave me a good hiding. This was a regular occurrence. Between hidings, I had to be occupied with 'doing' something. Chatting to my father, reading or playing with Gyuri counted as 'doing nothing'. I was quick to develop a few strategies to protect me from Erzsi's nagging and her punishing hands. Some worked better than others. To keep out of my mother's hair for a few hours, I didn't come straight home after school but spent the afternoon with my friend, Kati. Frequently there was a price to pay.

Kati lived with her widowed mother, Rózsika, and her grandmother, Nagyi. Her father had died during the War, but she was too young then to remember

Kati Szenes at 10

Vera at 10

him, and didn't seem to miss him. I asked what had happened to him, but no one said. With the exception of Erzsi, who, on rare occasions obliquely referred to the past when I was a bit older, the entire War was airbrushed out of existence, and it stayed like that for the next 45 years. Kati and I grew up in blissful ignorance of a War that had wiped out so many members of our own families in our own lifetime.

In school, we learnt about the proletarian heroes of the Great Russian Revolution of 1917 and about the huge strides the Soviet Union had made since then. We were encouraged to not look back on the dark bourgeois past, and to only celebrate the glorious present.

* * *

Kati's grandmother, Nagyi, seemed ancient to us, but was probably only in her 60s when we were at school. Nagyi was short, a little corpulent, always wore black and had very sad eyes. Kati's mother, Rózsi, was the breadwinner – away all day, nervy, uptight, and never without a cigarette in her mouth. I didn't see much of her because I always left the Szenes' before Rózsi returned home from work.

After school we invariably ended up at Kati's. Granny had responsibility for her granddaughter and took this task seriously. She escorted Kati everywhere and Kati hated it; she was the only girl with a granny in tow. She took out her humiliation on the old lady and I aided and abetted my friend. We both tried to disown Nagyi – we walked way ahead of her, pretending she had nothing to do with us, and that she was merely an old woman out for her daily stroll. We didn't talk to her in public nor include her in our activities.

The Szenes' rented a flat which had its own bathroom and government-installed tenant. The cheaper courtyard units had no bathrooms and people living in them had to share the one toilet on each floor. The Szenes' toilet was regularly out of action, and at those times we had to use the smelly, overflowing, paperless common toilet, which invariably had a queue in front of it.

The kitchen, a small, narrow room with a sink, a table and a sideboard, was Nagyi's domain. Apart from her chaperoning duties it was up to her to prepare the meals. This is where she busied herself, out of sight and earshot, occasionally offering us a cup of cocoa or a slice of home-made cake if she had any. Kati and I spent all of our time in the large lounge, around the table in front of the bay window, where we could sit and survey the grey world outside.

Kati was learning to play the violin, and had to practise every afternoon, so I had to endure all the back-shuddering screeching of the strings, all the discordant high-pitched sounds. Soon she improved and the experience became less painful, then pleasant. The rest of the afternoon we spent daydreaming and giggling. If Granny complained that we were chatting too much we shooed her away.

'Don't worry, Nagyi, can't you see we're doing our homework?' Of course she couldn't, but she shuffled back to the kitchen to her chores anyway.

So very little happened in our daily lives that I wonder how we found so much to talk about. We hardly ever went to the movies or to any shows and never to a restaurant. Occasionally, the school took us on an excursion.

We did not have any other friends and there were no computers, computer games, TV or mobile phones; hardly even any toys or books. But there were always boys.

We spent a lot of time daydreaming about the husbands we would have. I had reluctantly given up on Jancsi Valkó. Both Kati and I decided we'd marry a Péter – we liked the name. And one of us discovered that the name originated from the Greek *petros*, which means rock, and we thought how strong and secure a rock would be to have around as a husband. And Peter sounded good in English; in Russian it became Pyotr or Petya, and we liked that, too. In Italian it changed to a romantic Pietro. And the French Pierre was something to die for! A few years later we both married Péters (and a few more years later, we both divorced them).

We discussed our classmates. What they looked like and what they wore, even though their clothes were as drab and uninteresting as our own. We repeated what other girls had said to us – about the boys who were (or were not) interested in any of them, how well they did at school, and whether or not they were nice. At the end of these discussions, we invariably came to the conclusion that no matter how attractive or pleasant other girls might be, we were going to be friends for ever, because none of them were as good as us.

One summer holiday, I gleaned some mind-shattering information whispered in my ear by an older girl. She enlightened me about what boys and girls do when they marry. Needless to say, I did not believe her. But on returning home, I relayed my new-found juicy news to Kati. We chewed over the possibilities. We knew babies had to be made somehow. We knew they grew in their mothers' tummies, but how did they get there in the first place? Boys and girls do that? Really, how could they?

After spending many more hours – days – discussing in detail the hows and what-to-wheres, and, even if they could, why on earth would anyone do such a filthy thing?, we agreed that others could do whatever they liked, but we would never sink so low. Not us. Never.

My nightly curfew was 6pm. As it took ten or so minutes to walk from Kati's to my home in Váci Road, and I always left at the last possible moment, I needed to run all the way, with anxiety and guilt rising to a crescendo just as I pushed the doorbell at home. I never knew what mood Erzsi might be in. I steeled myself for the worst, and Erzsi rarely disappointed. Often, she would come to the door, but not open it.

'Do you know what time it is?' she would bark.

'I suppose it's about six. Remember, I don't have a watch,' I would answer indignantly, trying hard to sound innocent.

'No, it is not! You're late again. If I tell you to be home by six, it means you be home by six. Not five past, or ten past, not even one minute past!'

One night, Erzsi was working herself up into an explosion, but I could not leave well enough alone.

'I'm bursting to go to the toilet.'

Now totally out of control, she screamed without holding back. 'You should've thought of that before! This door closes at 6pm sharp. If you're late, it's your own stupid problem!'

'But I'll wet myself!' I whined.

'Don't you but me! If you can't be home on time, you're on your own!' she continued yelling.

'I am always on my own,' I muttered, safely out of earshot.

I danced around cross-legged, banging on the door, whimpering. It was to no avail. I could hear her storm back into the kitchen. Then I skulked down the stairs and asked the concierge if I could use the toilet.

'Why don't you go upstairs and use your own?' Mrs Kovács asked, none too pleasantly.

'I would, but Mummy's not at home,' I lied. My statement puzzled her. She knew all the comings and goings of the residents. At last she opened the door while mumbling something about her home not being a public toilet.

When I left, I stood by myself crying quietly. What next? As the reality of what had happened took hold I thought, How dare she? It's my home too! I considered spending the night on the street, or going to one of my grandmothers.

I was sure that, though Cina lived a fair distance from us and I had to walk past a horrid pub on the way, she would give me a loving welcome. Gizka was closer but would ask too many questions. I couldn't face the pub that night so, buttoning my coat, wrapping my arms closely about me, with gritted teeth I headed towards Cinka's. To hell with the dark!

It took less than 15 minutes.

'Oh Veronka! What are you doing here?' she opened the door, surprised.

'Can I come in?' I asked, tentatively.

'Why aren't you at home?' Gizka probed further.

I didn't want to answer. I was ashamed of having such an angry mother and ashamed of myself for precipitating her anger yet again. But my grandmother kept on looking at me, and eventually I had to confess. 'I was late home and Mummy wouldn't let me in,' I snivelled.

Gizka did not like this answer. She was cranky, but I didn't know whether it was with Erzsi or with me. She said nothing, but grumbled under her breath and shook her head from side to side. As she left me to take off my coat I thought I heard her mutter, 'This is not right. You shouldn't lock out a child.'

My grandmother may have had daggers in her eyes for Erzsi, but I was the one who received them. Auntie Stefka, who was quite bent and nearly blind, shuffled out into the hall. 'Is there something wrong, Gizinko? Who was that?' she queried.

I blended into the background. She continued, more loudly, 'Gizinko, where are you? Is everything all right?'

She had to be answered, so I carefully stepped forward, trying not to scare her. 'It's me, Auntie Stefka, I came to stay with you and Gizka!' I enthused as if it were the most natural thing in the world to do.

Her face dissolved into a relieved, welcoming smile. 'Oh, it's you, Veronka! You came to stay the night? So what's wrong with your own bed? Heh?'

'There's nothing wrong with my own bed,' I mumbled. 'I wish I could be in it tonight.'

'Speak up girl, I can't hear you!'

'*Lass Ihn, Csupka, lass Ihn!* ('Let her be, Csupka, let her be!') Don't ask so many questions!' Gizka interrupted.[21]

Grandmother spoke to her little sister (whose affectionate nickname was Csupka) in German so I wouldn't understand. Of course I knew exactly what they said. Auntie Stefka didn't like being left out of anything, I could hear Gizka telling her quietly in the other room what had happened.

And now I had two old women shaking their heads. 'Tssssk, tssssk.'

I felt like a traitor. It was all right that I hated Erzsi and her temper tantrums, but it was not all right for me to tell anyone else about it. Then Stefka suddenly thought of something, and shouting to Gizka, she ordered, 'Gizinko, make up a bed for the girl!'

She turned to me and asked, 'Have you eaten anything?' and thinking she was facing my grandmother, said to the wall, 'Gizinko, I have a little jam left in the

---

21 'Lass Ihn' translates as 'Leave him', but Hungarian doesn't differentiate between 'him' and 'her', so I expect the German was used incorrectly by my grandmother, or my memory is flawed.

jar, and I still have a couple of slices of fresh bread. Get some food ready for her, the poor child is starving!'

She wasn't wrong; I was always starving in my teen years. With the two old ladies hovering around me, I enjoyed my jam sandwich. Then there was a knock on the door.

'It's your daughter on the phone, Auntie Gizka, she wants to talk to you,' the voice said.

Gizka hurried downstairs with the woman.

I was afraid that Gizka may not be allowed to keep me for the night. What would I do then? I had no money. I couldn't possibly go to Kati's. I didn't want to cause any problems for Erzsi, and besides, the shame of anyone knowing I had been locked out would kill me. In all the years of Kati and I spending every spare moment together, she didn't know of any of my problems with Erzsi and I didn't know of any she had with her mother. Apart from my two grandmothers, I couldn't turn to anyone. I waited anxiously for the answer.

'She just wanted to know that you're safe.'

I was furious with Erzsi, but relieved. Now I could enjoy my grandmothers and be well looked after; a little spoilt, maybe. I knew that though the grumblings and head-shakings would continue, it was going to be pleasant evening. And best of all, I wouldn't have to face Erzsi until the next day. I was happy.

Gizka and Stefka shared one room, which was both bedroom and lounge. I had a bed made up on the floor from large cushions and slept comfortably on that. One of the nice things at my grandmother's was the fresh smell of the sheets – a unique, clean aroma. A special Gizka-household smell.

The next morning I went to school leaving Gizka with the tidying up and washing.

* * *

Of course by the time I was ten I was as big as Erzsi and could have fought back or at least restrained her. But I was petrified of her. I knew that a child couldn't possibly lay hands on her mother. Yet the fury of the words she spat out had the strength of a river in flood, ripping me away with rage, jetsam and flotsam hitting me hard. I had nothing to hang onto.

37

GOING TO CINA'S

For the next few weeks I was more careful to be home on time, but one evening I found myself late again. Being aware of all the questions and disapproving tut-tuts at Gizka's, this time I started out in the opposite direction – to Cina's house. She lived a fair distance from us, and we would normally get to and from her place by tram. In fact, that is how she got her nickname – the tram's bell made the 'tzin, tzin' or (*cin, cin* in Hungarian) sound, and as a little girl I had named my grandmother 'Cina'. But that evening, it took me a good half an hour to walk. In the dark.

Cina lived at Angyalföld, Angel's Place. This was a misnomer, really – angels seemed to have left the place quite a while before. Unlike the area where we lived, which retained its architectural dignity and character, here at Angyalföld most of the houses were single-storey, lime-washed cottages built directly on the street, as was the custom in Budapest. The gardens, if any, were in the back and were mostly overgrown and neglected.

Cina at age 55

Many houses had cracked windows, some held together with sticky tape. The venetian blinds had broken cords, and the formerly pretty lace curtains were torn and holey. Rusty, leaky guttering was held more or less in place with bits of string or wire. Large patches of wall were bare and exposed where plaster had fallen off, and many walls had evidence of rising damp and mould. And everything needed painting.

The people also seemed to have suffered from neglect, and were dressed in hand-me-downs, with clothes and shoes that didn't fit and were often dirty. Some of the former cellars, now used for housing, had no bathroom or washing facilities. No one appeared to be happy. I regularly heard angry, raised voices, people shouting abuse at each other, swearing; Hungarian is a good language for that.

*   *   *

A few blocks before Cina's house there was a pub. The acrid smell of spilt wine, beer and urine hit me as I passed this establishment, which was always full of unshaven, loud men staggering around drunk and bad-tempered. Normally I was not exposed to this kind of behaviour and it frightened me, particularly as their expletives exploded into the otherwise quiet street: '*Az Isten bassza meg azt a rohadt disznót! A rohadt kurva anyját!*' ('Fuck that rotten stinking pig. His rotten whore of a mother.')

The drinking men in Hungary, many of them cart drivers, had trained their horses to stop at all the pubs at the end of each working day. I pulled my hat down over my face, hoping to become invisible, wanting to slide past them unnoticed. But they always saw me, and nastily offered to 'show me a good time', with hands on the buttons of their flies, rubbing their crotches, '*Gimbelem, gombolom, légy enyém, angyalom,*' ('Bittening, buttoning, be mine, my angel-ing') they chanted while laughing lewdly.

I was too young to know exactly what they meant, but my whole body shuddered. Their words and actions seemed to cover me with shame, even though they never actually laid a hand on me. Sometimes I crossed to the other side of the street. Nearly every time, unperturbed by my presence, at least one would be standing exposed against his patient horse, urinating under it.

My heart still pounding, I arrived at Cina's. At that time, all blocks of flats were overseen by janitors; they kept the streets clean, shovelled snow in winter for access, operated the lifts and locked the gates at night for security. For a nominal fee, they could be buzzed at any time to open up.

As much as I would have loved to sneak in quietly, the gate to Cina's was shut and I had to call the concierge, Mrs Süle. Auntie Süle, a busybody but not ill-intentioned, rattled her large bunch of keys as she greeted me. 'A young girl shouldn't be walking alone at this time of night! Tell your mother to take better care of you!' As if I could tell Erzsi anything!

I thanked Auntie Süle for opening the door and apologised for the inconvenience. In the morning my grandmother paid her a bit more than the agreed fee.

When Cina saw me, she clapped her hands together and sighed happily, 'Oh, Verácska! My dear, how lovely to see you!'

Then, realising that there had to be a reason for my visit, she asked, 'Is everything all right at home?'

'Well ... I was late home this afternoon and Erzsi was angry with me. I decided to come to you for the night.' I didn't want to elaborate on having been locked out.

'But you come so late! It's not safe for you to walk alone in the dark.'

'I'm not afraid of the dark, grandmother!' I said quite cockily, not mentioning the pub and its clientele.

Cina made a call from the phone at Auntie Aranka's to let Erzsi know of my safe arrival. I resented the call; as Erzsi had locked me out, I wanted her to be punished by spending the night worrying about me.

My grandmother was short and plump, with a smooth, unwrinkled forehead and rosy cheeks, the latter of which I have inherited. I was very pleased to look like her. She always wore black, probably still mourning her beloved husband, my grandfather, Rudolf. Her skirt was long enough to cover the top of her footwear – ankle-high soft leather lace-up boots. Her grey-white hair was cut short in the back with longer strands at the sides neatly curled into snails over her ears and held in place with invisible bobby pins. She wore it that way all the years I knew her. And she never had a hair out of place. I didn't ever see her rush or hear her raise her voice. If she was ever angry, she did not show it. Cina always displayed an air of acceptance and serenity. And sadness.

Her smile showed her white even teeth, more regular and perfect-looking than dentures. In fact, she would often be called on by Bella Kovács, our dentist, for whom Cina occasionally worked as a receptionist, to model for the patients Bella wanted to shame. 'Come in here, Auntie Gizike,' Bella would call. 'Please show your teeth. See, Mrs Szabó, this is how well-tended teeth should look.'

Cina heated a pot of water on the gas cooker and poured it into a basin. She dipped a washer into it, wrung it out, and handed it to me to wipe myself with after going to the toilet. It was soft and warm; the height of luxury compared with the harsh and skimpy bits of toilet paper or torn bits of rough newspaper I normally used.

She placed the basin on the floor so I could soak my feet in the warm water. It relaxed me and, somehow, also melted the shame and dirt of the pub. Before the water had a chance to cool, I had a hot mug of cocoa in my hands. Auntie

Aranka arrived home from work. The two old ladies turned their full attention to me. What had I learned at school? Did I have any homework? If so, I'd have to do it after supper. What was my little brother up to? Was he eating properly? How was my father? Whatever my answer to this last question was, Cina always followed with, 'My poor, darling son, God bless him, he's working so hard!'

We all ate supper together. Each time I was there, I was offered a slice of bread with salami or cheese, if they had any, or if their pantries were empty, a jam sandwich. The two sisters kept me company while I ate, urging me to eat more. Compared with Erzsi's preoccupation with my weight and consequential admonishments to not gorge, this was heaven. No one yelled at me here; I didn't even have to do any chores.

Cina still had some copies of *Women's Weekly* from World War I – large-format, black and white magazines with pictures of soldiers going to war in the uniforms of the day, and ladies in long gowns with bustles and corsets sporting fancy hairdos. I never tired of looking at these pages, though was quite annoyed at myself because I had scribbled over some of them when I was little.

When it was bedtime, my grandmother arrived with a heated lid of her cast iron pot and placed it between the sheets to warm the bed. As I jumped in, I was swamped in an ocean of feather doonas and down pillows. I asked for a bedtime story and my grandmother gladly obliged. Our favourite was *The Lady of the Camellias* by Alexandre Dumas. It is a tale of a painful true love and, though I heard it many times, I cried each time. Unlike Marguerite Gautier, the heroine, I was healthy and robust and did not want to become sickly, even less to die … but, like her, I wanted to find my great love. Would any man ever love me, truly?

By the time the story was told, it would be late. But I never wanted the magical evening to end. 'Please, would you sing to me, nagymama? Please Cina, pleeease?'

She had a soprano voice, thinning and a little wobbly, but still clear and melodious. It wasn't difficult to wear her down. Soon she sang songs from her girlhood, or arias from the popular operettas – *The Gypsy Baron*, *The Merry Widow* or the heart-wrenching *Liliomfi*, which was later rewritten in English with the title *Carousel*.

After Laci, I was the apple of Cina's eye. She spoilt me whenever she had the opportunity, but equally, if I did something wrong she did not let it pass. On those occasions she told me unequivocally what I had done wrong, and then firmly suggested what I had to do to make it right. Her method was much more effective than Erzsi's ragos, which simply needed to be endured and then could be ignored. Erzsi's outbursts were so unjustified that I fought them bitterly, and

learnt nothing from them. If I was in trouble with Cina, my own guilt took over
and the lesson was never forgotten.

One example involved my 'playing' one Sunday afternoon. Having nothing
to do, I leant out of the window and started to spit. I was targeting a crumpled
bit of paper on the footpath, but as my aiming skills were none too finely honed,
I rarely hit it. Every so often someone would appear from the cellar dwellings
below the house, the underground dark, dank rooms which were rented by
the worker comrades (*prolis*, when out of earshot). Now and then I hit one,
unintentionally, but not wanting to be caught, I quickly disappeared behind the
curtain, squatting low. It was not hard to find the point of origin of the spitting
and soon someone complained to Cina.

She called me to her, looked me in the eye and said, 'Shame on you, Vera.
The people who live below may be poor and not well educated, but every human
being deserves to be treated with dignity. Don't you ever forget it!'

And then she made me knock on their door, face them by myself and
apologise.

Most of the time, I behaved well. While Erzsi was quite adamant that I should
not be spoilt and develop exaggerated ideas of my own worth, Cina spoilt me.
It was the best thing she could have done, because it made me feel a worthy
human being. I could let my guard down when I was with her, while with Erzsi I
needed to be constantly on my toes; she could lose her cool at any moment, and
I needed to be on alert to duck her hands. The irony, perhaps, was that spending
time alone with Cina, being treated like a princess, always came as a result of my
having done something wrong in the first place.

I never told Erzsi how much I enjoyed staying at Cina's, how well and
tenderly she attended to my every need. And I never told Cina how much Erzsi
had yelled at me or how often and regularly she hit me. There was no love lost
between these two women, and I wasn't going to pour oil on that fire.

But it wasn't all bad. I learnt that there was a silver lining even in the worst
storm clouds. On many an occasion, an argument at home led to my ending up
at Cina's and being spoilt. Rotten.

38

AUNTIE ARANKA AT WORK, HER HOUSE AT ANGYALFÖLD

(A peasant woman standing on the scale, while others are bringing their produce to be weighed by the Co-op)

'Why are you standing on the scale, Auntie Borika? You are not a vegetable!'
'That's true. But I like to weigh myself here, because these scales always show a bit underweight!'
Ludas Matyi, 26 January 1956

A textile outlet, a supermarket and a men's toilet, all with large signs posted on them: 'Closed for stocktaking'.
Ludas Matyi, 26 January 1956

Auntie Aranka's corner grocery shop was at street level, directly under her flat. As a special treat, whenever I went to visit my grandmother Cina, my auntie let me help in the shop, and at the age of five or six I already showed great promise as her junior assistant. Under her close supervision, I served the customers, took money and carefully counted out change. I thought it was fun, but my main interest was in the cakes and sweets on display. I was not allowed to sample any of the wares, but in the evenings there was always a little something for me. Then the shop was nationalised.

The youngest of the grandmothers, Auntie Stefka, was already frail and nearly blind. Because of her disability, she received a minimal allowance from the Jewish community, to whom she had donated generous amounts of money throughout her life. Cina, with her high blood pressure, was not able to work either, and was not eligible for any pension. Both Auntie Aranka and Gizka had to return to work.

With all the stealing that was taking place, new positions were created: controllers. Soon deliveries were made by pairs of employees – one wearing overalls carting the stuff, the other in a grey twill coat checking the delivery, weighing and recording. There were now twice as many jobs – under the communist regime there was no unemployment – but as both the overalls and the coat stood to benefit from short deliveries, not much changed.

At the age of 66, Gizka became a controller on a coal cart. She had to get up at five in the morning, travel to the coal depot, keep an eagle eye on the coalie as he loaded up his horse-drawn cart and then sit all day with him in the open on top of the cart, in rain, hail or snow, until he finished his deliveries. If she caught him cheating and told him so, a violent spurt of expletives would hit her pink lady ears. At each day's end, she returned to the depot and handed in her sheet of checked weights. After two years of this, she was finally entitled to a small (and inadequate) pension. She was a strong woman, and took it all in her stride. But it did affect her health, and after a couple of years she needed a pacemaker.

Auntie Aranka owned not only her shop but also the house she and her sisters lived in at Angyalföld. Originally, this had been a lovely single-storey villa with a sunny courtyard in the middle and six small self-contained flats on each side. Mrs Süle, the concierge, lived with her husband and grown-up son next to the gate.

Aranka's unit was the one closest to the gate, and was a little larger than the rest, with a lounge, a bedroom, a kitchen, a bathroom with a deep bathtub and a separate toilet. Next to her was Auntie Jolánka, one of the middle two of the four Heimler sisters. Two doors down was my grandmother Cina in her bedsit. The other places were rented out.

The garden was a romantic little green space with a small pond and fountain in the middle, and lilac bushes and snails. I spent hours collecting and examining these creatures with their houses on their backs, fascinated by the slime they secreted to help their progress in the world. The large fancy ironwork gate was kept locked, but once a month a gardener came and tidied up.

When the shop and the house were nationalised, all the other residents cheered, because now they too would have access to this lovely garden. The gate was left open and they could come and go as they pleased. Very soon the goldfish in the pond died, the fountain was vandalised, the garden became neglected. It was full of rubbish, overgrown with weeds, and stank of urine. It was decided that the gate should be kept locked at all times, and in the end no one at all used the garden.

The garden could have been a metaphor for the whole communist system – everyone owned everything, but no one had the responsibility, the knowledge, the money or the will to look after it.

*   *   *

Auntie Aranka found employment in a small chocolate shop in the city. Now she had to travel to work, and her hours were quite long, but the job was not as physically demanding as Gizka's. She was soon asked to become manager. I visited her a few times and was quite taken by the fact that an old lady had been given such an important position.

Auntie Aranka, 1968

She took command of the shop in her spotless white coat and ran it as if it were her own. Her customers, many of them regulars, appreciated the old-fashioned manners not found in the new government-owned stores and treated her with kindness and respect in turn.

I figured that being the manager's grandniece entitled me to sample every item in the shop, but was quickly put in my place. At home, however, I was still the recipient of an occasional small brown funnel-shaped paper bag containing two or three of the yummiest chocolates.

My great-aunt was a calm, elegant lady. She had a straight back, gentle and kind eyes and a pleasant smile. I admired her independence.

Her only luxury was having the hairdresser, Rita, home-visit her every morning to do her hair. Mostly it was only a comb-up, but once a fortnight Rita washed and set the thick silver halo that surrounded my auntie's head. It was a self-indulgent, almost wicked waste, and I decided that one day I too would spoil myself like that. But I never did. Maybe my upbringing wouldn't let me accept this manifestation of bourgeois decadence.

In communist ideology, the ownership of property was considered to be theft. However, this did not apply to the government. In the early 1950s the living conditions were so hard, and there were such gross inefficiencies in the running of businesses and organisations, that everyone stole from all government-owned ventures. Official business would have ground to a halt if it hadn't been oiled with bribes and short-changes. The system worked like this.

You bought, say, 10 dkg (100 grams) of salami. The employee in the delicatessen placed what he thought was about the right number of slices on a skimpy bit of paper and then threw it on the scale. Quickly he whipped it off the balance, while the needle was still wildly oscillating, wrapped it and handed it to you. If you wanted to get your blood pressure up, you could re-weigh it at home, where, to no great surprise, you found it was only 87 grams. A half-kilo of meat weighed barely a pound and much of it was gristle and fat, a tonne of coal was probably only three-quarters of a tonne and lower in quality than what you had ordered and paid for.

It was no use complaining, because the shops or warehouses which short-changed you were short-changed themselves. And the factories that sold it to the distributors or warehouses had an equally raw deal on the materials. Nearly all professional and qualified tradespeople had been labelled 'reactionary bourgeois elements', and consequently sacked. Many ended up in labour camps, breaking stones or building roads. The country was run by former factory workers and peasants who had neither training nor experience. Nobody had enough money to survive. Through corruption, one could make ends get a little closer together. Once such a system is in motion, it is as good as impossible to not be part of it.

Auntie Aranka, like everybody else, couldn't trust the delivery men. She regularly found that she was one or two boxes short, or the chocolates were not quite the stated weight on the box. When she protested, the men shrugged their shoulders and told her that this was what they had been given, and it had nothing to do with them. If she then insisted on writing out the receipt for the actual quantity of goods she had taken possession of, she not only made enemies of the delivery men, but from then on nearly everything she ordered became 'out of stock'. And if she took her eyes off the men, they quickly smuggled a box or two out of the shop back into their cart. To ensure any delivery at all, she had to take what she was given, and even reward them with a tip.

Had she given the correct weight to her customers, she would have been found short at stocktake time – stocktaking became the rage, a national pastime, and this constant administration kept everyone on the verge of a nervous breakdown. Had Auntie Aranka been short, she could well have been accused of embezzling the great Hungarian workers' chocolate, of being the enemy of the proletariat and of class struggle. This was cause for disciplinary action, with a possible jail sentence. All this gave Auntie Aranka a headache, as she had been brought up with different values.

In the end, she decided it was best to simply aim for a small loss, and she ran the business accordingly. So now Aranka néni, like every one else, weighed the small bags of sweets by throwing them on the scale. Sometimes she was lucky and under-weighed just the right amount, and if she was a bit short at the end of the month, she managed to talk her way out of it with only a rap on the knuckles. Finding herself with a surplus was a potential disaster. All excess had to be quickly removed and made to disappear. At those times Gyurika and I were the lucky beneficiaries of her miscalculation.

39

THE PEASANT AND THE CHICKEN; LACI'S TRAVELS

I loved stories, stories of all kinds, including stories by the Grimm brothers, full of little abandoned waifs and wicked, ugly stepmothers. I read *Sleeping Beauty* over and over again – it took 100 years, but her prince did come. I loved folk tales where the ignorant but clever peasant triumphed over the powerful king or prince. One of my favourites was this one:

Once upon a time there was a king who lived in a palace with his queen, two sons, and two daughters. Once every year, just after harvest, the peasants queued up in front of the King with gifts for him. Each brought whatever he felt he could spare. One of them, a very poor fellow, gave the King only one chicken, for that is all he had. The King was furious. This was an insult, hardly a fit offering for his Royal Self.

'You brought me only one chicken? You impertinent fellow! How am I and my family to dine on that? Eh?'

His Highness glared angrily at the man. 'I'll teach you a lesson, you ungrateful minion. Tonight you will divide up and serve this one chicken among all of us – fairly, mind, or you'll pay with your head!'

The peasant bowed. 'As Your Majesty pleases.'

In the evening all the members of the Royal Family gathered in the royal dining room and took their seats. The chicken had been roasted to perfection by the Royal Cook and was placed on a silver platter in the middle of the table.

The peasant rolled up his sleeves and, concentrating on the job and on his head, he began to carve. 'I am your humble servant, Majesty,' said he. 'You, Majesty, are the Head, not only of your household but of the whole realm. You deserve nothing less than the head.'

And with that he served the head of the chicken to the king.

'And the queen must always support the king,' he continued, *'just as the neck supports the head. So, Your Highness the Queen, allow me to present to you the neck.'*

'Hmm', the King cleared his throat.

'Now the two beautiful princesses are nearly at an age where handsome suitors will ask for their hand. They will soon leave the Royal nest to fly to faraway lands. To assist them in a safe journey I give them the wings.'

'Hrrmmmph', harrumphed the King.

'The two princes will stay here by your side, Majesty. They will fight many a battle bravely in your defence. They will need to stand their ground firmly. To them I therefore give the feet.'

'And, Your Majesty, what's left of the chicken I will humbly take for myself.'

The King laughed heartily, slapped the man on the back and after a right royal banquet, let him go home to his family.

And then there was Scheherazade and the 1001 Arabian nights. I was on familiar ground with the folk stories and the Grimm brothers, but the Arabian nights took me to magical lands unknown to me, full of mystery and treasures, lands resplendent with gold and syrup. Although I had read about the Ottoman occupation of Hungary – the courts of Baghdad and Istanbul with their caliphs, Ali Babas and Aga Khans – I couldn't imagine that any of it had actually existed. But my father travelled widely in the Middle East and made it real for me with his postcards and stories.

In 1945, Laci left the employ of the Reich brothers, where he had worked in various responsible positions. Later, these large, efficient, privately owned companies were nationalised. Their experienced workers were dismissed, and the factories were restructured. They were then run mostly by untrained workers and peasants.

Laci was lucky, because he found a job in a newly formed government-owned company, Hungarotex, where he was employed as a section head in 1949. He was later promoted to be the director of the piece goods department. Hungarotex sold textile products to foreign countries at competitive prices. Laci's job was to design narrow fabrics such as elastic bands and trimming, as well as curtain laces. These fabrics were then made by the factory to his specifications.

After the War Hungary was desperately short of hard currency. It had traditionally relied on mineral exports, agriculture and light industry for its wealth, but now the economy was in ruins. Agriculture initially continued to do well, due to the fertile land between the two rivers, the Danube and the Tisa. But later, the new co-operatives, run by inexperienced management, had very low productivity. The peasant workers did not own the land, did not benefit from working hard and so had no incentive whatsoever to over-exert themselves. With massive sums of money going to the Soviet Union, and with having to pay for raw materials for the new heavy industry, Hungary was broke. The two most profitable ventures were the chemical and textile industries, both of which became a source of foreign revenue.

Laci found himself well placed, in a key position in the textile industry. Because he was fluent in German and had some understanding of French, he was asked to represent the company to foreign countries and sell its products – on condition that he learn English as well. He studied hard and passed his exams.

It was the not-yet-tapped markets of the Middle East that he had to win for Hungary. He travelled to Cairo and Alexandria in Egypt, to Saudi Arabia, Lebanon, Syria and Turkey. He did well and was sent back over the following years, until 1952. It was an extremely important job because he was not only trading textiles and bringing in hard currency; he was also acting as an unofficial diplomat, selling the ideals of communist Hungary. The country needed both the trade and the goodwill of states outside of the Eastern Bloc.

Laci was away several times a year for two to three months at a time. I would watch him get the light, soft-leather suitcase from the secret compartment of the wardrobe in his bedroom in preparation for his journey. Erzsi packed – six ironed and neatly folded shirts, sufficient underwear for a week, two tailor-made, well-cut lightweight suits, a number of appropriate ties, and official presents for clients from the Hungarian Government. They had the packing routine down pat. I was not taken to the airport to see him off, but he would hug and kiss me goodbye at home, with a mutual promise that we would write to each other.

Regularly, though not often, he did send postcards to me and I to him. Here is a translation of one I sent for his birthday in November 1951:

Dear Daddy, we have received our ¾ yearly report it was quite good. I'll write it down for you.

Behaviour:	3
Conversation:	6
Reading:	7
Writing:	6
Composition:	6
Grammar:	6
Mathematics:	6
Drawing:	5
Singing:	5
Gymnastics:	7

They signed it: Vera is trying hard and is behaving well. Mrs Konrád.

Daddy I am already a much better little girl. I am helping Mummy and am more diligent. I'll write about Gyuri as well. Daddy, you know that Gyurika can already reach the door handle and if I am doing my homework he comes in and disturbs me. Today Mummy found the key to my room and the door has to be locked. Anyway, he is full of mischief. Daddy are you well? We are well. Write.

Many kisses

Vera

It was a delight to receive his cards from exciting places. There were pictures with palm trees from Syria or cedars from Lebanon, sand dunes and Bedouin tents from Arab lands, bustling bazaars from Egypt and Turkey.

The pictures of bazaars fascinated me the most. They were bursting with people and goods of all kinds, and the colours had a cacophonous vibrancy. In Hungary, the shops were almost empty and the little that was there was boring, utilitarian and grey. Laci took many photos with his beloved Leica, some of which I have in albums. Of course they are in black and white, but the postcards were in colour. Would I ever experience anything as exotic as these places? For ordinary citizens, there was not much coming in and absolutely nothing going out from behind the Iron Curtain.

I kept the cards until he returned and asked him to talk about the places he visited. Laci was not a particularly willing teller of tales, but there were a few. The most memorable was the time when he was invited to a Bedouin tent, where they treated him to a dinner fit for a foreign dignitary. On the menu were roast lamb, flavoured with the herbs of the Dust, shish kebabs on skewers and, as a *pièce de résistance*, the special delicacy of the Arab world, sheep's eyes. Laci had difficulty bringing himself to swallow one, but taking a deep breath and holding it, with his eyes closed, he managed to get it down. Then he squeezed out a thin smile, more out of relief – mission accomplished! – than out of enjoyment of the experience. Everyone present cheered.

All this exquisite food had come at a price, though – the obligatory loud burping required of guests to signify appreciation. Those present quickly and easily performed this, but Laci simply couldn't. All around him froze, as if in suspended animation. They waited, and waited, and waited. The burp was not forthcoming. Every man in the tent had his eyes fixed on him. As guest of honour he *had* to produce the sound or risk seriously offending his hosts. Not good for business. The others looked at him expectantly, patiently, encouragingly, until, at long last, he managed a good one. Then, courtesies having been observed, with jubilant approval from everyone, the meal continued. Strong local coffee was served with an assortment of Turkish delights, baklava and loud chatter. And the business deal was done, the Arab way.

Following this story I practised my burping skills just in case I found myself in a similar situation in the near future.

Whenever Laci came back, his suitcase was full of gifts for us children and Erzsi. For her he brought back the finest of fine silk material, brocade from Damascus, feather-light exquisite leather sandals from Turkey or, occasionally, when he managed to save enough on his hotel expenses, a small gold bracelet or a necklace. Later, on special occasions Erzsi still wore an emerald-green blouse Laci had bought for her in Syria, more than 50 years ago. At times he didn't get the size right. Erzsi was very disappointed at having to sell these beautiful new acquisitions.

Once he bought a wonderful 'spinning skirt' for me; a skirt so full I could sway and spin to my heart's content. Erzsi hated it; she only liked well-cut tailored clothes, 'The English Look', even for me. She had been a tomboy, and didn't like anything 'girlie' or pink or frilly. A tailored look came closest to the practical, serviceable clothes she wanted. It did not occur to her that I might not be the same. Anyway, my joy didn't last long, because by the time Laci delivered it I'd just about outgrown it, and it too had to be sold.

At times Laci arrived home with some real treasures. Once, a small mysterious packet materialised from his suitcase. It was jelly crystals from England. I had no idea what jelly was, or what to do with it, but was certainly curious.

'Daddy, what is this yelly?'

'It's *jelly*,' he corrected me. 'You'll like it, I think.'

'Do we eat it?'

'Yes. But why don't you wait and see? We'll make it together, right?'

Laci and I commandeered the kitchen as Erzsi had no appreciation for the finer points of jelly making, and considerably less for the mess we were likely to create, which no matter how well we attempted to clean up would not be to her standards.

First, with appropriate ceremony, Laci carefully translated the instructions. We didn't want to get it even slightly wrong, did we? I was proud of him. Everybody spoke German, but English was something special. With great precision, we measured the requisite amount of water, brought it to the boil and then I energetically dissolved the jelly crystals. When it was done, Laci added an exact amount of cold water. It was lucky he had a measuring cylinder at home from his old chemistry set! A bit more stirring and it was ready. I had to try it, of course, by dipping my specially 'designed' cake-bowl-licking little finger. I am very pleased with my little finger because it has a small bend in it so it can hold more than my share of secretly pilfered goodies.

The hot jelly liquid was nothing to write home about, but I didn't say anything so as not to dampen our enthusiasm. We waited. Though I didn't know exactly what was meant to be happening, I kept on sampling. After an interminable time, it finally set. It was red, comically wobbly and absolutely delicious, and Laci, Gyurika and I pigged out on it. Erzsi wasn't interested even in tasting it, and reckoned it wasn't worth the mess.

Returning home from another trip, he brought a small metal pot with a long handle from Turkey, a Turkish *ibrik* or coffee pot. I didn't drink coffee but loved the aroma and the ceremony, and Laci appointed me as his assistant while he fussed around.

First, the coffee beans had to be roasted in a frying pan to just the right colour, not too dark and not too light. The aroma infused the whole neighbourhood with an exotic feel, which it could well do with. Next, in my role as chief assistant, I hand-ground the beans in an old-fashioned coffee grinder. With the movement of the turning handle, the lumpy and crunching sounds of the beans gradually became smoother, the effort less, and the smell saturating my nostrils hypnotised me.

Laci then took the *ibrik*, filled it two-thirds full of water, added two teaspoons of finely ground coffee and the same amount of sugar. He gently heated it over the gas flame until it started to froth, then quickly lifted it from the heat before it had a chance to overflow. When the froth subsided, he repeated this last step twice more. After removing the pot from the flame for the third time, while gently swirling it he sprinkled cold water on top. It was allowed to stand for a couple of minutes to settle the sediment. Finally, we served it in tiny espresso cups.

I had a sip. It was comfortingly sickly sweet, and strong enough for the spoon to stand up in.

From another trip, Laci produced a pair of slippers for me from Turkey. They were made of shiny pink and green and gold silk brocade, and had turned up toes like the ones in the fairytales. These too were too small for me.

On a later occasion, he brought home a Meccano set from London for Gyuri, and demonstrated some of the wondrous creations he would be able to make when he was older. When Gyuri was older Laci still supervised his son, which meant that he played and Gyuri watched. It was only several years later that my brother finally had his chance to assemble magnificent creations of his own design.

From his last trip Laci brought home a calendar. I had not seen one before – with the dire paper shortages, it would have been a luxury in Hungary. It was really only an ad for some textile product or other. It showed an English family with a mother and a father, a small son and an older daughter. Erzsi named them the Tumb family. This was pronounced Toomb with a short 'oo' and the 'b' sounded.

Gyuri, too young to understand that it was not a storybook, insisted that Erzsi read it to him and she reluctantly gave in. She believed she lacked imagination, and she lacked the confidence to make up a story. She did not live in fairyland the way I did; she was too bogged down trying to survive in the real world.

The Tumb family's 'story' was the only one that Erzsi ever told us. It became Gyuri's favourite because, of course, Gyuri Tumb was the hero, always naughty, always in trouble, barely out of one scrape before getting into the next. The calendar was 'read' over and over again, forever changing as it incorporated the latest misdemeanours of my little brother.

The calendar was in English, so we couldn't understand it, and Laci wasn't around to translate because he was away yet again. This time he had gone on a trip not of his own making, not one anyone would choose to go on.

40

LACI'S FINAL TRIP

In 1952 I woke up one fine morning and found my father gone.
'Where is Daddy?'

Erzsi looked as if she hadn't slept all night. Her eyes were bloodshot, there was something wrong. 'He's gone.'

'Gone where?'

'On one of his trips.'

That was not like Laci. He would have kissed me goodbye. But Erzsi was not in the habit of making up stories and I believed her.

Over the next few weeks I missed Laci. I felt excluded from this trip. Erzsi was always tired, extremely irritable, and I was continually on the wrong side of her hand. She yelled at me and slapped me if I as much as blinked the wrong way. I did my best not to rile her, and tried to keep out of her way. I didn't succeed, and the slaps continued coming, with ever-increasing force.

Erzsi's behaviour changed in other ways too. Laci

She spent ages on the phone. Her voice had lost its sparkle, and the light-hearted teasing she normally adopted with close friends was gone. There was no joy in her. With most people she became evasive and secretive, and she snapped at the slightest provocation.

She now spent ages talking to Éva Fenervary, a colleague and very close friend of Laci's. I liked Éva and adored her husband, Uncle Ali, but was not allowed to stay in the room when they visited. I could hear from behind the door that they spoke seriously, in hushed voices.

There was something very wrong. I knew it, and I wanted Erzsi to tell me, but she was evasive.

Then, a few days later, Erzsi produced a letter. It was a plain note in Laci's writing, not the usual card. No picture and no stamp.

'Where's the stamp?'

'I accidentally opened the envelope and threw it away.'

Erzsi would never throw out any stamps. She knew I collected them. 'Mummy, I know there is something wrong. Please tell me, I am not a baby, I am already ten!'

She took a few deep breaths,

'Well … Well … Your father made me promise not to tell. I suppose, seeing you're asking so many questions, it's better if I do. But not a word to Gyuri!'

'No, I promise.'

'Your father is in jail.'

I fell silent. I was trying to digest the information, but it made no sense. Laci was in a high government position, he worked hard, and was often praised. His colleagues and the labourers in the factory treated him respectfully and looked up to him. I knew that. I also knew that, although a reluctant party member, he could not have been sent to other countries if he weren't trusted. He believed much of the ideology – we had had a few discussions about it. Above all, he was scrupulously honest. Even if he had wanted to, he wouldn't have known how to cheat anyone. I knew my parents' ethics. Neither of them would give a millimetre when it came to their core values. After a long time I asked, 'Why?'

'I don't know. He was framed. Someone else did something wrong and your father is getting the blame. We are trying to get a lawyer to help us.'

Naïve as I was, that cheered me up. 'Oh, don't worry, we know he didn't do anything wrong, and so they can't find him guilty. He'll be back in no time, when they realise they made a mistake.'

But the books had to be balanced, no matter what. If the real culprit could not be found or if he was out of reach, someone else had to be nominated to carry the blame. Scapegoats were Hungary's most prolific product for the internal market. And my father's status had changed overnight, from respected, highly valued director of the Hungarotex factory to criminal. He was now about to be put out to graze for a long while in the less than green pastures of Ajka's jail.

There was a joke going around at the time. It went something like this:

'How many types of people live in Hungary?'

'I don't know. How many?'

'Three.'

'Three?'

'Yes, three. Those who had been in jail, those who are in jail and those who will be in jail.'

In those months, the joke did not seem funny to us.

Some time later Erzsi had a conversation with a party official that was as surreal as that joke.

'My husband is innocent and yet he's locked up,' she said.

'Guilty is whoever is thought to be guilty,' he answered.

'Then is it right that 99 out of 100 people are found guilty?'

'Yes, it's better to have 99 innocent people in jail than one guilty person going free.'

My mind was whirring with all it had to take in. 'Mummy, have you visited him in jail? When will you go again?'

'Yes, I have, and I am going to see him as soon as I am allowed.'

'I am coming with you.'

'Your father will be upset. I wasn't even supposed to tell you! My God, he'll be upset with me.'

In a matter of days, I changed from a child to a grown-up. There was absolutely no question in my mind that I would visit him. He had to see my face, to see that I believed in him. My heart was full of love for him, and he had to know it. I wanted to tell him that on his release I would still be his little girl, proud of him, that I didn't doubt his innocence.

But we had to wait for months, until after the sentencing. When the time came, we left Gyuri with Gizka, and Erzsi and I set out on our trip. Ajka is south of Budapest, not very far, but there was no direct train line there. We travelled at night and changed trains several times, walking along the tracks from one platform to the other. Erzsi carried provisions for Laci. We arrived at Ajka at about midnight and waited in front of the gates until they let us in at 9am.

When we got past the security check, we were led into a very large rectangular courtyard. There was a balcony above us, where the cells were. I looked up, feeling very small. I saw men wearing grey stripey prison garb. Would I recognise my father? My throat tightened, my heart pounded. I was standing a little distance from Erzsi when I spotted him. In the stripey clothes. My father. My father. When he saw her, his whole being lit up. He walked with a spring in his step.

Laci smiled, and indicated with his chin, while gesticulating with both hands towards the reception area, where prisoners were allowed to talk to their visitors.

He didn't see me. Then Erzsi, also looking more cheerful than I'd seen her for a long time, pointed to me with a guilty look. Laci turned ashen, his arms went limp, his body collapsed. The spark of life visibly left him; the shame was too much for him. Not looking at me, both of them started to walk towards the visiting area.

After a minute or two, Erzsi called out to tell me that only adults were admitted to see the prisoners. I had to wait outside. She returned an hour or so later and we travelled in silence all the way home.

We never spoke of this visit again.

And for my family, time became irrevocably split into *before* and *after* 1952 by the fault line of Laci's term in jail.

41

AND SOME MORE POLITICS: COMMUNISM
IN ACTION

(A dishevelled, angry man is waving his arms about in a room he's just trashed.)

'They dared to tell ME that I can't take any criticism!'
Ludas Matyi, 29 January 1953

Mrs Tito: 'Why did you nominate yourself to be President of the Republic?'
Tito: 'I tried on the crown, but it did not look good on me.'
Ludas Matyi, 29 January 1953

In the summer of 1948 the Hungarian Workers' Party (MDP) was formed. Their proclaimed aim was to build communism after the principles of Marx and Lenin, but in practice they followed Stalin, concentrating all power with the leadership of the party. Over the following few years, banks, industry, businesses, education were nationalised and all agriculture was collectivised into co-ops. There was no compensation for the property taken and the co-ops were set higher and higher production quotas and paid lower and lower prices for it.

To ensure the MDP's hold on power, they ruthlessly weeded out the 'class enemies'. To this end, more than 10,000 of the former nobility, plus the high flyers and the intelligentsia, without even being charged, were deported from their Budapest residences to allocated accommodation in distant villages. Justice was meted out not according the severity of the 'crime', but according to the social standing of the person who had supposedly committed it, and to ensure that the 'wrong' ideology was not perpetuated, these people's children were barred from higher education. Once they had been removed from the city, their empty apartments were ready to be used by the party elite.

The elite, the replacements for these 'class enemies', were the workers and peasants who might have been ignorant of how to run a factory, or a bank, but were faithful to the party and open to learning the new ideology. Soviet advisors stationed in Hungary taught them the ropes. The churches were dismantled, their leaders dismissed, often jailed, and new party-compliant leaders installed.

Fear, intimidation and terror kept these policies working. Denunciations of those with views different from the officially acceptable ones were not only encouraged, but became the 'duty' of good citizens.

New courts were created to enact the party's wishes. A judge trained in law and in party politics was at the head, flanked not by a jury, but by a people's tribunal consisting of workers and peasants, some illiterate, and all with no knowledge of the law. Often the verdict was handed to the judge before the trial even began.

Party secretaries became the most powerful people in society, intimidating workers and controlling their lives. They initiated 'character-building criticisms' and insisted on applause whenever Stalin's or Rákosi's name was mentioned.

The ÁVO, which was initially set up to deal with war criminals, expanded its role (and changed its name to ÁVH) to include spying on those thought to be against Sovietisation. They fabricated accusations and backed them with false evidence, arresting and torturing their victims until they obtained a 'confession', which was followed by a jail term or hanging. These are now referred to as 'show' or 'conceptual' trials. There was never any shortage of invented indictments.

A particularly significant show trial in 1949 (which a few years later became the trigger for the 1956 revolution) was that of László Rajk. Rajk, a home-grown – that is, not Soviet-trained – and charismatic government minister, was popular with young communists, but a threat to Rákosi. By getting rid of Rajk, Rákosi would remove a potential rival and at the same time show solidarity with the Soviet Union against Tito.

Tito, the Yugoslavian leader, unlike the leaders of other satellite countries, remained independent of the Soviet Union, and even had the temerity to have 'visiting' Soviet officials followed by his own spies. This put the Kremlin into a rage.

Rajk denied all the fabricated charges against him, naturally. But his 'friends' and comrades in the party convinced him that the trial was only intended to be a show trial, to discredit Tito. Yes, he would be sentenced as part of the charade, but after a short while he would be exonerated. Rajk had little choice but to agree. The ÁVH then tortured him physically and psychologically until he admitted to everything they wanted him to admit to. Rajk's confession was broadcast on radio – we heard him duly denounce Tito and the Yugoslav Communist Party. For his troubles he was executed on 15 October 1949.

The trial was the start of large-scale 'cleansing' in Hungary. Between 1950 and 1953, the government initiated more than one million law suits, of which about half went to court (in a country with a total population of only 10 million!); 400–500 were executed and hundreds of thousands were detained. They arrested tens of thousands of communists, socialists and members of trade organisations, as well as members of the middle class, peasants, workers and civil servants, who were then interned and tortured.[22]

By now we all saw through the sick hoax, the duplicity and unreality around us, but we were terrorised into noisy admiration of this dictatorial system.

---

22 Laci was one of those removed. While serving, true to the communist work ethic, he 'consistently achieved 176–212% of productivity results'. László Káhn, private letters.

42

AJKA

The significance of an incident which occurred before Laci's arrest became apparent only later on.

Whenever Hungarotex sent anyone to a foreign country, it was always in the company of another person, so they could keep an eye on each other; this time it was the Assistant Foreign Affairs Minister, a friend of Laci's.

At 11 o'clock at night a few weeks before the fateful trip, there was a loud knock on our front door. Erzsi opened it to two men.

'Is comrade Káhn at home?' one demanded to know.

'Yes, but he is in bed.'

Erzsi did not like the look of the men, and had no intention of letting them in, but they pushed their way past her. Laci woke up with the noise and came to the hall in his pyjamas. 'What's up? Who is it?'

'Get dressed, comrade, you're coming with us,' the men stated.

Laci quickly threw his clothes on and went with them. Later it emerged that they were from the secret police. He was taken to the Deák Square Police Headquarters in the city. After several hours of questions and answers, everything seemed to be in order, but just before they let him go the inspector asked him to 'keep an eye' on Hungary's commercial attaché in Egypt. Laci knew the attaché: comrade Kallós, a well-educated man and a Jew. Although under the communist regime there was no official discrimination based on religion, unofficially, just like under the Horthy regime, it was not to a person's advantage to be Jewish.

Laci was quite taken aback by this request. He was oh so naive! He explained to the men that he was a good citizen, he loved his job and always did it to the best of his ability. He was proud of his country, and when abroad always tried to do the best trade deal possible for Hungary. And then he added that although he was willing to take full responsibility for himself, he could not do that for others.

In other words, Laci refused to spy. Later, at his trial, this counted strongly against him and landed him a sentence.

* * *

A woman, Emerencia, or Enci, as she was called by everyone, had the supremely powerful position of Party Secretary of Hungarotex. She was an avid communist, and to add to her power, her brother, Tibor Pőcze, was the Assistant Chief of Police. Enci was to be feared. A person in her position, especially with a direct connection to the police, could effectively denounce anyone.

One day at a productivity assessment ceremony, she received commendations for work well done in the narrow fabrics section of Hungarotex. Despite all the propaganda, the workers were not held in as high regard as those managing them, and the highest commendations were always for the party representatives. After Enci had received her ribbon, she noticed Laci, and hugging him said, 'My dearest Laci, you should have got this. You earned the Certificate for Exemplary Work, you are the one who deserves it!'

Officially she proudly accepted the praise in his stead, but privately she acknowledged Laci's achievements. A few weeks later Enci was not feeling well, and had to go to hospital. There she shared a room with a young woman called Blanka. The two women didn't get on well. They had an argument. Soon after that Blanka landed a position at Hungarotex. On her first day at work someone explained to her that she would be working with Enci. Blanka commented that she already knew Enci and that she couldn't stand her.

'Blanka, for heaven's sake, be careful of what you say! Enci is extremely powerful. Watch yourself!'

When she realised how much power Enci had, Blanka's face paled. She thanked the person for warning her. Soon, Enci and Blanka bumped into each other in the corridor. Remembering the argument they had had at the hospital, Blanka fainted and had to be scooped up by those near her.

Every so often, Hungarotex put on a social evening of music and even dancing, to which spouses were invited. Erzsi didn't go because she liked to call a spade a spade, and had to watch her every word among the comrades. It was simply too dangerous to talk to anyone, as every conversation or, even worse, part of conversation, could be reported to the authorities.

On the Friday night just before Erzsi's birthday in October 1952, the Káhns and their closest friends, Ali and Éva Fehérváry, had tickets to a Russian ballet,

The Fountain of Bakhchisarai. The same evening there was one of the office social evenings, but they declined their invitation. Laci went to work in the morning as usual, and in the evening, all dressed and ready to go, Erzsi waited for him at home. He did not show up. It was getting late, time to leave for the ballet, and he had still not arrived. She was worried, but thought he might have gone to the party for a bit and lost track of time. She tried to phone, but there was no reply. She rushed in to the office and cornered the director. He was surprised that Laci hadn't gone home already and equally intrigued as to his whereabouts, but couldn't help her at all. They missed the ballet. The next morning he still hadn't arrived home. Worried sick, she went to the police to enquire. There was a guard at the door. He couldn't let her in without an appointment or special permission from his superiors, but tried to cheer her up.

'He probably just went on a boys' night out. It's Friday night! It happens all the time. Don't worry, Madam. You'll see, he'll soon be toddling along!'

Erzsi knew this was not the case. Her husband was a considerate, thoughtful man who never stayed out late or strayed away from home. He was far too much in love with his wife! On seeing Erzsi's obvious anxiety, the watchman whispered, 'We have to be very careful what we say. There are many secret agents coming and going here. They listen to every word we utter.'

He pointed to a nondescript man and added, 'See, there is one right here.'

Erzsi had a really good look at the agent as he walked past. By this time Erzsi feared the worst, so she went to Hungarotex to see Enci. Even if no one else knew what was going on, the Party Secretary would.

Enci had an office upstairs. There was a uniformed man guarding her door, and Erzsi was kept waiting downstairs for quite a while. As she stood there, she recognised the detective she'd seen at the police station the previous day. He brushed past her and went directly up the stairs. Erzsi was instantly on red alert. That's where Enci's office was. Finally, she was asked to go upstairs.

'Encike, do you know where my Laci is? I am very worried about him, haven't seen him since yesterday morning.'

Instead of answering, both Enci and the agent interrogated Erzsi. Where could he be? What did she know of his activities? Does he visit anyone on his trips abroad? What did he bring home from his last trip? Does he know so and so? But Erzsi was on her toes and wasn't going to say anything. To every question she answered that she didn't know, or that she herself was about to ask them the same. She left Enci's office no wiser, except that by now she had more than a strong inkling that Laci was in serious trouble.

On arriving home, she phoned Éva Fehérváry. She asked Éva to see if it was possible to find out anything from the 'inside'. Éva, at great risk to herself and her position at Hungarotex, managed to take a look at the daily records, where she found papers that indicated that Laci had indeed been arrested on Friday. It was only much later, at the court hearing, that they found out why.

* * *

One of Laci's jobs was to design and oversee the manufacture of net nylon bags for onions, other vegetables and fruit for the foreign trade. Holland was their largest customer for these. A sample was sent to the would-be purchasers, who were satisfied with the quality. However, when the full consignment arrived in Holland, the customers saw that it was not up to specifications, and the shipment was returned to Hungary. The problem was not the design, but the quality of materials used.

New, improved bags were made and Laci wrote an explanatory letter to accompany them. To make sure it was party-politically correct, he submitted the letter to the Chief Director of Hungarotex, Erzsébet Farkas. For his own protection, he also showed it to Leo, a lawyer in Hungarotex's legal department. They both approved it. When everything was in order, the new bags were sent to Holland with the explanatory letter.

With all the to-ing and fro-ing, the shipment was not on time according to the original contract, and the customers demanded a large sum of money, hard currency of course, from Hungary, where money was already extremely scarce. Apart from the financial cost, this was a huge blow to communist Hungary's ego, as the country was desperately trying to carve herself a niche as a fully functioning, reliable trading partner for Western countries.

To make matters worse, the Hungarian ambassador to Holland chose to defect at that very time. Hungary had lost face and credibility. The ambassador was out of reach in the West, and a scapegoat had to be found. Laci was it. And it was at this point that his firm and uncooperative stance against spying on a colleague counted heavily against him.

Laci was told nothing about the 'crimes' he had supposedly committed. In fact, the prosecution found it difficult to find a charge against him. Apart from his professional ability and integrity, he was a model employee, not a troublemaker.

Once in custody, Laci had naturally asked for a lawyer. He was told 'not yet'. So in effect he was denied legal representation. He still did not know what the charge was or even if he would be allowed to have a defence.

Until the trial Laci was in Budapest's Markó Street jail, in the company of some real – that is, non-political – criminals. He had to stay there for about seven months, from October 1952 to May 1953, when his case was heard.

During his time in Markó Laci wasn't allowed to communicate with the outside world. This included Erzsi. Laci was desperate to let her know that he needed a lawyer. There were eight men in his cell, one of them due to be released within a couple of days, and Laci asked him to go and see Erzsi with the message. The released inmate was a farmer, a simple man and not a criminal. He had been arrested because he slaughtered a calf, when, according to the law at the time, only fully grown cattle could be killed for meat.

Erzsi was hugely relieved to hear from her husband, to know he was well and that, though worried, his spirits were up – mostly, the man said, because of her.

'Why is that?' she asked.

'Well,' the man answered, 'this is what Mr Káhn told me: "Please ask my wife to get a lawyer for me. If she takes my affairs into her hands, I know I will be well looked after."'

Erzsi was not used to responsibilities of this magnitude – the house and home were her domain. Though way out of her depth, she immediately set to work to find a lawyer for Laci. This proved to be extremely difficult, because this was not a simple criminal case, but a political trial, and lawyers were afraid of the implications of representing a political prisoner. Once again, Éva Fehérváry came to the rescue, finding someone through a friend of a friend.

When Erzsi met him for the initial consultation, she reported her 'conversation' with Enci and the undercover agent. The lawyer blanched and said, 'Erzsi, had you answered even one of their questions, we would both be in jail now.' But he did continue to represent Laci.

Now Erzsi had to let her husband know that she had managed to arrange for his defence. She could neither talk to him nor send messages. She called Laci's former 'criminal' inmate, the farmer, who had an idea. He drew a diagram, showing the exact position of Laci's cell, his own former cell. He suggested she stand there with a message on a large cardboard sign until he spotted her.

After collecting the laundry, Erzsi stood under Laci's cell window and held up a placard with the message in large black letters: We have a lawyer. She stood there until there was some movement behind the window the farmer had marked on the diagram. Laci had seen the sign.

Erzsi attended the court hearing, and to her horror, found that Vilmos Olti was the judge. This was the judge who had sentenced Cardinal Mindszenty just four years earlier. A former Nazi, but now an avid communist, he was known as the Red Government's *vérbíró* (hanging judge). He presided at many a show trial and had no qualms about pronouncing death sentences. It turned out that Laci's case had to be taken to the High Court, this time with a Judge Jónás. It was conducted behind closed doors – no one was allowed in or out until the case was over. For the whole time Erzsi sat outside the courtroom, but as the walls were thin she could hear much of what went on inside.

Unfortunately, one of the potential witnesses for Laci, Leo from the legal department of Hungarotex, had died just before the hearing. The other, Erzsébet Farkas, Laci's superior, was called as a key witness in Laci's favour. On her way out of the courtroom, she spotted Erzsi, hugged her and said, 'I am so sorry my dear Erzsi, they want to sentence Laci.'

The judge started his sentencing speech with the following: 'Comrade Káhn, it is well documented that you had always worked conscientiously and enthusiastically in the interest of the Hungarian People's Republic ...'

Laci was given two years. In a letter dated 1954 he stated, 'In May 1953 the Highest Court sentenced me for two years of jail for a crime unknown to me.' He had not even been given the respect of being told what the exact charge against him was. The kind of serious political disloyalty we assume he was charged with carried a sentence of life imprisonment or death. The judge was politically pressured to give a sentence, but the lightness of this sentence attested to my father's innocence.

After the hearing, he was allowed to write and to receive letters. This is the only one that has survived:

IGA 234 III / 12

My dear Mother,

I received your card on the 24th. Your encouragement helped me regain my strength, especially for Erzsi's visit. I never really doubted that you're doing whatever you can in my interest, though somehow after such a long time of being here, it's hard to imagine that justice may prevail. But I have not given up hope; I only wish I knew why I am in here?

It's important that all of you at home remain strong, then I won't be disheartened either. I am very worried about how you can survive [without my income] and I was very touched that Bella is such a wonderful, kind soul. I won't forget it.

My dear Erzsi,

It happened once again that we were unable to use your time with me to our best advantage. We love each other much more than to need words to express ourselves. You sent a very good parcel. They opened it in front of me and everything was really nice. I'm sure it will last me for three weeks. I will ration it well, and with this the food is sufficient. I'm sorry that you sacrificed your Sunday morning for me, but believe me ... I'm a little selfish. I'd love you to decide that once a month you'll write about the kids. I'm thinking of them a lot. Many kisses for the children.

Lots of kisses,

Laci

After the sentencing, Laci was transferred to the prison in Ajka. Visitors were only allowed once a month, and could bring only one suitcase of clean clothes and food per prisoner. Cina filled the suitcase to the brim for her beloved son. It weighed a ton, but of course it was Erzsi who had to carry it. Luckily, she was exceptionally strong, particularly in her arms and hands. Erzsi had to drag the full suitcase from the station along the tracks and down the brightly lit path to the jail's front gate. Other women were not as capable, and she would double back to help them.

On her first visit, Laci didn't seem too distressed. He was delighted to see his wife and receive all the goodies his mother had packed. He had all he needed, except for his freedom.

Laci's sentence was two years, but he was out in 10 months, thanks to the death of Stalin in March 1953. The amnesty granted all political prisoners in August the same year meant that he was released, and that he had no criminal record.

While Laci was in jail we had no income. To add to the problem, the hefty legal fees also had to be paid. Erzsi was desperate for money. Éva, the best of friends, came to visit us one day and left an envelope full of money, tactfully hidden out of sight, to be found after she was gone. It was a sizeable sum.

Postscript

I wanted to know what the exact charge against Laci was. And what did he actually get convicted for? What was the precise wording of the verdict?

When I returned to Hungary in 2006, after a few phone calls I found the offices of the Historical Archives of the Security Services in Budapest. With my head pounding and heart thumping I fronted up at the Eötvös Street office in the city centre. There was no one at the front desk. When I rang the bell a friendly-looking woman, sandwich in hand, came out of a back office asking me my business. She excused herself, saying it was her lunchtime, but meanwhile there was a form I could fill out with all the known details of my enquiry. She would attend to me in 25 minutes. I could barely stop myself from screaming at her.

How dare you not tell me what happened to my father this very instant? How dare you keep me waiting another second longer? I thought as my anger rose to my throat.

But, even managing a smile, what I said was, 'Please take your time, I've waited for this for more than 50 years now, a few more minutes will hardly matter.'

I started filling out the form. Name, mother's maiden name, nature of the enquiry plus a list of all known details. I breathed heavily and swallowed deeply, trying to remain calm. In all the years since 1952 I had not ever spoken to anyone about Laci's arrest – not to Gyuri, not to any friends, not even to my son David. I only told one person, Peter, after we were engaged. Now here it is, on an official piece of paper, that could be viewed by anybody. How do I inform the authorities in cold black print on a pre-printed form what it was like watching the life go out of my father when he saw me when he was in jail?

The woman returned in 15 minutes. She read what I wrote and while wiping the last crumbs off her lips casually asked, '*Egy koncepciós per volt?*' ('Was it a conceptual trial?')

I had never heard the term before. 'What do you mean?'

'Well, conceptual, you know.'

Her question was so matter-of-fact, so mundane, just as if she'd asked, 'You say you had toast and marmalade for breakfast this morning?'

I didn't know but said yes, I supposed so, guessing it meant a political case. But it meant a bit more than that. It was a show trial, a mock trial that devastated the lives it touched for the sake of propping up the ideological principles of a regime that operated with no principles.

I became very, very angry. To take people, make them disappear until their pretend show of a trial, to change the lives of generations thereafter and make it all seem normal, acceptable, everyday, enraged me.

The woman behind the desk must have seen the clouds gathering in my eyes. 'I'm sorry, really sorry. There are so many of you coming back from all over the world trying to find out where your family is, what happened to your loved ones. Unfortunately I can't give you much hope. All we can do is try. At the end of the communist era, when the change of regime seemed imminent, documents were burnt by the truckload – the documentation of entire departments was shredded. Whole sections are completely gone.'

Gone? Gone? I live on the other side of the world because of Laci's jail term and it was all a bad joke, something for entertainment, and there is not even any record of it? Our lives, our shame, permanently deleted from the official history? Did all of this not happen?

After giving me a minute to digest what she'd just said, the woman continued: 'Unfortunately, that's how it is. Please try to think of anyone else who was involved with this case, any names, places, dates, associations. It would give us a greater chance of cross-referencing. I promise we will try, but please don't expect too much.'

When I arrived back in Australia, I asked Dudi to think as hard as she could and try to recall every detail. She came up with some new information and I emailed it to the office with a note from her:

I am over 92 years of age and to this day I don't know what exactly happened to my husband, László Káhn. I would be very appreciative if I could find out as soon as possible. I hope you will be able to help me.

A year later we had a letter saying they had no information at all about Laci's case, but we should resubmit our request in about two years, as they were computerising all their records and maybe by then something would have turned up.

In 2007 I returned to Hungary and went travelling around the country with Kati Szenes. We passed the township of Ajka, where Laci had been in jail. I asked Kati to stop there on our way back. We veered off the main road into the small industrial town. It was drab, and seemed not to have much to recommend it. There wasn't anything on the map marked as a detention centre, nor was anything listed in the phone book. As it was Sunday, the police station was closed. At the service station they knew nothing about it, and at the railway station not even an older man had ever heard anything about it. How could it be?

We drove back to Budapest and in the following days I phoned the police at Ajka, the office of local courtrooms, the Town Hall and Council of Ajka, the district criminal justice office. The jail did not exist, and as far as anyone knew, it never had.

The council advised me to call the Ajka library, as they had all the documents relating to the local history from the year dot. The girl at the other end of the phone promised to do a search. When I rang her back a couple of days later, they had absolutely no record of a jail having ever existed in their town.

'But please, I visited my father there in 1953. I was there. I remember!'

She sounded distressed for me, and was lost for words. I could then hear her call across the room to a colleague, the curator of the local history section. I could hear his answer: he couldn't think of anywhere else to look for information. Once again we had been obliterated from history.

And then, in the background, I heard a gruff old voice pipe up. The girl listened and passed on to me what the man said. 'There is an elderly gentleman here in the library, one of our regular readers. He says he can remember the jail, a large rectangular building. It was a demountable, erected by the inmates in the early 1950s, but it was later taken down. It's long gone, there's no trace of it left now.'

I am grateful to that old gentleman, who, it seems, is the only witness to our reality.

43

OPERA, VIOLETS, LÁNGOS AND CHESTNUT AUNTIES

There was a silver lining to even this darkest of clouds. My parents had season tickets to the opera. So as not to waste the tickets, while Laci was in jail I went to some of the performances.

The Opera House is beautiful and impressive from the outside, similar to its counterpart in Vienna. This was not new to me. I'd seen it before, but had never entered it.

On passing through the doors, a pure white marble foyer opened up, with a high ornate ceiling and sparkling crystal chandeliers. Shiny ladies and gentlemen, not the usual grey comrades, filled the space, parading their jewellery, perfume, fur stoles with stuffed fox-heads and sharp claws, or dark suits and well-polished shoes from a near-forgotten era. A broad red-carpeted staircase led up to our balcony, which boasted plush red velvet seats, gilded carved chairs and a teal duck-and-gold embroidered ceiling. It was like being right in the centre of one of my many magic carpet trips from the Arabian nights. All this at a price a factory worker could afford.

The orchestra tuned up – strange sounds – then came anticipation, a momentary silence and then, with sharp precision, the first notes of the music sliced the air. A few minutes later, the curtain glided up and we were transported to a colourful, buzzing piazza in old Italy.

Rigoletto, the ugly, bitter, crippled hunchback, was acting the fool for his debonair master, the Duke of Padua. From the very first notes, I was aware that something terrible was going to happen. I could feel the tension in the music, from Rigoletto's mock tragi-comic limping signature tune to the overly light lilting of the 'La Donna è Mobile' of the Duke. Disaster was inevitable. As the story unfolded, I realised it was about hatred, jealousy, love, pain.

I could not get the music out of my head, and the story opened up a Pandora's box of emotions in my ten-year-old self.

*   *   *

There were many other wonderful things to enjoy in Budapest.

I took to walking after my first outing in the Buda hills. One year at the end of winter we went to Hüvösvölgy. The hills were covered in snow, but there were proper paths and it was an easy walk. I loved the fresh air, the naked tree skeletons against a crisp sky, the cool white snow. Against the bare trunks, violets were showing their velvet heads, well protected from the winter's cold by the snow.

I picked a small bouquet of the violets. They were Erzsi's favourites and I loved them too – their colour, their vulnerability, their delicate perfume. At home, they went in the special vases – a pair of dainty, ten-centimetre-high silver vases shaped like Greek urns, with handles on both sides. The bulging body of each urn had been polished to a high shine, but the intricate work on the handles had accumulated patina, and it gave them a sense of age and respectability. They set off the violets wonderfully.

My other special flowers at the time were snow drops, with their heavy green-and-white heads bobbing on skinny stalk necks, and lily-of-the-valley, the tiniest of heavenly perfumed white bells, Cina's favourite.

As I grew up I learnt to love many other flowers. I was taken by the vast fields of raggedy blue cornflowers, *búzavirág* (wheat flowers in Hungarian) mixed with white daisies and the brightest red floppy-petalled poppies. I knew they were all considered weeds, but I didn't care. My dream was to marry in a meadow full of them.

Florists were virtually unknown in the poverty-stricken 1950s, but in early spring there were women standing on street corners selling violets in small neatly tied bunches, carried in woven baskets on their arms. They had picked the violets themselves, and for a few fillérs one could buy a little sprig of hope and beauty.

During the winter months, street vendors sold freshly roasted chestnuts on city corners. The 'chestnut aunties' were short, stout, middle-aged, wrapped up to their noses in heavy coats and rugs, and with more rugs on their knees to keep the cold at bay. Woollen scarves covered their foreheads, and only their noses braved the cold. They wore thick fingerless hand-knitted gloves, and sat by their brazier with the chestnuts, five in each brown paper bag.

I liked the whole chestnuts, but the purée was even better. The chestnuts were roasted, peeled, mashed, flavoured with good old-fashioned 65 per cent rum and forced through a press into long worms, onto a generous bed of whipped cream. This luscious cholesterol bomb was decorated with a few more artistically arranged dollops of cream and sported a cherry preserved in brandy on top. Chestnut purée was more a dream than a reality – cream was often unavailable, and in any case, we had better ways to spend our money.

Lángos was another street specialty. This is a bread roll's worth of dough, pulled into a 20-centimetre-diameter circle and deep fried, with a clove of garlic rubbed into one side. It was sold with a paper napkin wrapped around part of the edge. Sometimes sour cream or cheese were used as toppings, but for me heaps of garlic was always the winner. I smelt for at least a day afterwards.

The cafés had for decades been the places where people relaxed and caught up with each other, enjoying a strong espresso and fine pastry. But they closed down one by one, because, according to the propaganda, the busy workers of that great country had no time to spare for sipping coffee.

44

ANTAL; ERZSI GOES TO WORK

During the ten months Laci was in jail, Erzsi became independent, albeit reluctantly. She had responsibility for the whole family. She worked extremely hard, and slept extremely little. Much of the time she was tired and irritable, but she managed well. For the first time in her life she went to work, looked after us, made all the decisions about our upbringing and care, ran the household, organised Laci's affairs and visited him in jail, and looked after the finances.

She rented my now tiny room to a man, Antal. He was a country person from a well-to-do former land-owning family, but his father had been denounced as a *kulák*. He was scared of the system and kept a very low profile.

Our tenant was a serious stamp collector, and this gave me a good opportunity to learn how best to display my own collection, a gift from Auntie Stefka for my tenth birthday. First, the stamps had to be soaked in lukewarm water until they floated off the envelope. Then they were dried and pressed flat between tissue paper in the phone book. The following day they were placed on an appropriate piece of black cardboard, each stamp exactly in the middle, and finally they were covered individually with cellophane. It had to be right, perfect, each stamp in its own little world. It was a very fiddly job, but one I was allowed to do without too much nagging from Erzsi.

But the most perfect thing about Antal as a tenant was that he was a butcher. Once in a while, he was able to get us a half a kilo of good lean pork, veal or beef.

However, we still could not make ends meet, so Erzsi urgently had to get a job. She found a position in a shop at the *Maradék Feldolgozó Kisipari Szövetkezet*

(Remnants-Utilising Small Business Co-operative), a government-run chain store. She had to start at 8.30am sharp.

At the shop they custom made men's and women's fashions from left-over materials. Although Erzsi could sew, she was employed as an assistant window-dresser. There were eight outlets altogether, seven in Pest and one in Buda, and she followed her boss from shop to shop, ironing the display items. When she started, in November 1952, it was already bitterly cold, and she had to stand behind the window working in the draught. Afraid that the iron would fall out of her frozen hands, she decided to wear gloves. This went into the report about her: 'Mrs Comrade Káhn is a good worker, but she wears gloves while ironing.'

A bad mark against her name. A working-class woman's hands would be tough enough not to have to be pampered by gloves. Every worker was reported on regularly. If they were not up to scratch, a central committee reprimanded or sacked them, and if they did well, they received commendations and maybe a ribbon or two. Erzsi was conscientious, and they kept her on.

Her earnings there were not enough, though, so she needed a second job. Knitting machines at the time couldn't knit to shape. The fabric was produced as a continuous piece, which then had to be cut out and sewed together to form garments. There was a lot of waste produced by using this method, which the country couldn't afford. Every Saturday afternoon, on her way home from the shop Erzsi went to the factory to collect a bagful of waste, then at home she unravelled the knitting, tied the bits into a continuous thread and wound it into balls. These were sold. Each week she returned the balls of knotted wool as she picked up her new batch of work. Quite often Gizka was there to help her.

The waste was weighed on its way out and again on its way in. The pay for this mindless work was pitiful, but each week Erzsi was able to pinch a few metres of the wool until there was enough for her to knit Gyuri or me a jumper of many hues. Erzsi's designs were a great success: she used a variety of stitches to create interest – garter stitch, moss stitch, plain or cable. She knitted my monogram into one nifty little vest. The multitude of colours produced joyful pieces. I was constantly stopped on the street by total strangers enquiring who made the jumper. I answered with pride, 'My mother knitted this for me.'

Would she knit one for their little boy or girl? They'd pay her well. But Erzsi didn't have the time or the inclination.

One day in the summer of 1953 we received a notice from the local post office that some money had arrived. Erzsi was puzzled, and raced there after work to collect it. Noting the sender and the address, the clerk behind the counter commented, 'You must have an exceptionally talented husband if he can send you money from Ajka jail!'

And Laci was. He was an innovator and inventor, and he continued to work while locked up. As he was the foremost expert in Hungary in his field, they sought his advice even there. Kábel weaving factory asked him to design the rope, and work out the machine settings, for the parachutes they were about to manufacture. So then Laci could, in a small way at least, contribute to our finances, and at the same time keep up his skills and reputation.

Meanwhile, Erzsi kept working. The Co-op had two shops next to each other – they were internally connected. When the manager of the women's shop left, Erzsi was promoted to take her place. Szidike was in charge of the men's shop. She was a pleasant, talkative woman, and the two of them got on well. In their spare time they often chatted.

Szidike had two children, a boy and a mentally somewhat slow girl whom she used to spoil, perhaps to make up for the girl's problems. One day Szidike said, in passing, that oranges were available in a large Co-op on the boulevard, and that she had bought some for her daughter.

'They're very expensive, don't you think?' Erzsi commented.

Then, on a different occasion, Szidike told Erzsi she had bought a fine, large, hand-embroidered tablecloth for her daughter's trousseau.

'That must have cost you a bit!' Erzsi commented. Then she started thinking out loud. 'Szidike,' she said, 'you and I are getting the same wages. Neither of our husbands is earning much. We have similar size families and similar expenses. I don't know how you do it, because I certainly couldn't afford the luxuries you're buying for your daughter!'

'Well, I am good with money,' the other woman answered, turning red.

Even though a quality controller checked up on the shops regularly, the chief accountant, György Erős, noticed that the books were not in order. It turned out that the controller and Szidike had a deal: they both stole from the shop. No wonder she could afford all the finery for her children! They were both dismissed, and Erős, who was now in charge, appointed Erzsi to run the menswear department as well. Erzsi knew him well from her single days, when they were both members of the canoe club and used to go on camping excursions together.

'But comrade Erős, I know nothing about menswear!' she protested.

'You'll quickly learn,' came the pragmatic reply.

When Erzsi took over, there was a large deficit in the books. She was livid when she saw this, and immediately called him on the phone. He was adamant that the money had to be replaced, and as Erzsi was now in charge, it was her responsibility to do so. To make the books balance, Erős simply deducted the missing money from her wages. Erzsi protested the unfairness of it and then informed him that she would simply steal it back. György assured her that she would never get away with it: he would go over every account, every piece of paper, with a fine-toothed comb from then on.

'By all means, go ahead!' said Erzsi and slammed the receiver down.

The following day a woman came in to order a dress, wanting it made from a lovely piece of black crepe fabric. The measurements were taken for the job and the order was completed within a week. The dress was well made, looked beautiful and the customer was satisfied. But the material was 'black' in more than colour. It was, in fact, stolen by Szidike. Erzsi knew this and in turn took the hidden material, leaving no record of it, together with all the accessories – the thread, buttons and zip. When the whole transaction was finished, she called György again and said, 'Don't bother any more with the checking. I have already taken back my share.'

He was flabbergasted. After some weeks she bumped into him in the city. His first question was, 'How did you do it, Erzsi? You must tell me.'

She did no such thing, but instead gave him a talking to and assured him that she had no intention of ever enlightening him. He was really annoyed.

About twenty years later, in 1975, Erzsi was visiting Budapest for the last time in her life, and they bumped into each other. After all these years his first question was still how she did it. Yet again the answer was, 'You were extremely unfair and out of order, as I told you then. As far as I am concerned, nothing has changed.'

And she did not tell him.

45

MORNINGS BEFORE WORK AND SCHOOL

While Erzsi was struggling with work, Gyuri and I did not make it easy for her. This is how a typical day started.

'Cinike, time to wake up!' I heard the quiet call.

I didn't move a muscle; only my ears were alerted to the new day. As quickly as Erzsi's temper flared the rest of the time, in the mornings she was as gentle as a lamb. A sleeping person was sacred to her. As this was the only time I could count on a loving voice and soft touch from my mother, I made the most of it. The delaying tactics became a bad habit and stayed with me into adulthood.

Erzsi had been up for ages, preparing breakfast, making her bed, tidying and getting herself ready. I heard the clatter in the kitchen, I heard her go into the pantry to take bread and jam for our sandwiches at morning break. She returned to my room and playfully called again, 'Cinike, wakey, wakey!'

This time I grunted, but still did not stir. She'd woken Gyuri with no trouble at all. Quickly jumping out of bed, he was already making noises – 'Brrrrmm! Brrrrmm!' – as he steered himself towards Erzsi.

I listened to my mother struggling to get him dressed as he constantly wriggled, playing at being a car, or kicking a fallen button on the floor, or trying to catch a moth. Everything was a game to him. While she attempted to put his jumper on, he bent over, following a dropped marble that had rolled under the chair.

'It's time to go to school, we have to leave in 15 minutes!' Erzsi came to me again, and this time gently tickled my toes in the hope of stirring me into action.

I yanked my feet under the blanket.

Gyurika was having breakfast, one slice of bread with jam, and it had to be cajoled into his mouth bite by bite.

'Come Gyurikám, another little bite. Hummm, there it goes. Look, it's disappeared into the big black hole.'

Gyuri laughed delightedly and started to play with his chocolate-flavoured drink, which was made from something other than chocolate.

'Drink it, little son. Drink it while it's still warm.'

Her temper fraying, she now clumped her way from the kitchen back into my room. 'Vera, get up! You'll be late for school,' she said loudly, '*Now!*'

While Gyuri was still staring into his cup, my mother stormed in, scooped the blanket off the bed and looked on ominously while I jumped up.

'All right, all right, no need to fuss. See, I'm up already,' I growled.

I threw my clothes on and was at the breakfast table in two minutes. Erzsi was already washing up, Gyuri was still sitting at the table playing with his fake cocoa and I gobbled up whatever food Erzsi had readied for me and enquired about more.

'That's enough for you,' she said. 'If you don't curb your appetite you'll get fat. You'll thank me one day for not allowing you to stuff yourself,' she prophesied.

'If I don't starve to death before then,' I mumbled inaudibly.

'Have another bite, Gyurikám,' Erzsi wheedled.

One child didn't eat enough fast enough, the other ate too much too quickly.

We had our winter coats on ready to go, but Gyuri was still staring into his drink.

'Come on, son!' Erzsi was getting anxious by now. 'We have to leave!'

With his attention focused on the cup, he was totally oblivious to Erzsi's growing agitation.

'But I have to wait until the little boat reaches the edge! I can't leave it in the middle of the ocean to get shipwrecked.'

Erzsi looked at whatever Gyuri was looking at. A fluff of a froth ship in his chocolate-flavoured ocean was sailing towards safe harbour at the side.

By now Erzsi's every nerve was jangling, and though she felt guilty at always having to rush him, she had no more time to wait for the froth to drop anchor; it could sink for all she cared. She grabbed hold of Gyuri by the hand and off we went.

Before she could start her day at work, Gyurika had to be delivered to his kindergarten. The two of them walked to St István Boulevard and took the number 4 or number 6 tram, and then at Jászai Mari Square they changed to a number 2. The trams were always full at that time, and people hung off the open doors. While Erzsi struggled to get in, Gyuri wriggled between the legs of the other passengers to the back of the vehicle and hopped off at the other end.

Naturally Erzsi, too, got off, and the whole game had to start again. Gyuri's infectious laughter filled the air, while Erzsi was jumping out of her skin.

Later, when Gyuri started school, which was only a few blocks away from home, it was my job to pick him up at noon. Erzsi always prepared our lunch the previous night. I fed my brother and we entertained ourselves all afternoon, until she came home after 5pm. I was twelve, Gyuri six.

Erzsi constantly worried about her son's eating. He was fussy and ate little, too little. Breakfast was no problem, apart from the time he took to finish it – he loved his chocolate-flavoured drink made with milk. But the other meals were difficult.

Erzsi tried to tempt him with whatever she could get hold of: cheese, salami, chicken liver, bread, home-made jam. She made a sandwich and cut it up into one centimetre cubes. Each cube became a soldier. A plain bread-and-jam bite was a private, a salami and capsicum-topped cube became part of the cavalry, some had thin slivers of carrot swords, or wore a jaunty cap of a tomato slice. The soldiers walked, sometimes limped or galloped on horseback into my little brother's mouth. It was a lot of fun – for Gyurika, anyway. But he could still counteract the attack by snapping the gates of his mouth shut. Then the army had to retreat and try storming the fort again.

When Erzsi was at work, the job of feeding Gyuri fell to me. He prolonged the game as long as he could, objecting to any fallen majors, captains without their proper weaponry or injured privates. I was happy to play with him and we often roared with laughter, but if his mouth-gate was shut, I employed an expert new military strategy, whereby the soldiers were immediately deployed in a different direction, and without any resistance at all they marched straight into my mouth.

After the first few times Erzsi was amazed how Gyuri's appetite had improved for dinner, and with what little fuss he ate whatever she put in front of him. Then she became suspicious, 'Did you make his sandwich?' she asked me.

'Yes, of course.'

'Did you cut it up into soldiers and feed it to him?'

'Yes, Mummy.'

Luckily, she never asked what the army's final destination was, and I didn't volunteer this information. Meanwhile, Gyuri had cottoned on to this new manoeuvre. He made suitable adjustments to his game plan and ate his fair share much more quickly.

46

ERZSI THE BLOCK COMMANDER; FIGHTS

While Laci was in jail, Erzsi was out of control. Anything could set her off: if I left a book lying on the table, didn't take the garbage out, pulled a face when she talked to me. Erzsi knew for a fact that there was only one correct point of view, *hers*. She knew that all things could only be done the right way, *her* way. She was angry at having to single-handedly bring up two kids she didn't want in the first place, at having to take charge of finances, at being the main provider for us all, at having to work so hard. Perhaps she was simply over-tired. To add an extra burden when she least needed it, the local district party secretariat appointed her 'block commander'.

Although Laci believed in social democracy, he didn't go along with the communist ideology, but in order to be appointed as a director and especially to be able to travel, he had to join the Communist Party. Probably under duress, he signed Erzsi up too, and this is how she became eligible for the onerous task of running the 'block'.

A group of houses, maybe two or three buildings with approximately 100 or so residents, were deemed a 'block'. They had regular meetings organised by the party secretariat and led by the 'commander', where general information coming from above was disseminated: the need to immunise, the need to conserve coal and the need to organise for May Day celebrations and to ensure there were enough flags, banners and uniformed 'pioneers', together with their parents. In the name of the proletariat, we all had to attend and enthusiastically cheer at the rallies. It was the block commander's job to pass on the latest slogans and propaganda.

So while her genuinely idealistic socialist husband, Laci, was cooling his heels in Ajka, Erzsi, who had been completely disillusioned by the new government only a couple of weeks after it came to power ('Lacikám,' she said to Laci, 'this can't be a good system. They all cheat and lie'), was now in the hot seat as the trusted mouthpiece and disseminator of propaganda. With the risk of being thrown in jail herself, she could not refuse the 'honour' of being appointed to this hallowed position.

Though Erzsi was prone to fearlessly giving her opinion to all and sundry, whether they asked for it or not, she turned to jelly in front of an audience of more than two. Never before had she conducted a meeting or spoken in front of a crowd. She coped by keeping her head down, and when she had to look up, she imagined herself to be talking to a field of cabbages. She could just bear it that way. To protect herself from voicing her own opinions, even if only by an accidental slip, she opened the sealed envelope containing the evening's instructions and read these out without further comment. Once her duty was complete, she left no time for questions or discussion, having to 'race home to look after the kids'. Gyuri and I had our uses. Miraculously, she managed to survive her commandership.

For many months, Erzsi only had about three hours' sleep a night, and it was not enough. We had no cat to swing or dog to kick, so I was the punching bag, and often when she came home tired and irritable I felt the back of her hand in a rage that I was not the cause of. She raised her voice to a scream and went purple in the face, gesticulating wildly, her whole body taut and ready to pounce. She hit whatever part of me was within reach – my bottom, face, anywhere. Gyuri cowered in a corner, and I was scared out of my wits and wanted to run, but had nowhere to go. I soon learnt that it was best to get it over with as quickly as possible.

Once, my grandmother Gizka tried to stop her. '*Lass Ihn, lass Ihn!*' ('Leave her, leave her!') she said, in German so I wouldn't understand.

Erzsi snapped back, 'Butt out, Mother. You had your turn, now it's mine. I can do exactly as I please with my own brats.' And she kept on yelling and hitting me.

Gizka tutt-tutted disapprovingly but did not dare confront her daughter any further.

When her rage was spent, Erzsi calmly commented, 'Well, that's that,' and then, as if nothing had happened, called us to dinner, and the conversation took on an ordinary tone.

'What did you do at school? Did Auntie Emma call you to recite the poem?'

I was still shaking with fear, and resentment was brewing inside me, and often I was bad-tempered, surly, petulant or passively resisted Erzsi's requests for help, making it difficult for her.

The only person who seriously stuck up for me was my uncle, on one of his rare visits to our place. Before his arrival Erzsi had yet again lost it with me, and Feri walked in on all the shouting.

'Stop it, Erzsi!' he ordered.

She paid no heed. He did not waste words arguing, but calmly grabbed her wrists and clamped them in his iron hands. Making the most of the opportunity, I quickly slid away. Erzsi flailed around in utter frustration, unable to get free.

'Mind your own business,' she screamed at him. 'When you have your own brats you can treat them as you like. This is my turn. Let go of me!'

Although still scared and deeply ashamed that someone had witnessed me getting thrashed, I watched with glee as she who always had her way, who was a law unto herself and made my life hell, was handcuffed, immobilised and disempowered. I felt, for once, vindicated.

Feri did not say a word to Erzsi's squirming. He stayed quiet and still, continuing to hold her until she calmed down, though she was still defiant and unrepentant. Then, before letting her go he demanded, 'Promise me you'll never do this again! Vera doesn't deserve this, no child does.'

'Like hell I will promise! I am her mother and I can do what I want when I want.'

'You do wrong, Erzsi,' Feri said in parting.

'Huhh!' she responded derisively.

I found Feri difficult to warm to, but am deeply grateful to him for bearing witness to my woes and for trying to protect me. Now I knew that there was at least one other person who thought Erzsi was out of order and who was prepared to stick up for me.

＊　　＊　　＊

Erzsi generally didn't go berserk when Laci was home. At those times, she no longer had to shoulder the burden by herself. Laci knew nothing of Erzsi's temper, of her fierce and sudden anger or the beatings. None of us ever told him. On the few times she started picking on me in his presence, he had words with her out of earshot. Then, if she insisted on her way, in a huff he locked himself into his study and sulked for days.

'See what you have done!' Erzsi said, blaming me. 'We finally have your father back, and you have upset him! For once, just once in your life, you could do as you're told!'

After a few hours, even the blame was forgotten. We wanted Laci back. The three of us were tense and spoke in a whisper. Then we would start feuding with each other, hoping something would entice Laci out of the room.

'Daddy, I did very well at school. I was the fastest girl to answer the maths problem in class today!'

'Good.'

'Lacikám, I cooked you pasta squares with cabbage. Your favourite! Open the door, I'll pass in a plate.'

'I'm not hungry.'

'Daddy, would you like me to get you your slippies? I can bring them for you,' offered Gyuri.

'Thank you, son. I don't want them tonight.'

There was no way of coaxing him out until he was good and ready. By that time, we were all so glad that things were back to normal that the reason he went off in a huff was forgotten and never mentioned again. It offered me no protection and it did not help my mother get her anger under control.

✻   ✻   ✻

All of this had an effect on me. While Laci was still in jail I cried a lot, lost all my things and although already ten, wet the bed. My recurrent nightmare started in that year, 1953, too. It haunted me for a long, long time and only let up after my marriage, when I slept next to another body:

> *I am 11–12 years old, standing somewhere in the bombed city of Budapest amid rubble and destruction, my family behind me. I am protecting them – Erzsi, Laci and particularly Gyurika, who cringes behind me, shielded by my body. Facing us is a German, his raised gun pointing at us. I am staring at the soldier with anger, defiance and fear while screaming at him not to shoot. With a face devoid of expression he readies his gun, aims, pulls the trigger and shoots. Before the bullet has a chance to reach me, I wake up with a start.*

I regularly lost my homework book, pencils and gloves. I couldn't ever find my morning tea sandwich, which somehow slipped out of the bag, just as bobby pins fell out of my hair, disappearing without trace. Often I left my hat and scarf somewhere at school, never to find them again, and some days I arrived home with only one sock after a gym class. Once, when the elastic gave way, even my undies disappeared.

Erzsi was going out of her mind. She spent so much time and energy trying to keep us clean and neatly dressed, and nothing could be replaced because nothing was available in the shops. And we had no money. I was constantly fuelling her anger.

And then there was the crying. I cried if someone teased me, if anyone raised their voice to me, if I was even just gently pulled up, or if I didn't get praised. I cried if someone didn't want to lend me a ruler or if they didn't hear me when I spoke to them. I cried for all the slights, some real, most imagined.

Word got out that Laci was in jail. Kati knew, though I certainly didn't tell her. She looked at me with compassion and said it didn't matter, but just the fact that she knew mattered. I wanted to hide in a cupboard and never come out again. But that would have meant running away, admitting shame and defeat. So I gritted my teeth, and with my 11-year-old head held high, marched to school every day and challenged the world simply by being there.

One day I was chastised gently in class, and as usual, I started to cry. By now, the whole class was sick of it, and they all chorused, 'Cry baby, cry baby!'

Auntie Marika put a halt to the name calling immediately, with unusual sternness, and asked me for a word after class. I stayed back and told her she need not worry, I'd never cry again. And I didn't for the next 40 years, not even at Laci's funeral, which was, until then, the saddest day of my life. I couldn't shed a single tear.

I also started to steal. My mother was called in and the three of us stood in the classroom, I at a little distance from the two adults, my head hung in shame. Auntie Marika informed Erzsi of my pilfering activity and suggested that this should stay between us, and that she thought no further punishment was needed at school or at home, under the circumstances. Erzsi agreed, and never mentioned the incident again.

In 5th class, I had Auntie Emma for Hungarian and she regularly gave us compositions to do at home. Grammar was no problem at all, but what to write was. I nagged my mother into helping me with the story, but after a sentence or two she gave up.

'Stop pestering me. It's your homework, not mine.'

'But Mummy …'

I retreated to my room and somehow, anyhow, finished the composition. It was not good.

Auntie Emma called my mother to school, and forbade Erzsi from helping me, regardless of the amount of whingeing I inflicted on her, or the poor marks I might get for a while.

In retrospect, I realised it was fear of what I might say that caused the writer's block. I couldn't talk about getting into trouble with Erzsi, which was by then an almost daily occurrence, and I was afraid to report anything in case it was against the communist spirit and would get all of us in trouble. Hungary in general, and the home Erzsi created in particular, were not places that welcomed ideas or feelings. There was a constant fear of retribution hanging in the air.

The only times I felt happy, content and relaxed with Erzsi were in the mornings and some rare evenings. She regularly worked at home, sewing or knitting. When Gyuri was in bed, I sat with her doing my homework, the two of us working side by side in silent harmony. They were good times.

47

SPORTS, PUSKÁS AND SOCCER

Like books, the radio and movies, sport was a suitable medium for ideological indoctrination and was encouraged by the communist government. Most popular were fencing, athletics, volleyball, table tennis, gymnastics and handball, as well as wrestling, boxing and swimming. But it was soccer that kids played on every patch of green in every city, town or village. In the late 1940s, it became more organised through football clubs, many run through trade or professional associations.

All of us loved soccer, and no wonder – we had Puskás!

Ferenc Puskás was born in 1927. When he was about ten he was already playing for the local team, coached by his father. The soccer team was taken over by the Hungarian Ministry of Defence in 1949, and the football club became the Hungarian Army team, *Budapesti Honvéd*. Ferenc's name fitted in with the team, as it means 'Gunner'. The Army used conscription to acquire the best Hungarian players, who were then given military ranks. Puskás became a major.

In 1948, he was the top goal scorer in Europe. In the 1950s, he was the captain of the Hungarian national team, the legendary Mighty Magyars. They were unbeaten for a world record of 32 consecutive games. They became Olympic champions in 1952 in Helsinki. In 1953, they became the first non-UK team to defeat the English national team at Wembley, then in 1954 they beat England 7–1 in Budapest, which to this day is England's heaviest ever defeat in international football. The whole of Hungary was glued to the live broadcast on radio.

With a population of about ten million, Hungary won ten gold medals at the London Olympics of 1948, and four years later in Helsinki they won 16. In those years, Australia, with a similar population, won two gold medals in 1948 and six in 1952. Hungary was good! And the propaganda worked well for communism.

＊   ＊   ＊

In schools, sport became compulsory. I did not enjoy physical activity. My only interest was ice-skating, though I had no great talent for it, and swimming – I trained three times a week.

By 1955, Erzsi was not working full-time, as Laci was back in his job. She was in the kitchen when I came home too early one day from swimming training.

'What's up?' she asked. 'Why aren't you at the pool?'

'They sent me home.'

'Why? Did you do anything wrong?'

'No. My blood pressure was too high and the sports doctor said I couldn't swim like this.'

'Why on earth is your blood pressure high? Has anything happened?'

'I didn't get into high school.'

'What?! You're one of the best students in your class!'

The next morning Erzsi came with me to see the principal. Comrade Hegedűs said sorry, but Huba Street High School did not have a place for me.

'But that is Vera's district school!'

He shrugged his shoulders with a doleful expression. 'There's nothing I can do. You have to accept that they have no place for Vera in Huba Street. You know the situation, comrade Káhn.'

Comrade Káhn was not the accepting type. 'No place for one of your top students? We'll see about that!'

There was a shortage of schools, but that was not the real reason I was left out. I couldn't get into high school because of Laci's stint in jail. Through the amnesty, he had been fully pardoned, but his daughter had not. Under communism, the children carried the sins, real or otherwise, of their parents. I was last on the list for a high school place.

During the next few days Erzsi made appointments with the principals of all the nearby schools. They were empathetic, but none of them could accommodate me. One even sighed, 'Madam, I would like to help, but I can't even get my own son into university.'

'University is one thing,' Erzsi snapped, 'compulsory high school is another.'

After her failed attempts at local schools Erzsi's hackles were up and she thundered back to Huba Street. 'Comrade Principal. My daughter has good marks in every subject, except in singing, gymnastics and art, because her father wasn't a Caruso, a Puskás or a Picasso. She has not only a duty to study, but also a right to do so. I will not leave your office until you give me in writing why you cannot fit her in at your school. I will then go and enrol her in the Jewish school, where they will gladly accept such a good student.'

Now under the communist regime, no one in their right mind would put anything in writing unless absolutely forced to. With a slight change in the direction of the political wind, a person could be made responsible for a statement and pay for it with his liberty or his head. Erzsi used the system against itself.

Religious schools were in direct opposition to communist ideals. The principal could have been seen as condoning or even encouraging religious education. Realising this, he calmed Erzsi down, and she went home with the promise that he would see what he could do. The next day, during one of my lessons they called me to the office to say that I had been successfully enrolled in Huba Street.

My blood pressure quickly settled and I didn't miss another swimming session. For the rest of my stay in primary school, I absolutely blossomed.

48

AGAIN POLITICS: A CHANGE OF GUARD AND THEN THE REVOLUTION

High school started in September and I loved it from day one. Things were changing – Kati and I had grown apart. Kati was blossoming into an artist, becoming more flamboyant, and she had developed an interest in boys and socialising. She had a new best friend. I became more serious, withdrawn and cautious of people, though there was a new friend for me, too: Emese Papp. I threw myself into my studies. Reading and learning gave me pleasure and, more importantly, felt safe. Books could not leave you or betray you.

The school's cellar had a room full of books. The teachers asked for volunteers to help dust them and establish a new library. I was first to put my hand up. Three or four of us were led into the dingy cellar, which was full of boxes and cartons. Paradise.

After the death of Stalin in 1953, the Kremlin quickly turned its back on the old policies, and the faithful-to-Stalin Hungarian regime became a liability to them. Imre Nagy was ordered by the Kremlin to lead the party but Rákosi, the deposed First Secretary, undermined him at every step. In the end Rákosi had to be whisked away to Moscow 'for unspecified prolonged medical treatment' – permanently.

With Rákosi gone, the people felt freer, and immediately demanded a proper state funeral for László Rajk, the scapegoat sentenced and executed in a show trial in 1949. The people's wish was granted early in October 1956, when Rajk and his supporters were exhumed and re-buried in marked graves. The public's discontent with the government was clear when more than 200,000 people walked silently, defiantly, past Rajk's coffin.

At home we were excited, but our enthusiasm was mixed with a goodly dose of fear. We were thrilled about the political changes, but feared that new atrocities might be in store for us. On hearing the news about Rajk, Erzsi's comment was, 'I always knew they were a lying bunch of scumbags, these communists. They're full of great slogans, but their actions tell a different story.'

The Soviets thought their policies kept us happy, but everyone was grumbling, the young especially. A couple of weeks later, on 22 October, students of the Budapest Technical University formulated an agenda, which, importantly, demanded that the Soviet troops be withdrawn from Hungary and reparation payments be stopped; it also demanded that Imre Nagy return as Prime Minister and that we have free elections, with genuine choices and a secret ballot.

The following day they marched to honour the Hungarian heroes of the past, General 'Papa' Bem[23] and Sándor Petőfi in particular. An actor recited Petőfi's (banned) National Poem. The crowd, of about ten thousand students and their professors, swelled to several hundred thousand by the evening. They were joined by workers, soldiers, anyone who happened to be around. The people chanted, as they moved towards Parliament House, '*Nagy Imrét a kormányba, Rákosit a Dunába!*' ('Imre Nagy in government, Rákosi in the Danube'), and then, with heartfelt passion, '*Ruszkik, haza!*' ('Russky go home!')

Meanwhile, the ever-swelling crowd toppled the statue of Stalin. We all loathed this oversized bronze Stalin in his 2-metre boots, especially as it was made from the melted-down statues of former Hungarian statesmen.[24] The people reached the radio station, where they shouted to have their demands read out, but instead were blocked and labelled 'counter-revolutionaries' – and threatened with retribution.

Then a shot was fired into the crowd. The peaceful, albeit noisy, gathering instantly changed into an angry mob, and in the blink of an eye weapons appeared from nowhere and were used against the hated ÁVH. By the end of the day, the people had won, and Nagy was back.

So in a matter of minutes, a peaceful march of students demanding freedom for their country had erupted into a bloody revolution. Their hatred of the Soviets, repressed until now, had finally been unleashed. And all of us Hungarians were united as never before in the country's long history.

The official government, in a panic, sent for the Soviets to rescue them, and sure enough, by dawn the next day, 24 October, Soviet troops had arrived in the capital. The Russian soldiers were puzzled and confused – why had they been called out *against* the Hungarian workers and peasants? Weren't they comrades? Some even joined the revolution.

---

23 József Bem, a national hero of Poland and Hungary, leader of the 1848 revolution.
24 With typical humour, the place where Stalin's statue had stood was thereafter referred to as Boots Square.

When the announcement came on 23 October that the freedom fighters had won, we were ecstatic. Then Erzsi, always the most intuitive and pragmatic, reminded us that we, as Jews, had not fared too well in pre-communist Hungary. Although there were no antisemitic slogans yet, they were sure to follow after the euphoria died down.

All this was further complicated by the freeing of Cardinal Mindszenty, a fierce opponent of communism. He had been arrested and sentenced to life imprisonment in 1948 for treason against the new government, but on 30 October 1956, he was freed. He promptly delivered a speech on the radio, demanding full restitution of the church's property and the resumption of its traditional role in Hungarian life. I watched Erzsi and Laci listen to him, pale-faced, trembling. Mindszenty was not only a royalist and fiercely anti-communist; he was also a dyed-in-the-wool antisemite. If the Hungarian Catholic Church were in power again under his leadership, it would not bode well for us.

We need not have worried. The Kremlin was vacillating between crushing the uprising or pulling out of Hungary, but it decided on the former, due to outside events. A few days after the initial heady days of 'freedom', on 4 November, Moscow sent in the troops.

During these days, like everybody else, our family was glued to the radio, listening to the ever-changing news and wondering what it would mean for us. Under an oppressive government you learn to listen very closely, to who makes the speeches, to how expressions change, to where in the sentence the emphasis is, and most importantly, to what isn't being said. We had quickly learnt that under communism most information was between the lines.

Our good old Orion radio managed to pick up shortwave. We listened illicitly to *Radio Free Europe*, which offered us encouragement and support. Some was for real, some was hype. Some of the messages were from disgruntled Hungarian ex-patriots. And there was the *Voice of America*. Laci's relatively new knowledge of English came in handy. Everybody in the house asked him for 'real' news, as nobody trusted Radio Kossuth's reports. What we didn't know and couldn't guess was that much of the hype was being orchestrated by the CIA and MI6.

The outside events that made the Soviets change their minds were first, that Britain and France were plotting to regain the Suez Canal; Soviet interests here were aligned with those of Egypt, which had precipitated this crisis by declaring in July that it would nationalise the Canal, which was a British-French enterprise. The British MI6 sought to incite the already explosive situation in Hungary. They vigorously urged the Hungarian revolutionaries to continue fighting – not for Hungary's benefit, but because this would tie down the Soviets and distract them from the Suez problem.

Meanwhile, General Eisenhower, the US President, saw that US forces might need to intervene on two fronts against the Soviet Union: in Hungary and Suez. Eisenhower was concerned that the Soviets might overreact and start a pre-emptive nuclear war. He acted quickly and decisively, defusing what was the most dangerous moment of the Cold War so far. Unfortunately, his actions tacitly indicated to the Kremlin that the US would not interfere with whatever the Soviets chose to do in Hungary. So in rolled the tanks.

The Russian tanks did unprecedented damage in the densely built-up city centre, but they were more than miffed at the persistent and annoyingly effective Hungarians shooting at them with old guns and exploding their tanks with their own invention, the daredevil Molotov cocktail. The 'revolutionaries', mostly students, were too inexperienced even to be afraid. They fought with fierce determination, letting loose a century of bottled-up resentment and hatred. Grudges against the Russians went deep, all the way back to 1848, when the Russian Tsar was called by his Austrian Emperor cousin to help defeat the revolution – and obliged enthusiastically.

Whereas the first confrontation between the Soviets and Hungarians was characterised by a feeling of confusion in the former and absolute euphoria in the latter, now it turned nasty. The Russian tanks ignored the white coats and Red Cross ambulances: they shot them mercilessly, and in return Hungarian medical students and doctors did not bother saving wounded enemy soldiers. The fight was for survival and freedom on one side, for annihilation on the other.[25]

What we Hungarians needed in this revolution was money, weapons and foreign troops. Our hopes were raised by enthusiastic messages beamed at us by foreign radio stations. And oh, how I remember the excitement at the whole world barracking for us, the anticipation of the imminent arrival of foreign troops to help us! Maybe today, definitely by tomorrow. However, as with other pipe dreams, nothing but encouragement and praise materialised, and we gradually realised that that was all the help we were going to get from the West. That and the prayers of the American people. Later the support of the West for us was described as something like the support the rope gives to a hanged man.

I was confused. At school, on the radio, in newspapers and books, all I learnt was how wonderful communism was, and how brave, just and fair the Soviets were. They were our heroes, our beloved big brother, but such cruelty by a brother was beyond my imagination. In my 11 years I had known only

---

25 The losses were great: 2000–3000 Hungarians dead, ten times that many wounded. Most were workers, most were young. The Soviet losses: about 700 dead, twice as many wounded and some missing. For an excellent account of the revolution, read Korda (see Bibliography).

one system, and now it was changing by the minute – this way and back, that way and back again. I was in the middle of history in action (and reaction). But most significantly, I learnt not to trust *any* history taught in schools or, for that matter, handed down by the older generation. Every story had another side, no description of history told the whole truth. In school I chose science and maths – they had strict rules and you knew where you stood.

＊   ＊   ＊

The Hungarian Revolution was not planned, it just happened. It did not aim to end communism, only oppression. Yet the retribution was severe. Nagy was deported to Romania, and two years later, in a secret court case, he was sentenced and executed. Both trial and sentence were announced only after the event.

Ten million Hungarians fought against the might of the Soviet Union; a few thousand civilians against half a million trained Soviet troops and their tanks. Inevitably, the Hungarian government toppled and we were back under occupation, our strings once again pulled by the Kremlin. We didn't win in the long run, and were back under occupation. But on those euphoric days at the end of October, the until then unassailable Soviet regime 'could no longer lay claim to invincibility, to the "inevitable triumph" of socialism, let alone to humanity and decency'.[26]

My account of the events is from a Hungarian perspective. Meanwhile, the Soviet press reported calm in Budapest, and, they continued:

> *On 23 October, the honest socialist Hungarians demonstrated against mistakes made by the Rákosi and Gerő governments. Fascist, Hitlerite, reactionary, counter-revolutionary hooligans financed by the imperialist west took advantage of the unrest to stage a counter-revolution.*[27]

And according to the West, the revolution was nothing but the collective suicide of a whole people.

---

26   Korda, p. 204.
27   Frederick Barghoorn. *Soviet Foreign Propaganda*. Princeton, NJ: Princeton University Press, 1964.

49

SACRED BOOKS

In 2004 my Hungarian friend Babszi was in Australia for the second time, and unexpectedly her friend Csaba joined us in the Blue Mountains. We had a great time sightseeing, bushwalking and dining. At the end of his stay, Csaba presented me with a book about the history of Hungary in the 20th century. It was a heavy tome, but turned out to be a wonderful present because, as I was working on my memoir it filled in the political, cultural, social and economic background to my family's story.

Unprepared with a return gift for him, I found an old children's book on my shelf and gave that to help him practise his English. I suggested he look up the words he didn't know and write their meanings above the text or in the margins. Csaba was aghast at the suggestion. 'I can't do that! Books are sacred,' he said. 'It is not possible for me to mark this, not under any circumstances.'

I, too, was brought up with a reverence for books. Erzsi taught me that books were the repository of knowledge, and knowledge was the *only* thing we could really own. It was a good lesson and I passed it on to my son. Laci taught me how to handle a book, to turn the pages carefully with freshly washed hands, gently handling only the top edge of the page.

I can see my father behind his big desk with compass and ruler in hand, concentrating on drawing something technical, or maybe writing an article for the bimonthly trade journal, *Rövidáru Technika* (Narrow Fabrics Techniques). Built into his glass-fronted desk were a couple of bookshelves where he had a red-cloth bound volume by Lenin and a 22-volume encyclopaedia. As a child, I would often be aroused on the floor in front of his desk browsing while he worked, taking pleasure in our silent companionship.

During the revolution, Kati and I had been under house arrest for a whole week – with all the racket of the guns, tanks and bullets flying everywhere and the political situation changing by the minute, our respective mothers kept us indoors. Then the noise subsided, and it was announced on the radio that the revolution had been won. For a moment we believed that Hungary had shaken off the Soviet occupation and was finally free! Being insatiably curious and quite fearless, we decided to go and see for ourselves.

We lived close to the city centre. Walking along St István Boulevard, we saw piles of rubble used as trenches, still occupied by snipers, and heard the occasional rat-tat-tat of guns not too far away. We couldn't believe the extent of the devastation – so many buildings gutted. A large, elegant six-storey corner house had collapsed into nothing, exposing wall-less apartments, dangling light fittings, odd bits of ripped up floor-covering and a kitchen sink full of washing up. Another building had a gaping hole in the middle: the floor was torn apart, Persian rugs partly covered in rubble dangled in mid-air, chairs leant over the gap, ready to topple.

It was surreal, Daliesque; everything was in limbo, solid objects dribbled down the cannon-torn spaces. We could feel our surroundings with every sense in our bodies – sight, smell, touch. Later our parents told us that Budapest was more damaged after this one week than after months of battle in 1944. The heavy tanks the Russians used were meant for field battles, not for narrow city streets, and their only aim was to destroy. There was an aching emptiness inside me that I could not name.

On the streets that day we thought we could taste the bitterness of the battle and the sweetness of victory. We were free! Yet we could not *feel* that freedom. A heaviness hung in the air, the uneasy tension of unfinished business. There was no jubilation, no victory march. In fact there were hardly any people around. The shops were closed, trams and buses were not running, the streets were dead but for a few people like us.

Then we spotted a large crowd milling about in front of a Russian bookshop that stocked language books, school, university and technical texts, revolutionary Red literature in both Russian and Hungarian, history books, communist-approved literature, books on the arts and music, including Pushkin, Chekhov, Tchaikovsky, Gorky. We drew closer.

On the street, piled up to over a metre high, was a mountain of books. Glancing into the shop, I noticed the stomach-churningly empty shelves. The crowd shouted in a frenzy. 'Freedom for Hungary!', 'Down with the Russians!', 'No more propaganda!' Then someone put a torch to the heap and lit it. 'Russky go home!', 'Long live Hungary!' The crowd shouted and people waved their fists angrily as they danced around the pyre. The *danse macabre* escalated. My heart sank. I wanted to shout, 'Stop it! You don't understand, it's *books* you're burning! Stop it! Stop it!' but I said nothing.

All that I was brought up to believe in, all that I held dear – equality, the rights of workers, the importance of ordinary people – was going up in flames too. And the books. The precious, sacred books. How could people be such vandals? How is it possible that they were my countrymen, that I was one of them? I couldn't conceive that anyone would not respect the written word, and yet here they were carrying out this pagan act. Why burn poetry and art and literature?

I was still young. I had not known anything other than communism, and was not brought up with hatred. I could not yet comprehend the extent of the rage of the conquered, the exploited, the unfree. I did not yet know that books, like people, can lie and betray.

Vera at age 14, graduating from 8 years of primary school

Although I understand now, I have never come to terms with that fire. I still cry inwardly for the burning of those books and part of me still wishes to resurrect them. But books are now a little less sacred for me. Unlike Csaba, I can, if I feel the need, gently mark them with a soft 2B pencil.

50

THE AFTERMATH OF THE REVOLUTION

It took the revolution a long time to peter out and for the country to get back to normal. Those who took an active part in the uprising were arrested, and more than 20,000 people were tried. Many were sentenced to jail terms and hundreds were executed during the next five years under the new Kádár regime.

People simply disappeared, without being able to notify their families. Sometimes the families did find out, but they were virtually helpless, as they could not attend court, could not see their loved ones or give them moral support. Even if they were able to raise the money for a defence lawyer – and the costs were prohibitive for most – it was useless, as the cases were all show trials with the outcomes pre-written.

The charges against the accused were never clarified. Notification of the judgement mostly came *after* the jailing or hanging. The sentenced were not permitted a farewell note, or any visits; they couldn't say goodbye to their wives and children. Even after death, their bodies could not be viewed by their family.

Without understanding what had happened, without a final farewell, and with the added burden of shame and guilt, it was not possible to properly mourn the executed. For many, it was still incomprehensible 30 years on. They were never told the truth.

Meanwhile, with the husband in jail, the families had little or no income. The wives of revolutionaries were not eligible for widows' pensions, so were forced to become the main breadwinners. This proved insurmountably difficult for some, because instead of support, they were often sacked or demoted from their current job or were blacklisted and couldn't find employment at all. Many, even professional women, had to uproot their families and find menial jobs in towns where no one knew them. Quite a few lived in dire poverty.

As a result, many of the wives became ill or turned to alcohol for solace. Without family support, their children were taken into government care, where siblings were systematically separated from each other. In 1957, according to an MSZMP (Hungarian Socialist Workers' Party) ruling, the label 'enemy of the state' of the Rákosi era was extended to the children of those arrested in 1956.

With a few exceptions, these children were not allowed into high school, let alone into a tertiary institution, no matter how well they did, so of course later in life they had to take low-paying jobs. The children were traumatised – they experienced nightmares, bed-wetting, stuttering, ulcers, problems with the heart, not to mention psychological difficulties. They did not know if their father was guilty or innocent or even possibly a hero, as the messages that came their way were contradictory. The official attitude was scathing and antagonistic, but occasionally there was some support from ordinary people. Teachers at school were expected to enforce the government view, which demeaned and punished the children. Yet the idea of a criminal father was traumatising enough on its own.

In trying to protect their children, some mothers didn't tell them anything. Those children grew up in fear and distrust, and spent the rest of their lives waiting for their father's return.

After a 1989, some revolutionaries were 'rehabilitated': they could apply to clear their names, but many did not – it was not worth the emotional trauma.

It struck me how similar all of this was to my own father's disappearance, arrest and show trial, only four years earlier. We never talked about it and it was kept a secret from my young brother. My closest friend, Kati, distanced herself from me for a while, and even when we re-met recently she referred to it as 'that unfortunate incident with your father'. Unlike our family, she may still be unsure of Laci's innocence.

When Laci was jailed, Erzsi's faith in her husband, her anger and her righteous indignation, as well as her refusal to be a victim, were extremely effective. She stood up to both the Nazis and the communists and won her battles – in life-threatening circumstances she became the attacker and went straight for the jugular. So many other mothers were unable to demonstrate to their children this firm, effective support and strength.[28]

*   *   *

These repercussions of the revolution did not occur until after I left the country. Meanwhile, we still had to live, and during the upheavals and the strikes the

28 Adrienne Molnár. *A hátrányt nem tudjuk soha behozni*, pp. 74–80, in Teréz Virág (ed.). *Elhúzódó társadalmi traumák hatásának felismerése és gyógyítása* (*The Recognition and Treatment of the Effects of Long Term Social Trauma*). Budapest: Animula, 1997.

shops were closed and deliveries were halted. Everything came to a standstill. We, like everybody else, had very little to eat. The shops opened only when there was something to sell, and queues snaked around many blocks.

As the schools were closed and we had time on our hands, Kati and I became closer again. Often we spent a couple of hours or more standing in front of the bakery, the butcher or the greengrocer. The queues did not bother us as long as our endless chatter could continue.

While in line for potatoes, listening to gossip, someone would mention that only two blocks away freshly baked bread was available. We devised a scheme: Kati, who was more of an extrovert and more chatty than me, would go and stand in the other line for a while and make friends with the women around her. After twenty minutes or so I would go over and join her, while asking the lady behind me to mind my place. The bread line moved faster, so with our loaves in the bag we raced back to the potato queue, which had hardly progressed at all.

After a few goes, we polished this technique into an art form and were simultaneously lining up in three or four separate queues. Nobody minded, and our parents were more than happy with the results, but of course there were the occasions when, by the time we reached the front of the line, everything had sold out and we had to go home empty-handed.

Meat was another story. It was simply unavailable, so, as happened before, the government sanctioned the sale of horse meat, which apparently has the highest iron content of any red meat. Erzsi tried to make soup with it, but even after hours of cooking it was barely edible. The butchers then started selling smallgoods using horse meat. It made the best tasting Csabai, a smoked sausage like Spanish chorizo. We liked it more than the traditional version made from pork.

51

LEAVING HUNGARY

It was a cold, bleak, December Tuesday in 1956. Hard bullets of compact snow hurled abrasively against the windowpanes. Gunfire had ceased and although order had not yet been re-established, we were back at school. In the morning Erzsi happened to bump into her brother.

'Oh, it's just as well you're here, Erzsi. It saves me having to come to see you before I leave. Tomorrow I will defect with my beloved Éva, if she decides to come with me. I will leave even if she doesn't,' Feri announced.

'Wow! That's quite a decision!'

'I have a favour to ask. I have a gun, wrapped in cloth, hidden in the hallway cupboard. Would you send it to a mate of mine in the country?'

Reluctantly Erzsi promised to take care of it. Then, while they were asking each other favours, on the spur of the moment, she blurted out, 'Would you take Vera with you?'

Feri shrugged his shoulders. He wasn't keen. We were not close, and the last thing he wanted in a foreign country was to be saddled with me and that responsibility. But he said yes, if that's what his little sister wanted, he would take me. Erzsi asked him for his belt so that she could sew in some jewellery to be used as emergency currency. The Hungarian forint was worth nothing outside the country.

Later in the day Erzsi went around, probably to friends and family, to collect the cash needed to pay guides. First, there were guides who would get us to the border. Other guides would be needed for the next part of the journey. All of them would need to be paid. She returned home a little after I did from school, looking serious, with an edge to her demeanour. Like a child with a secret, Erzsi approached me and surreptitiously asked, 'Vera, would you like to defect with your uncle?'

She didn't really ask me that, did she? I must have misunderstood.

'What do you mean?'

'I just bumped into Feri a little while ago and he told me he was leaving Hungary. I pleaded with him if he would take you, and – quite reluctantly, I might add – he agreed. Do you want to go?'

I heard. My breathing stopped, my heart sank, my stomach knotted. Erzsi wanted to get rid of me and this was her chance. But Laci wouldn't let me. He'd miss me too much.

'Why don't we all go together? You, Daddy, Gyuri and me.'

'The grandmothers. They have nothing to live on. We have to sell what we can to try to provide for them, and organise a steady income, and that takes time. But we'll join you just as soon as we have everything in order. Besides, Gyurika is too young. He is too highly strung, he could be scared. You know what he was like when he was frightened before – it brought on the stuttering. It's better if we leave legally, if we follow you.'

I had nothing to say.

'Well, if you leave Hungary and go to, say, Australia ...' Erzsi started to explain.

'Australia?'

Australia was even beyond my imaginary trips. That was the place where you fell off the edge of the known world, a vast desert with only kangaroos for company.

'Well, wherever,' Erzsi continued. 'If you decide to go with them, once you are on the outside [of the iron curtain] we will be able to follow you legally. Maybe. It is always much easier to get a permit to leave if it is to join a relative. A *close* relative. Of course, only go if you want to.'

'But what about Feri? He is your brother. He is a close relative.'

'Ah ... A brother may not work. He is only a brother-in-law to Laci and an uncle to you and Gyuri. But you, you are a close relative to all of us. Anyway, think about it. You don't have to decide this minute.'

She meant it literally. Was she really sending me away? Alone? I would be crossing the border illegally. In the middle of the night. Maybe with a border guard shooting at me. Erzsi never loved me. She didn't want children, she told me that. She didn't want a daughter, she told me that too. I was not a boy, not even a tomboy. At last she would be rid of me. Like lightning, these thoughts cut through my whole body, over and over again. I was not wanted. But Laci wouldn't agree to it, he would not let me go. I stood there stunned into silence.

'You will have to tell me what you want to do. I have to take you to Feri and Éva's place by midnight tonight. The train is leaving at 5am.'

'But what about Gizka and Cina? And my friends? And Gyuri? And ...? I won't even have time to say goodbye to them!'

'You couldn't anyway. We mustn't talk to anyone. After you're gone, I'll explain to them.'

And then the penny dropped. Leaving Gyuri, Laci, my grandmothers behind, the wonderful new school with all its books, my home, friends, connections, my future husband Jancsi (or a Péter), the whole fabric of my existence. I couldn't even bear thinking about it. I would be cutting myself off from the known world I had inhabited till then. From one minute to the next I was to be alone, belonging nowhere and with no one.

At least I would not be eating her precious food, I hissed in my thoughts. Well, stuff her. No more nagging, no more of her bad temper, no more being belted because she had had a difficult day, no more being locked out for being five minutes late. I'll be out of her reach. I won't ever have to feel the back of her hand.

'Sure, if that's what you want, I'll go.'

'It's not what I *want*, but what's best for this family,' Erzsi corrected.

And from that moment on I was a free spirit – it was all going to be a huge adventure. From Budapest to the whole world. From landlocked Hungary to the grand wide oceans. From a unique language incoherent to all but the natives to languages of world communication: German, English and French. From a blinkered history, I'd find out first-hand about the world. From secrets, hushed voices, not-to-be-mentioned thoughts and burnt books, there would be the possibility of free speech, loud voices, open minds. I was young and inexperienced in life. I didn't know yet how hard it was to give up hurts and secrets.

My mind raced with the idea of this new adventure. I gave no thought to what the consequences to anyone else would be. How would Gyuri, Kati and my grandmothers feel? I did not think of them.

So in less than twenty minutes it was all settled. Erzsi spent the afternoon sewing a gold chain and a bracelet into Feri's belt. But just before she did that, she phoned the tailor, Mr Kecskész. Having outgrown my last winter coat, he had already been commissioned to alter one of Laci's old coats to fit me.

'Mr Kecskész, we need to have my daughter's coat finished by dawn tomorrow morning. She's already had a fitting.' There was no need to explain why.

'Hmmm. Yes, yes, the last fitting was good ... it should be fine. I'll work through the night and you can pick it up by 4am.'

Meanwhile, Erzsi instructed me to go and visit my grandmothers, but not tell them that I was leaving. First I went to Cina, who lived furthest from us. I asked her to show me her treasures; it was a bit of a ritual with us. She told me where each piece of jewellery or memorabilia came from, who gave it to whom, what was the special occasion. Then I gave her a last goodbye, no words betraying my mission, no emotion on my face. At Gizka's I took a deep breath from her cupboard and for the rest of my life kept my grandmother with me on the waft of that scent. I surprised both Gizka and Auntie Stefka with a hug.

Laci came home and Erzsi conferred with him alone in his study. About twenty minutes later they both emerged, Laci upset. I glanced at him. He was very shaken, but said nothing. Until now I had gone along with this charade hoping that Laci would come to the rescue and save me. *C'mon Daddy! C'mon, say something!* But he just looked forlorn. He did not put his foot down with Erzsi, nor plead with me not to go.

He spent this last evening writing something in my memory book – a few lines from Eötvös, a Hungarian poet, philosopher and statesman. I couldn't carry the whole book, but tore that page out and took it around the world. It filled me with the love and warmth of my Dad on many a cold Canadian night:

The relationship between parents and children is similar to that of a tree trunk to its branches. No matter how much they depend on each other, the branches are separated from the trunk, and as the branches continue to grow in new directions, year by year they become further apart. The grown branches meet others, those of quite different trees, but they will never again be close to their own trunk. Yet it is the trunk that continues to carry the weight of the branches and with every blow that affects them, the trunk is shaken to its deepest roots.[29]

Later, when I became a parent, my views changed somewhat. I do not consider children a burden to carry, rather a gift on loan, as Kahlil Gibran suggests in *The Prophet*. Still, in Canada, in my isolation from my family, I treasured the knowledge that there was a solid trunk, in the shape of my father, supporting me.

Erzsi and I walked to Feri and Éva's during the night and she left me with them. Neither of us said anything. She met us at the station at dawn with the coat she'd picked up from tailor Kecskész. I took the coat and turned to look at some of the other dissidents, trying to find someone my age. I said goodbye to my mother, but did not look back.

After a week or so, Erzsi fronted up at Feri's abode, Aranka's unit in Ipoly Street, explaining that she'd come to pick up Feri's gun. Despite her promise, Erzsi had no intention of sending it to anyone; it was simply too dangerous. At nightfall she walked across the bridge to Buda, found what she reckoned was a good spot, squatted down and threw the gun into the Danube.

---

29 József Eötvös. *Gondolatok (Thoughts)*. Budapest: 1874. The passage is the author's translation.

52

CROSSING THE BORDER

The railway station was busy at that early hour of morning. We had minimal luggage. I had Laci's leather briefcase containing a change of underwear, toothbrush, soap, comb, a largish stamp album and Laci's handwritten page for me. The reason for the album was that the colourful Hungarian stamps were unusual and much sought after. Laci thought that the collection would be valuable anywhere in the world.

The journey, a mere 200 kilometres, took most of the day. Once we reached the border town of Sopron, we met the organiser of our adventure and handed over the money for the three of us. It was quite a large sum. Everything seemed to be in order. He was to take us by train right to the edge of Hungary, where a local guide, familiar with the area, would walk us across the border. We would have to pay him his prearranged fee separately.

We waited for nightfall and boarded a cattle train. All of us dissidents were herded into a single car. The tension wrapped itself around us and held us as a unit as we squatted on the filthy floor. We waited and hoped no one would inspect the carriage.

The train pulled out and stop-started its way to our destination. Then it came to a halt for a final inspection before the border. We could hear the guard shouting, insisting on having the carriage opened, we heard our 'guide' trying to brush him aside, 'There's nothing in there, comrade guard, let's not waste time. The train is late already!'

The guard wouldn't budge. His nose told him there was something amiss, and the man was protesting a little too much. He tapped on the side of the car, indicating which was the one he wanted opened for inspection.

This is it, we thought. For me it would've been a reprieve, and there was no great risk, because being a child I was not accountable for my actions, but for the adults, including Feri and Éva, being caught meant a jail term with a dose of re-education in communist philosophy.

The door was pulled aside. We sat there, teeth chattering, frightened. The guard looked at us, but before he could call up his full communist indignation in the name of the proletariat and shout at us subversive counter-revolutionaries, his palm held a fat envelope. He glanced inside, tapped the side of the carriage and shouted, '*Minden rendben!*' ('All's well'!) That was the wonderful thing about communism – just about everyone could be bribed.

The train continued to its final stop and we were disgorged into the deep night. Our local guide appeared and we crossed through open fields into Austria. Where we were, the border was not protected, but only a few hundred metres away we could hear gunfire – it was obvious that the guide was worth his fee, whatever it was. It is hard to remember how long we took – every fear-filled minute lasted so long.

After the border crossing, we waited for daybreak. '*Grüss Gott,*' the locals at the small Austrian village greeted us unenthusiastically. They were not unkind, but they had had a bellyful of Hungarian refugees. Their lives had been turned upside down with this influx: 130,000 Hungarians had crossed into Austria in six weeks, and a total of 200,000 Hungarians left illegally before this mass exodus was finally stopped.

We didn't stay long – a bus arrived and took us to a refugee camp nearby. It was a huge camp, already with more people than it should hold. We newcomers were in an adrenalin-depleted stillness, satisfied that we had made it safely to this place. In contrast, those who had come before us were mostly grumbling, and it did not take us long to become like them.

We were first 'processed' to prove our identities, then had our names entered on a tally sheet, then were taken into a large hall. The corridor leading to it was lined with people handing out a motley collection of things they thought we might like. I supposed they were donated by charitable institutions.

We were given very welcome biros and small pads of paper. Appropriately, the pens were invented by a Hungarian, László Biró, in 1931. St Vincent's handed out pictures of Jesus and the Virgin Mary, not particularly useful for atheist Jews, but many Catholics were deeply moved and grateful for the cards.

The Salvation Army in their uniforms and funny bonnets, looking as if they had just stepped out of a Dickens story, had an enormous pot of hot chocolate cooking on a gas stove. It was made with reconstituted powdered milk, and was lumpy and too sweet, with a horrible texture, but after a freezing night it was the best drink I had ever had.

The Salvos also had a roomful of warm underwear to give away, sorted according to size, displayed on open shelves. We were given a basket and told to help ourselves to whatever we needed. I had never owned any bought underwear before, as Erzsi made most of mine from Laci's or Feri's old singlets, so I had no idea of the size I needed. A lady helped me. 'Size 12 should fit you, my dear,' she suggested, showing the number on her fingers. I took three pairs of undies and two long Banlon singlets. The latter kept me warm for many, many years and even when they were worn to rags I was loath to throw them out.

I thought the hot chocolate and the warm clothes we were freely given – without any bureaucracy, without signatures or lectures on the greatness of the donors – was the kindest act. I swore to myself that as soon as I had money to spare, I would donate to the Salvos. I keep that promise to this day.

We settled on the overcrowded floor, wrapped in blankets and whatever clothes we had with us. It was here that I witnessed a couple having sex under a blanket – I had no idea of the configuration of the bodies, or the amount of heaving and ho-ing that went with it.

The food was horrible, and the conditions quite abominable, but then no one had asked us to leave our country, and we had come in such numbers that the authorities couldn't cope. I was glad they were organised enough to feed us at all. Many of my fellow refugees were bad-tempered, rude and argumentative, and

Feri Háber in Canada, 1960

Éva Háber in Canada, 1960

there were fights and angry shouting. A large number later returned to Hungary when amnesty was offered.

Luckily Feri decided that three days there was enough, and in fluent German he explained to the camp authorities that we had relatives in Vienna and wanted to join them. On being assured that we had our accommodation organised, they were glad to let us go – three bodies less to take up space, three mouths fewer to feed.

There were no relatives in Vienna. We arrived in the city at nightfall with nowhere to go and with no useful currency. It was far too cold to stay in the street overnight, so Feri marched us to the nearest police station, explained our plight and asked if they could provide us with something for the night. The policemen looked at each other questioningly, then the man in charge nodded and said, '*Komm, kommen Sie mit.*' ('Come, come with me.')

We were piled into the back of a police van and taken to a large brick building. At reception they asked for any ties and shoelaces, watches or other valuables, which we handed over. Then they searched us perfunctorily. I found all this curious, but I supposed they didn't really know us. All the while Feri was asking for assurance that we would get our possessions back.

'*Ja, ja, am Morgen*' ('Yes, yes, in the morning'), said the policeman.

We were then escorted to the cells. Feri and Éva in one, and I in another, by myself. The cell had a tiny window with metal grates high above a toilet, and a bunk on the floor. I was locked in for the night. Alone in a cell, like a criminal. It was scary, but also a bit of a thrill. It was as close as I would ever come to being on the shady side of the law. We saw or heard no one else, and I tried to assure myself that at least it was a disused jail. Eventually I worried myself to sleep. That was our first night of freedom in Vienna.

In the morning we were let out, and the three of us were led downstairs to a dining area, where breakfast was served by women wearing blue striped uniforms. The next day Feri sold the bracelet from Erzsi, so we had some Austrian schillings, but not enough to last us any length of time. The most immediate need was to apply for a visa to Australia, which is where we wanted to go, but its quota had already been filled. Why on earth did Erzsi and Feri choose Australia? Simple: it was the furthest away from home, from the gas chambers, from communism. I was quite relieved to find that we couldn't get in. Canada had a much more open policy, and they welcomed all of us refugees.

We were lucky in that we received our permits within a couple of weeks. However, generous Canada ended up with a mixed bag of refugees. Many of us were political escapees, on the whole well-educated, basically healthy, hard-working people. Many others were criminals, some violent, and many of them continued in the same vein in their adopted country. They gave us Hungarians a bad name worldwide.

While we were waiting for our papers to be processed and for transport to be arranged, we sought out the local synagogue – we hoped people there would find us somewhere to sleep. This they did. The synagogue itself doubled as a giant, overstuffed dormitory, with no beds and masses of people. I claimed a hard wooden bench for the night. It was tucked under a table, with no room to move it out, so every time I turned, my head hit the table.

The Jewish community had also taken up a collection, and a couple of times someone came in to distribute the money, Jewish fashion. It was a schemozzle – that is the only word to do the process justice. A man stood on top of a bench with a fistful of paper money and whoever could grab it from him got it. I was tall, strong and quick and we needed the cash. When we had our share, I grabbed some money for others.

After three sleepless nights, we managed to rent a room for the rest of our stay. Then we took a train ride to Genoa, where we boarded our ocean liner, the *Venezuela*. For our trip, there was a minimal crew, despite – or because of – our numbers. Once again we were overcrowded for a fortnight, with no escape. The food was awful, but it did not matter to me as I was slightly sea-sick. With the help of some antihistamine pills I became *really* sick, chundering my way through the first week. The boat creaked and groaned all the way to Canada. The company of fellow Hungarians was abominable, as quite a number of escaped criminals were on board. There were fights, some with knives, so the locked hold in the bottom of the boat was over-filled with prisoners. The language was coarse and violent, not fit for my young ears.

There was nothing to do, and I spent the whole trip sick and bored. We had an all-male Italian crew with song in their speech, and music in their feet. They spent the evenings dancing, and when I was up to it, I joined them, the only passenger allowed to do so. They were happy to have young, appreciative female company and quite likely were hoping for a bit more than my enthusiasm. If so, they were disappointed.

After two weeks we arrived in Halifax, where we were fingerprinted to check our identity and criminal status and were given a medical once-over.

※   ※   ※

Meanwhile, back in Budapest, for many months after my departure, Erzsi cooked and set the table for four every night.

EPILOGUE

Though Erzsi was overjoyed to have me back in September 1959, after three years, her only comment on seeing me was that I had put on weight and looked silly in the clothes I was wearing. I was 17, an adult in my view, but the criticisms and complaints continued. Gyuri, now 11, had grown into a tall, lanky boy. When he saw me, he smiled shyly and said little. He was distant, and we were never again as close as we had been before I left Hungary.

No one asked me how it had been in Canada, how I had managed on my own. There were no congratulations for the good results I'd achieved (I'd won a scholarship to the prestigious McGill University), or the loneliness I might have felt, no acknowledgement that I had left Hungary for the sake of the family. Sometimes words are not needed, but I felt abandoned, in a country I did not want to be in, with a family I still loved but was alienated from. Of course in time I did learn to love my new home.

On leaving Hungary, I had left everything behind. Everything. I didn't give a moment's thought to how others might be affected by my leaving. Kati Szenes had named her first daughter Vera and her son Gyuri. We lost contact for 40 years, and in those years she'd talked to her family so much about me that they were sick of hearing stories about this 'imaginary' friend of their mother's. It was a great relief to them when we finally met, and her stories were confirmed.

Did Erzsi scream at Gyuri after I was gone? Did she hit the vulnerable little boy that he was when I abandoned him? We never talked about it, but I don't think he ever forgave me for leaving him. I don't think he could trust me, and I never felt his love again.

I learnt English as quickly and as well as I could, so soon spoke with a kind of a 'You're not from here, are you? Let me guess – England? South Africa? New

Zealand?' accent. No one picked Hungarian. And when asked for my religion I said I was an agnostic/atheist. I avoided the company of other Hungarians and had no Jewish friends. My closest friend at university was a German girl. I married a Christian/atheist husband and still carry his last name because it's Anglo, so I don't have to spell it, and no one asks me questions about it. My son grew up with no stories about my childhood, or Hungary, and I taught him not one word of the language. If I heard Hungarian spoken at a party or on a train, I pricked up my ears, listened for a minute or two, then walked away. If people told anti-Jewish jokes with 'I hope no one here is Jewish', I silently swallowed, hoped it would be not too offensive and at least a little funny, and kept silent. A long way from home, in denial, I had nothing to do with any of it. The past was other people's problem, not mine.

I became outwardly unemotional, the Anglo way – 'No sweat, mate! No problem, she'll be right!' – while sweating blood and tears to get 'it' right, hoping to gain the elusive acceptance, the pay-off, the perfect fit, the belonging, the 'You're one of us, girl!' It never came. I remained the 'outsider', the person from somewhere else, the difficult one, the one who said things that are not spoken of in company. I could not (or is it would not?) assimilate completely.

That was me.

The years between his marriage and emigration in 1957 changed Laci deeply, but not to me. He was someone who was fluent in German, and whose life was saved by his knowledge of this language, but I never heard him utter a single word of German during my whole life. Also, I was shocked when, in 2011, 40 years after his death, I found his letters from the War and realised that he had had a deep belief in God, and that religious ceremonies such as saying kaddish (the funeral prayer) for his father, even in the harsh conditions of the labour camp, had been hugely important to him. In my teenage years we had had many conversations about 'big issues' in life, but he had never talked about his belief, or the loss of it, even though 'having God in his corner' played a crucial role in his survival.

And Erzsi? Well, she was Erzsi. She hardly changed at all over the years. Half a century after I left Hungary, I asked her why she sent me away.

'Because I hated communism and neither of you kids had a chance of an education in Hungary.'

She had never been academically inclined, yet to her education was the most important thing she could give us.

Much of Erzsi's character was evident already when she was just a little girl. Tidiness and cleanliness became life-long obsessions, at times taking precedence over common sense, and often making Gyuri's and my life a misery.

Her love of animals, already so strong when she was young, also remained into old age. When she moved into the nursing home, Erzsi was delighted to discover a duck pond at the bottom of the garden. With her walking frame she paid regular visits to the two resident ducks, throwing them a few choice morsels of bread and other delicacies. They became excellent friends and she was on first-name terms with them: Ducky and Duchy. Mind you, she did mention that she no longer felt the need to share the pond with them.

She was not deterred by mishaps as a child and that love of adventure lured her throughout her life, mostly into wonderful experiences, including travel around the world. Both my brother and I inherited Erzsi's intrepid spirit, Gyuri more so than me.

And though tiny and frail, she retained some of her strength into old age. After a stroke about ten years before her death the doctor examining her said, 'Come dearie, take hold of my hand.'

She did.

'Can you hold it stronger?'

'Yes,' she said.

'Now, squeeze as hard as you can,' he asked her with kind, patronising eyes.

'Are you sure you want me to do that, doctor?'

'Yes, dear, as hard as you can.'

'It's your call, doctor!' Erzsi warned.

As she squeezed, he let out an 'ouch' and sat there for a while nursing his sore hand.

* * *

A few years before Erzsi died, I told her how battered and bruised I had felt throughout my childhood.

'What, after all these years you're still holding it against me? You surprise me. How can you hold a grudge for so long?'

Then her mood changed and she lashed out angrily, 'Well, what do you expect? I was under so much pressure, I boiled over at times. So what? Anybody would have. You don't know what it was like! Those bloody communists!'

Erzsi's memory was quite exceptional. After starting to write this book, I gave her a rough copy of many of the chapters to make sure all was as she had told me, urging her to write any corrections in the margins. She found it virtually impossible to mark the 'written word', but complained of my mistakes. 'Róza's cardigan did not have six buttons, only five. No, it did not happen in Plitvice, it was in Stenovice. Why don't you ever listen to me?'

When she entered the nursing home she refused to move into a room below street level and, against Jewish custom, she organised and paid for her own cremation. Despite knowing her reasons, despite being told of her childhood trauma of seeing the village grocers buried up to their necks during the time of the White Terror in 1919, the rabbi in charge of the Jewish cemetery showed no compassion. Instead, he gave me a severe lecture on how my mother had 'broken the most important rule' in opting for cremation, and refused to bury her ashes with her husband's, so her final wish of joining her beloved for eternity was denied her.

Laci last photo

Erzsi came to Australia more than 50 years ago. Although she adapted well to this country, and came to love it, in her psyche she remained fiercely Hungarian all her days.

In old age Erzsi compulsively told her stories, the same ones, over and over again. Gradually I became interested and asked for more details, more memories, and she obliged. Like Ariadne, she led me back by the thread of her life, to the time and place that were the cracked foundation of who I am – to all that I feared, all that I ran away from, all that I couldn't (wouldn't?) remember, all that I denied. She pushed, forced, fought her way through the dark and dank corridors of her memories, which were for her a daily reality, and I followed like a little girl: I was scared, but finally, I trusted her. She took me back to the major earthquakes, the fault lines, the sharp discontinuities in my life. She took me on a journey I needed to make but could not have made on my own.

Through the stories, she became my mother. Her memories in writing this story were her greatest gifts to me.

Last photo of George, 2008, two months before he died

Erzsi at 93

APPENDIX I

Erzsi's only letter to the family (written in English, and uncorrected):

29 December 2001

Vera, Gyuri [Gyuri] and David,

I am not keen on writing, even less now, but I want to ask you a few questions. Do you know about your father's family or about my family? The tapes[30] are here, you Vera started it – I have the paper with your handwriting on it – till now not one of you was interested in it!

   Do you know what is to live during the Hungarian Nazi occupation? The German Nazi occupation? The war, the bombing? No food, no water, no window, no bunker for Jews, only for the Catholics. With a little girl who still needed nappies but no water to wash them? The war above our heads? Adolf Eichmann's occupation? He sent all the Jews from the country to Auschwitz, but had not enough time to collect the last lot from Budapest! In that time 11 people committed suicide. [I am guessing 11 people from the house we lived in.] Do you know what it was to live under the Soviet regime? You could remember a lot about it, Vera, but not all. Do you know what it meant to have my husband taken away from forced labour when you, Vera, were six weeks old? From forced labour to Bor, a Nazi camp in Yugoslavia, more than 12,000 killed, Cservenka, your father had a few minutes before he was shot with the remaining few who came back from Bor. He was in hospital in Baja and in Pécs too. What do you think why he died when he was 63 years old?

   I could write much more, but I lived through it all again and it hurts. Dr David Baron, the cardiologist, was interested in me and asked me many questions, I answered his questions and in the end he said, 'Why don't you write a book?'

---

30   Stephen Spielberg's collection of stories for Survivors of the Shoah Visual History Foundation.

The man who made the videos about the Holocaust survivors, he was not Jewish, said, 'How could you survive?'

I lived through all by myself, first with you Vera, after the war with the two of you, and it was not easy! But in Budapest and here in Sydney I had and have friends who care about me. One of them said, 'Your life is a Greek Tragedy!'

Sorry for the many mistakes, but I never learned English, and I did not check the spelling. I still love the three of you, but I am very bitter! As long as I live I am here for you.
Love Erzsi/Grandma

I am so proud of Erzsi: her knowledge of English is remarkable for someone who only came into contact with the language at the age of 45.

APPENDIX II

How could it all happen?

As I started to listen to Erzsi's stories and research some facts, my hackles rose – not just because of the atrocities committed, but also because of the premeditated, cold-blooded ruthless *lawfulness* of these acts. There is something else, too, that I expect had occurred to everyone who is familiar with Hungary's particular Holocaust – how could it have happened *there*, how it could have happened *then*? How could ordinary human beings be part of atrocities like the Holocaust, or, for that matter, communism? And why did the world stand by and let it happen? When Erzsi told me about how they rounded up the Jews for the final death marches in November 1944, she fumed: 'Those bloody Arrow Cross men! It was the *law* that anyone with a baby should not be taken. I was eligible to stay at home. Did that concern them? No! I hope they rot in hell.'

I was surprised at her ire. Not that it wasn't justified, but why would anyone dream of them taking a blind bit of notice of *this* particular law so late in the game? After all, they exterminated millions of Jews, and persecuted and killed homosexuals, gypsies and communists and others, with or without laws. And from all accounts, the Arrow Cross men were more dogged about sending the Hungarian Jews off to their deaths than the Germans were.

Hungary was Germany's ally, and by the time the deportations started, the War had already been lost by Germany. Why did the Hungarian Jews go? Why did they not resist, fight for their lives? I was filled with shame and anger.

'Why didn't you hide and not come out?' I asked Erzsi. 'Why did you all go like sheep to slaughter? Surely you knew by 1944 about the extermination camps, the Germans, and the Arrow Cross's intent to liquidate the Jews?'

'Are you crazy? Not come? The Arrow Cross had a complete list of everyone who lived in the building. Every Jew's name was on it, and it was posted on the gate. Besides, even if someone, very unlikely, but say that someone had escaped the list, the antisemites who lived there would have willingly denounced them. The non-Jews had much to gain. They could occupy all vacant Jewish homes, and the possessions within became "public property" in deed if not in law.' I now understand that resistance was almost impossible.

The *lawfulness* continued to rankle with me – how, lawfully, bit by bit, the Jews were led towards the gas chambers. The Germans knew that they could only achieve their aims if they did not scare or panic the population. It was so much more effective to gradually break them into submission, into losing any hope, any fight.

I was quite amazed when Erzsi commented that life was easier under the German occupation than under the Soviets.

'What do you mean? The Nazis killed millions, the Soviets just made everybody's life hell.'

'The Nazis had rules, they had laws, you always knew what was coming. The bloody Soviets just arrived in the middle of the night and took you. You never knew what was coming.'

Both Erzsi and Laci survived the war by refusing to be victims – Erzsi showed no fear and virtually thumbed her nose at the Arrow Cross, and Laci commanded the respect of his German officer. Why did they become so different after the War? Laci not only had a belief in God, but was also firmly anchored in 4000 years of tradition. He practised the ceremonies, the markers that had been passed on to him, and he had a very strong sense of who he was, where he belonged. It gave him a tremendous amount of inner strength. Even though Erzsi had so much courage, physical strength and stamina, she did not have a strong inner life to protect her; she appeared to always be only a reflection of her husband. I suppose that is why she fell apart every time he was away from her.

And to survive one had to be able to distance oneself from emotion. When Erzsi related the story of how more than a dozen Jews were shot down by the Arrow Cross right under our balcony, I was deeply affected – tears rolled down my face as she kept on talking in a matter-or-fact voice.

'Erzsi, how can you not be crying? This story is so sad!'

'Ah, in those years you learnt not to feel – you could not have survived otherwise,' was her reply.

The difficulty, of course, was how to be able to switch those feelings back on again after the War.

Of the approximately 750,000 Hungarian Jews before the War, 450,000 perished. And those of us who survived knew for sure that we did not belong. We had to admit that despite being proud of our country, of being the best possible citizens, trying so hard for so long, all was in vain because we were never accepted, never integrated at all. The last 100 years had been nothing but a one-sided pipe dream.

This great desire to belong was the real downfall of the Jews in Hungary. They accepted exceptions. We were so happy to be Hungarians that we accepted that as Jews, there would be constraints: at times we could not be elected to Parliament, at times some jobs were denied us, at times there would be limits on the number of Jewish students allowed into tertiary institutions, and at times we would be short-changed when buying goods at the local shops, even before communism. Historically, for the Jews this was not a big deal. It had always happened, and it had happened everywhere for the last 2000 years, so why worry? This too shall pass, we'll survive ... But if you are a full citizen of a country you must insist on being treated the same as everyone else, and if your country decides to accept you as their citizen, it *must* treat you the same. Naturally, for your part, you have to take on all the obligations that go with being a citizen.

After the War many Jews emigrated to the newly formed Israel, and many went to any place that allowed them entry. So once again, they had no roots and had to start afresh. Those of us who stayed also knew that we no longer had a home, that despite being citizens who had lived on Hungarian soil for many generations, we were viewed as different, as 'aliens'. We could no longer trust our fellow countrymen. But like a ray of sunlight, Marxist ideology promised the end of antisemitism, gave us hope for a new start, for equality, for a real acceptance of all, which this time included us. So once again we enthusiastically took part in building our new society. Little did we know ...

* * *

Studies have shown that, like Eichmann, ordinary people became killers by following orders, by doing small – and not necessarily evil – deeds such as directing someone to an office, filling in a form, or, as in Kamanets-Podolsk, transporting a person from one place to another, and by being bystanders. These people were often motivated by fear and, just like us, their victims, by a need to belong.

And among all this evil, there was so much good, so much humanity, sometimes acts on a large scale, as with Raoul Wallenberg, sometimes small acts, like the Swabian women throwing bread to the death-marchers or the kindness of the German officer who saved my father's life.

* * *

Most survivors waited at least 40 years, Erzsi closer to 55, until they began talking about their experiences; many never did.[31] For Hungarian Jews there was an additional reason for silence: the fact that up to the last minute the Jews had trusted their fellow Hungarians, and they could not face their woeful misjudgement and its consequences. And after the War antisemitism continued, and now, with the far right-wing party *Jobbik* and the rewriting of history, it continues – with a vengeance.

And finally, a wishful thought, a make-believe. Suppose we Jews had been accepted as fully fledged Hungarians, our education, jobs, wealth, or whatever else was envied, accepted not as Jewish assets, but as belonging to the whole nation. There would not have been a *them* and *us*, *theirs* and *ours*. All of us would have been richer.

In allowing the extermination and emigration of its Jews, Hungary lost some of its greatest talents in the sciences, arts, literature, medicine, engineering, mathematics, commerce, finance, journalism, and so on, and even in some branches of sport. They also lost much of the national treasure, some taken by the gold trains and some simply pillaged by the Romanians, Germans, Soviets.

And I, like so many thousands of others, would not have to live on the other side of the world in isolation from my roots, my past, my history. I am forever grateful to Canada for allowing me to take refuge there and later to Australia for giving me a home, a kind and generous home. But it is not my birth home, it is not filled with my childhood friends, my early memories.

There are only a few Jewish people, at most 1 per cent of the total population, living in Hungary today, and yet animosity, hatred and blame are alive and thriving. Even if it is not the Jews, there can always be an 'other'. There are the traditional outsiders, the Roma, and now the Hungarian-speaking Ukrainian 'peasants' and the 'thieving' Romanian guest workers. They are the new 'aliens'. But as there are not many of these people, not enough to dump all the current

---

31   A Hungarian Catholic priest, Károly Olofsson, or Father Placid as he was known in the Benedictine order, after spending a ten-year sentence for his faith in a Soviet gulag, distilled the essence of survival into four key factors. He suggested that you don't dramatise suffering, but use all your energy for survival; notice even the tiniest joys of life and make a game of it; do not be a victim; and finally, believe in something, have someone in your corner. A sense of humour could be added to the list. See Wikipedia, *Olofsson, Károly, Placid atya.* (in Hungarian) http://www.szepi.hu/irodalom/pedagogia/tped_053.html, 2014.

economic woes onto, other new groups are being created – the latest is the Syrian refugees.

When I visited Hungary in 2006, and again in 2007, I found the air thick with anger, riots, contempt, one Hungarian against the other, this time the FIDESZ (right-wing party) supporters against the MSZP (left-wing party) supporters. Division and separation make a nation weak, and use up untold amounts of energy and resources in squabbles, in hatred, in putting the 'other' down. Only opening one's heart can make a person or a nation strong.

As Viktor Frankl put it: 'the truth [is] that love is the ultimate and the highest goal to which man can aspire'.[32] And acceptance, I would add.

My poor little (birth) country, will you ever learn?

---

32   Viktor Frankl. *Man's Search for Meaning*. Washington, DC: Simon & Schuster, 1962, p. 36.

BIBLIOGRAPHY

Arendt, Hannah. *Eichmann Jeruzsálemben* (*Eichmann in Jerusalem*) (trans. into Hungarian by Péter Mesés). Budapest: Osiris, 2000. (Translated into English by the author.)

Barghoorn, Frederick. *Soviet Foreign Propaganda*. Princeton, NJ: Princeton University Press, 1964.

Békés, Csaba, Byrne, Malcolm and Rainer, M. János. *The 1956 Hungarian Revolution: A History in Documents*. Budapest: Central European University Press, 2000.

Bertényi, Iván and Gyapay, Gábor. *Magyarország rövid története* (*A short history of Hungary*). Budapest: Maecenas, 1993.

Borhi, László. 'Containment, Rollback, Liberation or Inaction?', (1999) *Cold War Studies* 1(3): 67–108.

Braham, Randolph L. (ed.). *The Destruction of Hungarian Jewry. A Documentary Account*. New York: World Federation of Hungarian Jewry, 1963, 62 dokumentum.

Braham, Randolph L. with Pók, Attila. *A népirtás politikája – a Holocaust Magyarországon* (*The Politics of Genocide. The Holocaust in Hungary*) Vols 1 and 2. Budapest: Belvárosi Könyvkiadó, 1997.

Caesarani, David. *Eichmann: His Life and Crimes*. London: Vintage, 2005.

Conversino, Mark J. *Fighting With the Soviets: The Failure of Operation Frantic, 1944–1945*. Lawrence, KS: University Press of Kansas, 1997.

Crampton, R.J. *Eastern Europe in the Twentieth Century – and After*. Abingdon, Oxon: Routledge, 1997.

Deutsch, Yehuda. *Rabszolgavásár a második világháborúban* (*The Slave Market in the Second World War*). Natanya, 1998.

Dirks, Gerald, E. *Canada's Refugee Policy: Indifference Or Opportunism?* Montreal: McGill-Queens University Press, 1977.

Epstein, Helen. *Children of the Holocaust.* New York: Penguin Putnam, 1997.

Europe Review 2003/2004, Walden Publishing Ltd/Kogan Page Publishing, 2003.

Fejtő, Ferenc. *1956 – A magyar forradalom (1956 – The Hungarian Revolution).* Budapest: Holnap Kiadó, 2006.

Fernbach, D. 'Introduction', in *In The Footsteps of Rosa Luxemburg: Selected Writings of Paul Levi.* Chicago, IL: Haymarket Books, 2012.

Frankl, Viktor. *Man's Search for Meaning.* Washington DC: Simon & Schuster, 1962.

Frucht, Richard C., *Encyclopedia of Eastern Europe: From the Congress of Vienna to the Fall of Communism.* Abingdon, Oxon: Taylor & Francis Group, 2003.

Gerlach, Christian and Götz, Aly. *Az utolsó fejezet (The Last Chapter).* Budapest: Noran, 2005.

Glantz, David M. and House, Jonathan. *When Titans Clashed: How the Red Army Stopped Hitler.* Lawrence, KS: University Press of Kansas, 1995.

Horthy, Nicholas, Simon, Andrew L. and Roosevelt, Nicholas (eds). *Admiral Nicholas Horthy Memoirs.* Phoenix, AZ: Simon Publications LLC, 2000.

Kádár, Gábor and Vági, Zoltán. *Aranyvonat (Gold Train).* Budapest: Osiris, 2001.

Korda, Michael. *Journey to a Revolution.* New York: HarperCollins, 2006.

Kramer, T.D. *From Emancipation to Catastrophe.* Lanham, MD: University Press of America, 2000.

Lendvai, Paul. *One Day That Shook the Communist World: The 1956 Hungarian Uprising and Its Legacy.* Princeton, NJ: Princeton University Press, 2008.

Levi, Primo. *Is this a man?* Abacus, 1987.

Majsai, Tamás. *A körösmezei zsidó deportálás 1941-ben (The deportation of Jews at Korösmező in 1941),* in Ráday, *Gyüjtemény Évkönyve* IV–V, 1984–85.

Makarenko, A. *Az új ember kovácsa. (The Road to Life)* Budapest: Új Magyar könyvkiadó, [No date] 3rd edition.

Mayer, Arno J. *Why did the Heavens not Darken?* New York: Pantheon Books, 1988.

Molnár, Adrienne. *A Hátrányt Nem Tudtuk Behozi Soha (We could never make up the losses),* in Virág, Teréz (ed.). *Elhúzódó társadalmi traumák hatásának felismerése és gyógyítása (The Recognition and Treatment of the Effects of Long Term Social Trauma).* Budapest: Animula, 1997.

Nazi Conspiracy and Aggression, Vol. III, 'Directive for the Handling of the

Jewish Question'. Washington: USGPO, 1946.

Prauser, Steffen and Rees, Arfon. *The Expulsion of 'German' Communities from Eastern Europe at the End of the Second World War.* Florence: European University Institute, 2004.

Ranki, Vera. *The Politics of Inclusion and Exclusion: Jews and Nationalism in Hungary.* New York: Holmes & Meier, 1999.

Romsics, Ignác. *Magyarország története a XX. században* (*History of Hungary in the 20th Century*). Budapest: Osiris, 2004.

Ságvári, Ágnes. *The Holocaust in Carpatho-Ruthenia.* New York: Memorial Foundation for Jewish Culture, 1998.

Szabó, Borbála. *Tények és tanúk: Budapesti napló (1944. november –1945. január).* [*Facts and Witnesses: Budapest Diary (November 1944 to January 1945)*]. Budapest: Magvető, 1983.

The 1956 Hungarian Revolution, A History in Documents. Gyuri Washington University: The National Security Archive.

Tibor, Frank. *Discussing Hitler: Advisers of U.S. Diplomacy in Central Europe, 1934–1941.* Budapest: Central European University Press, 2003.

Tokaji, András. *Mozgalom és hivatal. Tömegdal Magyarországon 1945–1956 (A New Movement: Mass Song in Hungary 1945–1956).* Budapest: Zeneműkiadó, 1983.

Ungvary, Krisztian, Lob, Ladislaus and Lukacs, John. *The Siege of Budapest: One Hundred Days in World War II.* New Haven, CT: Yale University Press, 2005.

Valent, Paul. *Child Survivors: Adults Living with Childhood Trauma.* London: Heinemann, 1994.

Yad Vashem (Arad, Yitzak, Gutman, Yisrael and Margaliot, Abraham (eds)). *Documents of the Holocaust – Selected Sources on the Destruction of the Jews of Germany and Austria, Poland and the Soviet Union.* Oxford: Pergamon Press, 1981.

USEFUL INTERNET SITES

Part II: The War years: 1942–45

13 My arrival, at long last
Foreign Broadcast Monitoring Service, Federal Communications Commission. Translation of Speech by Hitler made on 30 January 1942. http://www. worldfuturefund.org/wffmaster/Reading/Hitler%20Speeches/Hitler%20 Speech %201942.01.30.htm.

Wannsee Conference, minutes of discussion. http://prorev.com/wannsee.htm.

15 Uncle Feri and Laci in the forced labour service
The Labour Service System in Hungary. http://degob.org/index. php?showarticle=2032.

http://holocaustcontroversies.blogspot.com.au/2013/02/the-kamenets-podolsky-massacre_12.html.

http://www.zsido.hu/tortenelem/holocaust/chapter3.htm.

http://www.zsido.hu/tortenelem/holocaust.htm.

Kovács, Tamás. *Magyar munkaszolgálatosok Borban (The Experiences of Hungarian Slave and Forced Labourers in Bor).* http://antiskola.eu/hu/beszamolo-beszamolok-puskak/23970-magyar-munkaszolgalatosok-borban.

Holocaust Dokumentációs Központ és Emlékgyjtemény Közalapítvány Levéltára (HDKE), Deportáltakat Gondozó Bizottság (DEGOB), Protocol No. 3233. http://degob.org/index.php?showarticle=3233.

Memorandum from Rosenberg File Concerning Instructions for Treatment of Jews. http://www.phdn.org/archives/www.ess.uwe.ac.uk/genocide/ostland2. htm.

17 Life in Budapest, 1942–44

Memorandum from Rosenberg File Concerning Instructions for Treatment of Jews, 'Directions for the Handling of the Jewish Question', point 3. http://www.phdn.org/archives/www.ess.uwe.ac.uk/genocide/ostland2.htm.

The Argus, Melbourne, 4 April 1944. http://trove.nla.gov.au/ndp/del/article/11809123.

http://degob.org/index.php?showarticle=2021.

http://www.yellowstarhouses.org/chronology#main-content.

https://www.jewishvirtuallibrary.org/jsource/biography/wallenberg. htmlhttps://www.jewishvirtuallibrary.org/jsource/biography/wallenberg. html.

http://raoul-wallenberg.eu/home.https://en.wikipedia.org/wiki/Operation_Frantichttps://en.wikipedia.org/wiki/Operation_Frantic.

http://antiskola.eu/hu/beszamolo-beszamolok-puskak/23970-magyar-munkaszolgalatosok-borban.

Nuremberg trials, 119, 21 November 1945. http://avalon.law.yale.edu/imt/11-21-45.asp.

http://www.zsido.hu/tortenelem/holocaust/chapter3.htmHouse of Terror (Budapest): exhibitions, notes.

19 From Bor to Baja: 450 kilometres on foot

http://antiskola.eu/hu/beszamolo-beszamolok-puskak/23970-magyar-munkaszolgalatosok-borban.

HDKE, DEGOB, 3068. sz. jkv.

HDKE, DEGOB, 3454. sz. jkv.

HDKE, DEGOB, 3233. sz. jkv.

HDKE, DEGOB, 3199. sz. Jkv.

21 The War comes close to home; cellars

The Siege of Budapest. https://en.wikipedia.org/wiki/Budapest_Offensive.

Gosztonyi, Peter. *Fortress Budapest*. www.hungarianquarterly.com/no151/137.html 2005.

A personal story from a protected house (21 Katona József Street). http://nol hu/archivum/20090613-katona_jozsef_utca_21-336956.

http://en.wikipedia.org/wiki/Siege_of_Budapest#Civilian_deaths_and_mass_rape.

http://www.nationalarchives.gov.uk/education/worldwar2/theatres-of-war/eastern-

22 The tail end and the aftermath of the War

https://en.wikipedia.org/wiki/Mikl%C3%B3s_Horthy.
https://en.wikipedia.org/wiki/Adolf_Eichmannhttps://en.wikipedia.org/wiki/Adolf_Eichmann.
https://en.wikipedia.org/?title=Raoul_Wallenberg.

Part III: Communist times

29 Starting school, warnings

http://www.rev.hu/history_of_45/tanulm_muv/index.htm.
The Institute for the History of the 1956 Hungarian Revolution. https://www.dokweb.net/database/organizations/about/92283301-833c-4f8d-8c1a-8b83529a2501/1956-institute-budapest.
http://www.rev.hu/history_of_45/tanulm_muv/muv_e.htm.
http://www.rev.hu/history_of_45/tanulm_muv/index.htm.

35 Visit to a synagogue

https://en.wikipedia.org/wiki/Dohány_Street_Synagogue.
http://en.wikipedia.org/wiki/Joshua_ben_Gamla.
http://columbusjewishfoundation.org/irving-a-baker/.

41 And some more politics: Communism in action

https://en.wikipedia.org/wiki/Eastern_Bloc_politics#cite_note-crampton.
https://en.wikipedia.org/wiki/L%C3%A1szl%C3%B3_Rajk.

46 Sports, Puskás and soccer

http://en.wikipedia.org/wiki/Ferenc_Pusk%C3%A1s.
https://en.wikipedia.org/wiki/Golden_Team.

47 Again politics: A change of guard and then the revolution

https://en.wikipedia.org/wiki/Hungarian_Revolution_of_1956.
UN General Assembly Special Committee on the Problem of Hungary (1957), Chapter II.C, para 58 (p. 20), para 480 (p. 152) and para 600 (p. 186). http://mek.oszk.hu/01200/01274/01274.pdf.
UN Secretary-General 'Report of the Secretary-General Document A/3485'. http://www.un.org/depts/dhl/dag/docs/a3485e.pdf.
Time Magazine, 'How to Help Hungary', 24 December 1956.

ACKNOWLEDGEMENT

Where to start with the 'thank you' list?

Thank you Barry Kinnaird for eagerly reading one of the first rambling versions of the story and for being the collector and safe-keeper of a whole archive of its many rebirths – at first ever increasing in length, then gradually, at times painfully, slimming back down to a sensible size. To Joyce Kornblatt, who was the first 'professional' (Professor of English and Creative Writing at the University of Maryland and the wonderful author of four novels) who gave me the confidence and courage to continue by saying 'You are a writer!' after reading the manuscript. And, because what she read was a pre-edited version, her gentle comment, 'But where are my people?' when the family disappeared from the script and politics took over; her voice in my head throughout the editing process helped to keep my focus on the 'people'.

And more friends who gave honest feedback and continued enthusiasm on the various versions of the manuscript: Fiorella and Jim Pollack, Ruth Bennett, John King, Raya Gadir, and Alison Bremner, who listened to me endlessly and helped with some last-minute editing of blurbs as I sent them off to publishers. Yasmin Clemens for reading the first few chapters before there were any others and seeing a potential book. Dawn Mears with her enthusiasm and wonderfully encouraging comments. My gratitude goes to my Hungarian friend Margaret (Babszi) Balasi, who was always ready with the right book for me to read, and who, patiently and with many good laughs, helped me re-learn Hungarian.

I would like to thank my editor Shelley Kenigsberg, for trimming the book so skilfully and sensitively at the beginning, and Veronica Sumegi and her husband Andras Berkes for unhesitatingly sharing their years of experience in publishing with me, guiding me along the rough road of getting the book into print, coming up with new ideas when I was ready to give up. Thanks to Sarah Shrubb, for doing a great job on the copy edit, together with Victoria Jefferys of WriteLight Publishing, for hearing me, for being efficient and making this otherwise difficult process so easy. Thank you Lindena Robb for listening with your heart and painting the wonderful cover picture that captures the essence of the book.

A special thanks to my writing groups started by (the late) Walter Smith and another by Virginia King, both many years ago and continued later along similar lines with Jillian Salz, Anita Swanson, Judy Pinn and Margaret Rock. They forced me to tackle the emotionally challenging parts, encouraging me to rewrite those stories until they could 'feel' the characters, and they had the kindness to say not only what didn't work, but also what did. Without them this book would not have been written.

And finally, I'd like to thank those then 'strangers' who so willingly read the book, gave suggestions or helped me promote or 'blurb' it for the back cover: Diana Hill for her initial appraisal, Marilla North for sharing her experiences in getting published, husband Robert Gordon Jones for so carefully going over a still long manuscript and Dr Dasia Black-Gutman for her valuable suggestions. At the beginning of my venture into Hungarian Jewish history, Dr Tom Kramer, formerly of the University of Sydney, generously gave his time and warned me to be prepared for the emotional impact of what I would find. Nearly ten years later, Dr Michael Abrahams-Sprod, from the same university's Biblical, Hebrew and Jewish Studies, after carefully reading and correcting the now finished manuscript, so kindly made me aware of the emotional impact of language and of how sanitised expressions can become in translation.

My deepest thanks go to David, always in my heart, for being my son and for being so wildly proud of me when a publisher showed interest.

ABOUT THE AUTHOR

Vera Hartley is a passionate educator who has worked in schools and TAFE for most of her life. With the skills gained through her scientific training, she has researched the history of her childhood in Hungary. She presents that information with minimal sentimentality or commentary, as the context for the focus of the book: her mother's persistence and courage, demonstrated by the sharing of her powerful personal anecdotes and intimate, difficult memories. She lives in the Blue Mountains in NSW.

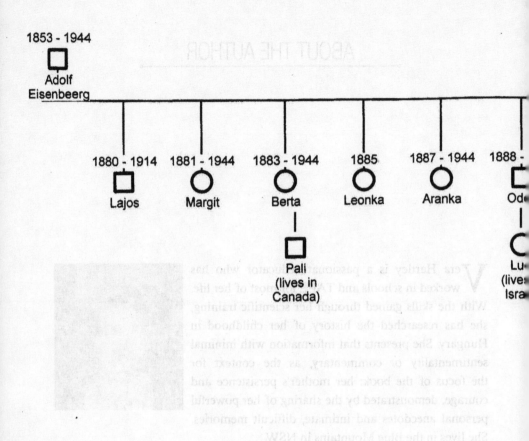

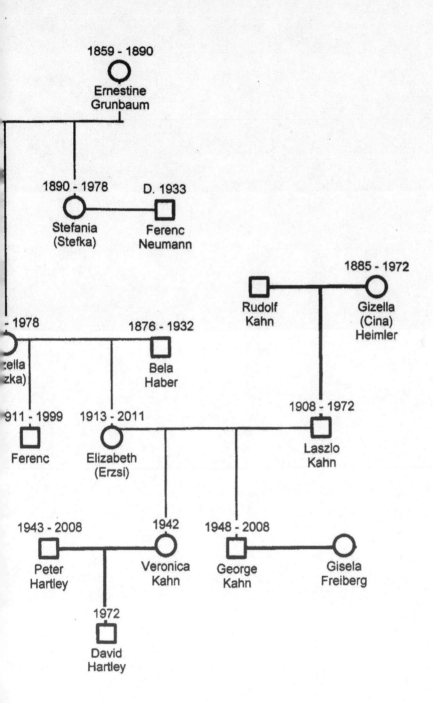

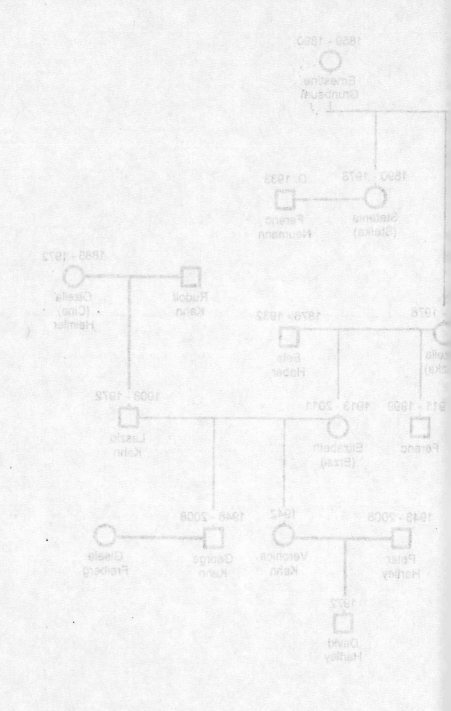